The Library Administration Series

Lowell A. Martin, General Editor

Organizational Structure of Libraries

Lowell A. Martin

Revised Edition

Library Administration Series, No. 5

The Scarecrow Press, Inc.
Lanham, Md., & London
1996

SCARECROW PRESS, INC.

Published in the United States of America
by Scarecrow Press, Inc.
4720 Boston Way
Lanham, Maryland 20706

4 Pleydell Gardens, Folkestone
Kent CT20 2DN, England

Copyright © 1984, 1996 by Lowell A. Martin

First edition published by The Scarecrow Press, Inc., Metuchen, N.J., &
London, 1984. ISBN 0-8108-1696-2

British Cataloguing-in-Publication Information Available

Library of Congress Cataloging-in-Publication Data

Martin, Lowell Arthur, 1912–
    Organizational structure of libraries / Lowell A. Martin. — Rev.
ed.
        p.   cm. — (Library administration series ; no. 12)
    Includes bibliographical references (p.   ) and index.
    ISBN 0-8108-3123-6 (alk. paper)
    1. Library administration. 2. Library administration—United
States. I. Title. II. Series: Scarecrow library administration
series ; no. 12.
Z678.M345 1996   96-273315
025.1—dc20   CIP

♾ ™ The paper used in this publication meets the minimum
requirements of American National Standard for Information
Sciences—Permanence of Paper for Printed Library Materials,
ANSI Z39.48-1984.
Manufactured in the United States of America.

CONTENTS

LIST OF FIGURES

Preface to the Revised Edition

Since the first edition of this volume over a decade ago, significant changes have occurred in the theory and practice of organization and administration and in the knowledge culture in which libraries function.

In both corporate and service enterprises, the trend away from centralized, autocratic organization has accelerated, and the move toward cooperative and participatory management has increased. The administrator is no longer boss and director but more stimulator and facilitator, releasing the energy within an organization. The manager who does not recognize this is destined to play an increasingly defensive and marginal role.

In business, manufacturing, and service enterprises, intensified attention is being given to quality of performance and to customer satisfaction with end products. The widespread downsizing of middle management in the corporate world is one example of this. The emphasis on quality in everything from automobiles to mail order catalogs is another example.

A pervasive change with profound implications for libraries is the opening of the information highway. While the term has become a cliché, electronic access to both facts and text moves steadily forward. A new culture for disseminating knowledge is at the end of the highway.

Participatory administration, Total Quality Management, and the electronic library—these open a new environment for libraries.

How have these and other changes affected libraries? What has been the library response? What is the prospect ahead? The present text has been brought up-to-date in light of such questions. The analysis here indicates that libraries face not just modifications in goals and practices but actual transformation in purpose and function.

This is the justification for a revised edition. It is hoped that the revision will help libraries over the next decade, which may be the most challenging in the history of the institution. The library will be a different agency in the twenty-first century.

Preface to the First Edition

Early in my library experience I was rather indifferent to organization. Clarity of purpose and quality of staff were what really counted. If I had to make a choice, I would still put these qualities first.

Over time, however, organization has moved up in my examination of libraries. Earlier it was almost a "given" of the enterprise, the bare skeleton, to be disposed of in an organization chart. But over the years the skeleton more and more proved to have flesh and blood and nerves. At its best it held a group of workers together, enabling them to achieve a group purpose. At its worst the arteries hardened in the flesh, and the organization held the enterprise back, preventing it from responding to change.

Organization also came to be more complex than appeared at first glance. It turned out to be not just neat boxes and lines on the chart. Third-dimensional relationships came into focus when the enterprise was analyzed for decision-making and performance. Organization emerged as a social structure, an environment, in which a library flourishes, drifts, or declines.

Understanding of that environment, and of how it affects both work and workers, is one important aspect of leadership. At one point the text states: "Together, in a suitable structure of relationships, a group can scale a mountain, make computers, put a man on the moon, and run libraries."

This volume seeks to present structure as a living, multidimensional body of relationships. If it succeeds, even in part, it should help administrators to use organization to further the ends of their libraries. This is quite different from the experience of many managers who find themselves imprisoned in a framework not of their own making. Organize and prevail.

Organizational
Structure
of Libraries

1 WHAT IS ORGANIZATION?

ORGANIZATION is an ambiguous term, difficult to define. Clear delineation is impeded both by variations in popular usage and by different emphases in the literature of administration. The meaning attached to the term in this volume must be clarified at the outset.

In popular usage we say, "I wouldn't join that organization." This could refer to any group from the local golf club to the Republican Party, from the army to the American Library Association. In this context the term is used in place of the name of a group entity, and has little if anything to do with how the organization functions, which is the concern of administration.

The term is also used to mean "Let's get something started." One can "organize" a ball game or a labor union or a revolution. In this sense my task at present is to organize a book on organization.

Or we say, "Let's get organized," meaning let's decide what we are going to do and how we are going to do it. This comes closer to organization as used in administration, focussing on planning or getting ready to act, but still is too narrow in what it encompasses and too general in where it can be applied. In this sense one could organize a desk drawer, a card party, or a convention of librarians.

The same phrase, "Let's get organized," is used with a somewhat different meaning, as a call for designation or election of officers. Once again this interpretation has some relation to the term as employed in administration, for it implies a hierarchy, a structure of responsibility and authority, which is

3

found in most organizations. But this meaning also is fragmentary, because an assemblage of people only begins to be an organization when it has a president or director.

Or still again the term is used as a synonym for "assembled" or "put in order." Disraeli was fond of the word in this meaning, as in "Party is organized opinion" and "Conservative government is organized hypocrisy." Libraries have been referred to as bodies of "organized knowledge."

These variations in common usage are confusing enough, but even within the literature of administration "organization" takes on different connotations. Thus, in the well-known earlier acronym POSDCORB, the first letter stood for planning, the next for organizing, then staffing, then directing, and so on. This sets organization as a distinct step apart, an action that is completed and then let stand, after which the administrator proceeds to locate personnel. Actually organization is recognized today as a continuing and changing set of relationships, and in any case organization does not exist separate from people; members *are* the organization, which they make and remake over a period of time.

Around the turn of the century, a classical school—as we will see later—defined organization as a hierarchy of job tasks. Like some of the other usages, this formulation has a considerable element of accuracy and relevance, even today. However, hardly had the concept been put forward before other management theorists attacked it on the grounds that only part of the functioning of a working group follows the established hierarchy or pyramid of authority. A significant part of the present volume will describe how the concept of hierarchy is modified and even negated in actual practice, in libraries and elsewhere.

More recent writers, such as Chester Barnard[1] and Peter Drucker,[2] stress organization as cooperative action, joint enterprise in pursuance of a goal. Now at least we have an organism, a living and changing entity, rather than simply a discrete step or a fixed structure. But other commentators, focussing on the individual caught in an organization for whatever reason (most commonly to earn a living), are less sure of the cooperative element. Pfiffner and Sherwood conclude, "The organization is really an uneasy holding company of individuals reacting as individuals."[3] Reading recent analyses of business and industrial firms by social psychologists, one is tempted to conclude that organization can be organized anarchy.

Each of these slants of insight throws some light on the character of organization; at the same time in their variety they underline the complexity of groups of people seeking to work together. We are not much nearer a definition, but it is now apparent that we are dealing with a complicated and many-faceted phenomenon. It would be wise to be wary of any neat and narrow interpretation.

Meaning of Organization

For this work a rather general and flexible definition is adopted. Organization is taken to mean the formal and informal structure through which decisions are reached and individuals perform job tasks that contribute to the goals of the enterprise. There are four elements here: goals which underlie the reason why the enterprise exists, decisions in pursuit of those goals, job tasks or assigned activities involving different responsibilities and specialities, and a pattern of associations that hold the group together. This model is found, with instructive variations, in the factory, the army, the church, the university, the hospital—and the library. This concept of organization, with its four components, will constitute the substance of the present volume.

This is not a model that can readily be set down in the typical organization chart. Such charts show neither what goals exist nor where decisions are made, nor how associations among members are maintained. Formal diagrams will be displayed in this presentation, but with recognition that they show only part of our topic, the part represented by the official hierarchy, the structure of authority and control. Our aim is to grasp organization whole, in all its subtlety, variety, and contradictions, to see it as interactions among individuals as well as relations between structural units.

Thus it is clear that organization is more than the skeleton or bare bones of administration. The formal structure of an organization has significance, but treated alone it tends to be lifeless, dealing with organization charts and fixed relationships. In this narrow view emphasis is placed on hierarchy, the chain of command, the scalar principle, communication through channels, and control. Each of these will be examined in the volume, but with recognition that this "anatomy" does not describe the full functioning of a group organism.

Seen whole, organization deals with flesh and blood relationships: planning, decision-making, specialization of functions, coordination, evaluation. It is movement as well as structure, human relations as well as authority, change as well as continuity. It is influence and power as well as authority. In other words, organization as used here covers the various systems and relationships that make the body of an enterprise work.

Organization touches on and relates to all functions of administration. Various of these are treated separately in other volumes in this series, on planning, communication, personnel, etc. This work will center on organization as a set of relationships designed to further the purposes of an agency, but will draw the connection to other aspects of administration where appropriate.

"The purpose of an organization," writes Peter Drucker, "is to enable common men to do uncommon things."[4] Organization enables individuals to accomplish goals beyond their separate capacities. Together, in a suitable structure of relationships, they can scale a mountain, manufacture computers, put a man on the moon, and run a library.

Pushing this concept further, perfect or ideal organization would be people working together without administrators. Objectives would be achieved without anyone either telling workers what to do or even establishing a structure in which they are to perform. But perfect organization may exist only in heaven; perhaps there are no administrators there. On earth, and in libraries, both structure and authority are needed.

This does not mean that organization is to be examined only from the top down. The former view was that there were a few decision-makers at the top and compliant workers below.

This missed the whole range of judgments actually made at the worker-product or worker-client interface. It lacked the valuable contributions to the decision-making process of both middle management and persons on the line. The authoritarian view disregards a host of informal relationships at every level that are part of organization. Perhaps most important, it fails to take into account the factors that motivate the contemporary worker.

It follows that organization as used here encompasses far more than the formal structure of departments. It includes, first of all, a variety of external conditions and pressures that create both opportunities and limitations. Relations of a library with City Hall, with the principal in the school, with the President's office of a university come first to mind, but extend well beyond, to library users, to faculty and community groups, to the "public" generally. Internally, organization includes all relationships which affect the performance and the product of the enterprise—those between administrators, between management and staff, among groups within the staff, and among individuals. A brief telephone conversation between two administrators may promote as much cooperation— or antagonism—as a two-hour "cabinet" session; discussion by staff at lunch may affect methods as much as a manual of operating procedures. In their places in the structure, individual workers react with enthusiasm, with indifference, or even with antagonism. All are part of organization; the whole web of relationships, if set down in a diagram, would not look like a neat organization chart but more like an abstract painting by Wassily Kandinsky or Jackson Pollock.

The many facets of organization complicate the task of preparing a book on the subject. Part of the topic can be captured in generalizations and even in "principles," but other parts escape because of the myriad ways in which people decide to work or not to work together. Order and harmony can usually be observed and recorded; lack of interest is less obvious, and opposition may actually be underground. This volume, like others on administration, examines in some detail the formal and repetitive relationships, treats more generally the informal aspects of people working in libraries, and no

doubt misses on some of the more subtle and occasional connections. But the effort is made throughout to go beyond the
visible and obvious.

Value of Organization

Why organize? Why worry about organization? Simply assem-
ble qualified people, inspire them with a mission, and let them
in their good skill and good will go about achieving the mission.
Would we not come out as well or better, and save the salaries
of general administrators and middle managers in the process?

Even the most democratically minded idealist is unlikely
to advocate such a formless pattern. Anarchy in organization
breeds failure in results. Some work would be duplicated and
some left undone. Special interests and capacities of individuals
would not be utilized, the pieces would not fit, in time a form
of gridlock would occur. Soon there would be an overwhelming
vote for the simple proposition, "Let's get organized."

The value of organization can be illustrated with the homely
example of the football team. Here if anywhere it would appear
that the essential ingredient needed for victory is not complex
organization but simple brawn. Recruit the biggest and tough-
est players, tell them to get the ball to the goal, and reward
them when they achieve the objective. The catch is that the
other side will do the same, with the result that a stand-off
occurs and both sides fail.

Which team wins? The one with the better organization
and the better spirit. With the goal of advancing the ball, a
sensible structure is adopted: a line of players to hold off the
opposition, a quarterback to call plays, and running backs to
carry the ball. Specialization of function is evident. Carrying
organization a step further, within the line the disposition of
tasks and the capacities of players differ: heavy guards to the
center, tacklers further out, and ends to range across the field
and catch forward passes.

But the organization of football teams does not stop with
this older model. Over the years various re-organizations and
additions of specialities have occurred, to the point where all

but the most dedicated fan is often confused by what occurs on the field and by the constant shifting in and out not only of individuals but also of whole "teams." There are offensive and defensive units, kick-off squads and run-back squads, tight ends and cornerbacks and safety men. A football game today is a succession of changes in organization to meet changing situations.

There is a further lesson in this football analogy. All teams use some form of modern structure, but some win and some lose. What accounts for the difference? Structure alone does not determine the success of an enterprise. There is more to effective administration than placing people in designated positions.

Two additional ingredients are clearly quality of personnel and team spirit. Given the same line-up, the winner of yester-year had a Red Grange, the winner of today a Dan Marino. It is interesting to note that as organizations become more complex, individual stars do not stand forth as clearly as in a simpler structure, an observation that applies to corporations as well as to athletic teams. We will be tracing at intervals the interplay of the individual on one side and group organization on the other.

The other animating ingredient is spirit, morale, team play. "We got it together," says the winning coach, explaining a victory. In technical terms he refers to coordination, the meshing of specialities to the achievement of a common goal. Another coach put it differently: "Our fellows have played together for a long time; they have an instinct for what their teammates are going to do." Here it is the informal organization that comes into play, the meshing that occurs without any coach or manager giving directions.

Even high-school teams have adopted some of these variations and complexities. Any team, amateur or professional, that stayed with the old, simpler arrangements would be doomed to defeat. Organization is not a once and forever thing.

Recently the championship of the National Basketball Association was decided with one final contestant winning a game by 35 points and then the other finalist coming back a few days later and winning by exactly the same margin. Same formal organization, same players. Why the difference in performance? Essentially it was team play, coordination in administrative terminology, which first one team and then the other achieved. Or to put it in the vernacular, as the losing coach said, "They killed us with the fast break."

The example from athletics may be far-fetched, but it identifies the four elements of organization that will occur and recur in this book: the formal structure of positions and operations, the informal relations and coordination that grow up in group endeavor, the decisions made by the coach and the quarterback, and the spirit or motivation of the individual within the group.

The example makes another point: without the team, the individual player, no matter how powerful, would not prevail. Organization enables libraries to achieve the goal of bringing seeker of knowledge and source of knowledge together. Without the group enterprise, the individual librarian standing alone in the stream of communication would be no more effective than the individual player standing in the path of the opposing team. In fact, librarians without a library are an abstraction, skilled workers without the means to exercise their skill. Librarians would do well to learn about organizations, because they will be spending their lives in them, and without them they cannot practice their profession.

Libraries as Organizations

The task of this book is to determine how libraries work as group enterprises. This will cover formal structure, the informal network of influence and communication, how decisions are reached, coordination, and the place of staff members within library organizations.

To help achieve this goal, we will draw as fully as possible on almost a century of successive theories of management; we will even come on a so-called "science" of administration. The theories and principles were based originally on burgeoning industry in the United States and Western Europe, with more recent attention to governmental and educational establishments. We will seek to apply to libraries what has been learned from other fields. There will be many parallels and legitimate applications.

At the same time the search will not stop with general theory. It must be remembered that the organizations that have been formally studied were more often manufacturing and not service concerns. It was the factory that first attracted the attention of the social psychologists and production engineers. Business organizations have been the focus of more recent examination of decision-making within group enterprises. Much of the study of schools, colleges, and universities, which are closer in character to libraries, has been done not by general management theorists but by educational administrators themselves, and this has resulted in a provincial rather than a universal literature. The same may be said of the analysis of libraries by librarians. We have the broad-view examination of economic enterprise on which to draw, and the narrow-view self-examination of service organizations.

All organizations are similar, and all are different: similar in that invariably human beings work toward some common goal, different in that neither the goals nor the human beings involved are the same. Every enterprise has its own personality.

It is indicative that many of the characteristics of organizations identified by students of administration do apply to libraries. These are basically scalar organizations, built on the hierarchical principle. They utilize specialization in work assignments and build departments on bases similar to other enterprises. Staff officers have appeared alongside line officers. Coordination is aimed at and sometimes achieved. Management experts find a counterpart within libraries for most of their categories.

Libraries clearly belong in the class of service organizations and the sub-class of educational agencies. This means that they cannot be measured either by tangible product or by profit, but rather by their effect on the people they serve, an elusive and nebulous outcome. At the same time, they are document-processing and information-processing agencies, which opens the prospect of measurement by success or failure rate in providing the documents or information sought.

After drawing on general knowledge, we must then look hard at libraries alone, to see what may be distinctive or unique about their organization. For any principle developed in other endeavors we must ask: does it apply to libraries? must it be modified in application? would wholesale utilization of findings from business and manufacturing concerns actually injure libraries? For the library director there may be limited benefit in learning how a shoe factory, or a bank, or a newspaper is organized. Librarians have their own tasks to perform and their own services to render. The organization of libraries is the center of the target.

It may therefore be useful at the outset to characterize the kind of enterprise we are dealing with. Libraries, unlike some other organizations:

- are service agencies and not profit-making firms;
- purvey information and not more tangible services or products;
- perform functions both of supply and of guidance, a kind of combination of what in the medical field is shared among the doctor's office, the hospital, and the pharmacy;
- provide professional service without in most cases having a personal and continuous client relationship, with the user depending on whichever practitioner is available at the time of a visit;
- for all their general acceptance, are currently marked by ambiguous goals rather than clear-cut objectives;
- in their long history, have accumulated set conceptions of function and method which make for rigid structure and resistance to change;
- respond both to resources on the one side and to clientele on the other, in a dual and sometimes conflicting orientation, with some staff characterized as "book-minded" and others as "people-minded";
- function as auxiliaries to larger enterprises (municipalities, universities, schools, associations, etc.) and not as independent entities in their own right;
- as a consequence of the auxiliary role, are subject to

external pressures, from political bodies, faculties, users, etc.;

- are staffed in the higher echelons by personnel with graduate training, making for a highly-educated core staff;
- are administered by professionals who move up from the service ranks, and not by career managers;
- seek identity and domain within a host of communication and information sources in the community at large and in their parent organization.

Librarians serve throughout their professional lives deep within one or more local library organizations that display these characteristics, and beyond that are members of a statewide and national library structure that reflects and reinforces the same outlook and traits. Librarians accept these attributes of their institution without hardly noticing them or reflecting on their implications. Some even react and object when the nature of the library is brought to the surface and articulated. When it is pointed out that libraries often have ill-defined objectives, for example, or that they lack continuing professional-client relations, the first reaction from the librarian is usually one of surprise, and then often of defense. Few practitioners can conceive of any fundamental alteration of the place of libraries in the larger social and communication complex, even though basic changes are occurring in the transmission of information and ideas outside of libraries.

Whether the present role is what should prevail, whether the place and function of the library should be or can be different, is not the province of organization. For the purposes of this volume the agency must be accepted as it is, and its proper structure and internal relationships worked out within these parameters. We are dealing with the organization of the contemporary library, and must take account of its special combination of characteristics. At the same time, the connection between organization on the one hand and purposes, objectives, and priorities on the other must be kept in mind and will be stressed throughout this work.

The book will be composed first of sections on organization

as understood by general theorists, and then of sections applying the general theory to libraries.

So-Called Principles of Organization

Are there really constants and common principles that apply to the factory, the insurance firm, the department store—and the library? There is some evidence that common elements do exist. For example, in large business enterprises executives move from one field to another, and from business to government and even to education, presumably because they possess a competence that can be applied to the production of educated graduates as well as to a government service or a market product. Such recruitment of what are seen to be effective administrators is not totally unknown in the library field, and the practice might be more frequent if the attractions of library directorships were greater. Further, there are management consultant firms that have successfully applied their expertise in widely different establishments, once again including libraries. Studies of communication and human relations within organizations have documented similar patterns in diverse settings. It is safe to say that analogous characteristics run through the fabric of group work.

At the same time we have noted that there are contrasts in management requirements as between the hospital, the university, and the textile mill. The same no doubt applies to the administration of libraries, which can be viewed as a combination of unique elements (bibliographic control, for example) and of elements shared with other enterprises, of which organization is one. We are dealing with both a broad genus and an individual creature.

The problem for library administrators is to identify and separate the two. Their knowledge of library matters derives from extensive professional training and experience, which develops competence in rendering library service. But they have no comparable background in administration. There is thus the danger that management concepts that happen to have grown up in libraries will be accepted as appropriate for the agency, when experience and research in other agencies have shown them to be less than effective. The librarian has a rich heritage of professional skills but only a small accumulation of management skills. The task is to examine the administrative methods that have been passed along within the profession in order to determine which have a tenuous base in library folklore and which derive from hard experience. For the former, the management practices that have grown with the institution, we must take a critical view to see which continue to be viable. And before that, it would be wise to look with equal care at the general precepts that have been developed in management as such, which will be done in the early part of the volume.

It would be a mistake to go overboard and assume that a definitive body of administrative principles exists, and that library managers have only to learn them and apply them to their institutions in place of the traditional patterns. The truth is that administrative theory has not advanced to this finished and universally-applicable stage. On the contrary, research in each generation since the new management approach around the turn of the century has raised basic questions about the "principles" enunciated in the preceding period. Closer examination of group enterprise has repeatedly shown its great variety and complexity. Although ours is a society composed of large-scale organizations, we are still short of understanding just how they work.

References

1. Barnard, Chester I. *The Functions of the Executive.* Cambridge, MA., Harvard University Press, 1966.

2. Drucker, Peter F. *Management: Tasks, Responsibilities, Practices.* New York, Harper and Row, 1974.

3. Pfiffner, John M. and Sherwood, Frank P. *Administrative Organization.* Englewood, N.J., Prentice-Hall, 1960, p. 34.

4. Drucker, Peter F. *Op. cit.,* p. 455.

II EMERGENCE OF A THEORY OF ORGANIZATION

SINCE THE TURN of the century, repeated attempts have been made to set down a body of theory which describes how large-scale group enterprises are organized and how they work. The purpose has been to analyze a distinctive contemporary social structure and thus to guide administrators of our various agencies in discharging their responsibilities. The search for principles began in the late 1800s as industries grew in size and complexity, and then was given impetus by the appearance of the large-scale commercial and governmental enterprises which mark the 20th century. In time attention was also given to service agencies such as schools, universities, and hospitals.

Many of the students of organization have been social scientists: sociologists, social psychologists, economists, and political scientists. They were attracted to the topic because the large work group became a characteristic feature of modern society. People were involved; they earned their livelihoods in organizations and spent significant portions of their lives in them. Their group endeavor produced the material culture and the governmental parameters of the developed nations. A standard of living resulted which was new on the face of the earth. What better topic for social scientists concerned either with group activity or with the role of the individual within large groups?

In recent decades some social scientists have devoted much of their attention to the functioning of organizations, making this the focus of their research and published output. Examples are Herbert Simon, with his analysis of decision-making in business enterprises (he won a Nobel Prize for this work), and Peter Drucker, whose writings have become a beacon light for modern administrators.

A smaller number of the theorists of organization appeared from within industry and business. Reflective individuals, they sought to stand back from the administrator's desk and to gain perspective and insight into what they had been doing.

Relatively few educational administrators have taken time out from their continuing tasks to pass on their experience and understanding, although John Gardner can be cited after he became U.S. Secretary of Education. From within the library ranks, only occasional contributors to the theory of organization come to mind (Erret McDiarmid and Ralph Shaw are examples), possibly because librarians are seldom drawn to their calling because of an interest in administration as such.

While the various theorists have built on the work of their predecessors, it would be a mistake to view organizational theory as a straight-line and cumulative progression from 1900 to the present day. More often than not, the take-off point for each commentator has been disagreement with what came before. Rather than accepting the established doctrine, each newcomer has been critical of previous theory, and proceeded to introduce or emphasize a fresh viewpoint. We thus have a mosaic rather than a single pattern, the pieces to a puzzle and not the completed puzzle itself. This follows from the fact that human organization is most complex and has not been fitted neatly into a finished body of principles. The study of administration is thus the consideration of differing and sometimes contradictory insights, with individual students and managers left to bring the disparate parts together for their own guidance. You can't graduate a certified administrator the way you can graduate a certified cataloger or computer programmer.

This means that library administrators should not skip over to the most recent theories of organization, avoiding earlier history because they consider it passé. There is value in each of the views, even the earliest, and limitations in each, even the most recent. Readers would be wise to extract their own lessons along the way and to attempt their own synthesis at the end.

The progression in organizational theory will be presented in four stages, covering almost a century: The Classical School; The Scientific School; The Revisionists; Students of Individual Motivation. The first two will be dealt with in this chapter and the latter two in the next.

The Early Classical School

Two names stand out in early analysis of contemporary organization: Max Weber and Henri Fayol. They had contrasting backgrounds and came at the problem from different angles. Weber, a German sociologist and economist, developed and analyzed the concept of bureaucracy. Fayol, a French mining engineer and industrialist, emphasized control in organizations. They and their contemporaries fashioned what can be called the "classical" school of organizational theory.

Max Weber and Bureaucracy

Max Weber observed the organizational structure growing up in industry and government at the turn of the century and labeled it "bureaucracy."[1] He did not use the term invidiously, as we do today. Rather he used it to indicate the order or pattern necessary to make large-scale operations work. He noted that those enterprises were productive and efficient that had a hierarchial structure of supervisors and subordinates, with the various superior-subordinate relationships fitted together into a chain of command from top to bottom.

Different degrees of authority adhere to the various levels. Weber noted that in time the authority inheres in the office and not in a particular incumbent. Within this structure, rules can be issued for proper performance, and control exercised to see that the rules are carried out.

Weber saw organization as a system of responsibility as well as of control. The very term "responsible" implies being answerable to something or someone. This may be the staff member's conscience, but more likely is his/her "boss." Both supervisor and supervised recognize this, he maintained, and the effectiveness of the enterprise is jeopardized if workers are unsure to whom they are responsible. Responsibility works both ways, from supervisor to subordinate as well as the other way around. The manager has a responsibility for getting tasks done, even as the worker has a responsibility to perform. If the cabinet fails in republican government, the prime minister has to go; if book processing does not get done within a library in reasonable time, it is the head of the processing unit or even the head of the library who is called to account.

Further, Weber observed that the concept of hierarchy provides for the expertise and contribution of persons of varying backgrounds—in the factory there are the manager, the engineer, the industrial designer, the maintenance man, and the fabricator on the line. In Weber's sense the library is a bureaucracy, with its hierarchy of positions, sections, departments and divisions, with its combination of non-professional, professional and managerial personnel, and with its various specialties of position such as cataloger, bibliographer, circulation staff, reference librarian, and so on. If the attempt were made to combine all these specialties in every worker, each one with the whole range of ability and responsibility, qualified individuals would be most difficult to locate. Even if they were somehow located, there would not be as much production in the factory or as much service in the library, because individuals would lose time in shifting from one role to another ("start-up" time), would have to function at different work stations, would probably lack full equipment at those stations, and would have to engage in some tasks in which they have little or no interest.

No doubt bureaucratic structures had existed long before Weber invented the term, way back to the armies of Alexander and Julius Caesar and even earlier in the building of the Pyramids. Certainly the Roman Catholic Church had long been a bureaucracy, with its system of a Pope, cardinals, bishops, priests and other functionaries. Weber's contribution was to identify, describe, and analyze a structure that had grown up over the years.

Weber saw the same design as appropriate both for the

manufacturing and the service enterprises that appeared with the 20th-century trend to urbanism and the spread of communication and transportation. By this means many people can be coordinated toward a given goal, whether the production of an automobile or the education of the younger generation, the making of computers or the provision of the information on which computer science is based. From this design, along with new technology, has come the prosperity of the industrialized nations and the rich variety of service institutions which we now take for granted.

From the workers' standpoint, the bureaucratic hierarchy provided a place where they could get jobs according to their abilities and could thus share in the new productivity. The structure provided workers with a degree of job security, and the prescribed rules guided them on how to perform. Weber felt that most workers of his time accepted and even welcomed the clear structure and the approved rules. As he saw it, employees tend to adhere to the established organizational structure as part of the bargain that gives them gainful employment. For the more ambitious, the hierarchy offered promotional opportunities.

The hierarchy also established a system of prestige and deference. More privilege and more reward attach to positions higher in the structure, up to the position of president of the corporation or director of the library. A certain allegiance is accorded to the office as such, and this deference applies no matter how worthy the incumbent, whether the head of a department in a library or the President of the United States. The worker looked up at this ladder of prestige and often aspired to climb it.

If bureaucracy had all these advantages, how is it that we now use the term in its derogatory sense? Have we simply rejected the original meaning? Not entirely, for there were seeds in the hierarchical concept that have since borne bitter fruit. While the concept prevailed and continues to our day, it had within it conditions governing work and assumptions concerning human motivation that have been challenged by subsequent analysts of organization. We will note these challenges as this account of organizational theory continues.

Henri Fayol and Control

Fayol took time late in his industrial career, just before and during World War I, to generalize from what he had learned in directing large-scale mining operations.[2] Plan and control were his watchwords. He broke the management function down into Planning, Organizing, Command, Coordination, and Control. His writing has an autocratic tone not in accord with the present-day literature of the field, but it exerted an influence when administrators were struggling to handle burgeoning industrial enterprises in the early decades of the century, and his methods are practiced today by some hard-driving managers who run a "tight ship." Fayol's emphasis can be gathered from the titles of various of his chapters: Authority, Discipline, Unity of Command, Unity of Direction, Subordination of Individual Interest to General Interest. While his views are out-of-step with contemporary theory, they still repay consideration by the administrator awash in permissive supervision, participatory management, and other views that have swung the pendulum from concern about results to concern about participants.

Thus far administrators had a recommended structure and guidance on control within that structure. While the works of Max Weber and Henri Fayol are seldom read these days, it is worth going back to this early foundation, if for no other reason than because much of what followed in organizational theory took off from this base.

The "Scientific" School

Parallel with classical theory there emerged early an effort to be more objective and experimental about how group enterprises function and how to get maximum production from them. Here again the work of two contrasting individuals stand out: Luther Gulick and Frederick Taylor. Again we have one theorist and one practitioner. Luther Gulick built directly on the earlier work of Weber and Fayol, seeking to reduce their ideas to principles. Frederick Taylor, by contrast, started on his own within the shop, studying individuals and their work methods.

Both sought to invest their concepts with the aura of science which was increasingly revered as we moved into the 20th century. Gulick claimed a "science of administration" and Taylor termed his contribution "scientific management." Whether either body of organizational theory deserved the term is a moot point—certainly they have not proven to have the permanence of scientific principles—but they did make a contribution under whatever name is applied.

Luther Gulick and the Early Formulation of Principles

Gulick picked up the hierarchical concept and went on to enunciate principles of organization that are still followed even though they have been subjected to pointed criticism in the interval. He was an influential figure not only in the academic study of administration but also in the actual organization of government in the early days of the New Deal, with its expanded activity to combat severe economic depression.

With such colleagues as Stanley Urwin and others, he elaborated on and systematized the bureaucratic structure. Principles were hopefully set forth as a "science of administration."[3] Gulick spoke of "scientific knowledge and control in the world of human affairs."[4] The principles were greeted with acclaim from many sides, and universities in the 1930s assiduously taught them. The practitioner had a guide to performance, and the university had a body of material that could be conveyed to aspiring managers. As we will see, the euphoria was short-lived.

Gulick elaborated on Fayol's functions of management and coined the well-known acronym POSDCORB, standing for Planning, Organizing, Staffing, Directing, Coordinating, Reporting, Budgeting. There was value in such an approach for it broke down a complex activity into component parts: dissecting and labeling is one of the first steps of science. At the same time one can ask exactly what is gained by putting names to functions.

The so-called "science" of administration rested on a half-dozen concepts, which Gulick and his colleagues tended to call "principles" but which some of the later critics call "proverbs." The most important of the concepts were unity of command, limited span of control, specialization of tasks, line and staff officers, and departmental structure by purpose, process, clientele, or place. All were designed to maintain control and to coordinate workers and sections into a unified whole.

Unity of command simply prescribed one designated superior for each subordinate, with both boss and worker knowing who was who. This avoids the uncertainity and confusion when one boss or foreman with a degree of authority tells the worker to do one thing, while another authority figure tells him/her to do another. Designated supervisors know they have responsibility for instructing certain individuals and for checking on their performance. Subordinates have the advantage of knowing where they stand and who to turn to for further guidance.

How many individuals should the administrator supervise? The principles did not prescribe any exact number for the span of control, but stressed that the span must be kept small enough so that adequate control could be exercised. When numbers were mentioned they were often in the range of six to eight, with smaller numbers recommended for the higher echelons (director, president, general manager) and larger numbers for lower down the line (foremen, supervisors, department heads). Thus a pyramid was formed, narrower at the top and wider at the bottom. Caution was recommended in simply adding to the span of control as an enterprise grew in size; this would weaken the supervision exercised. Growth in a business or agency called for reorganization in order to adhere to the principle of limited span of control.

But reorganization without broadening the span of control usually means adding to the pyramid, to the point where administration becomes top-heavy. Therefore we now know that it is worth considering a broader span as enterprises grow, an alternative not approved by Gulick. The human factor that must be taken into account is how closely it is necessary to supervise staff members. If proper motivation and communication are maintained, we have since learned, the span of control can often be increased, with attendant advantages. Indeed, this insight has resulted in recent years in widespread "downsizing" in the managerial ranks of business corporations. The Gulick concept of the "tight ship" had resulted in an excess of middle managers, some of whom could be dispensed with when more reliance was placed on individual workers.

Within the hierarchy, according to the principles, individuals and sections were to have special skills and distinct responsibilities, each part of a mosaic that together makes a pattern, a team of specialists coordinated to pursue a common end. One has only to look around at large-scale enterprise, whether the General Electric Co. or the United States Department of the Interior, to be impressed with the wide range of specialties involved, and impressed also that for the most part they seem to be working together, thanks to the bureaucratic structure.

One of the categories of specialization introduced by the early theorists was that of line and staff officers. This had developed in armies, with combat units at the front and planning, engineering, supply, and other support units behind them. The same structure came also to apply in the factory, with workers on the line, and accounting, personnel, and maintenance units backing them up. The purpose is to extend the executive's capacity to coordinate a large and disparate enterprise; specialized assistants to the chief are to help with record-keeping, fact-finding, and planning, in essence expanding the chief administrator's intellectual resources. Some staff units engage directly in research and planning, while others carry responsibility for parts of the administrative function, such as accounting, personnel, and physical maintenance. To retain control and unity of command, authority was to remain and reside in the line, with the staff units limited to serving, advising, and reinforcing the line. Staff officers theoretically function only through the chief executive.

As enterprises grow, not just a superior-subordinate relationship is necessary, but this scalar principle is to be extended in a structure of departments. The purpose of departments, according to the "science of administration," is to be clear and distinct, each constituting an identified specialty needed by the agency. The theoreticians identified departmentalization by purpose, by process, by clientele, and by place or territory. An agency might well need more than one of these types. In a latter section we will analyze the mix of departments found in libraries.

Gulick's formulation was extended and refined by several contemporaries, particularly two General Motors executives, James Mooney and Alan Reiley.[5] Their model stressed four of the "principles": the coordinative principle, the scalar principle, the functional principle, and the concept of staff and line. By the 1920s the hierarchical structure was firmly in place, and accounted for the high productivity of American business and industry.

One can see that the developers of a so-called science of administration were seeking neat and clear organization in the face of mounting and sprawling growth in manufacturing and service activities. They sought control of escalating complexity. To a considerable degree the structures advocated came to prevail and are familiar to us today. Whether the pioneers actually provided new insight which then influenced subsequent development or whether they simply described a system that had grown naturally and would have prevailed in any case is a moot point. What is clear is that the hierarchical structure, despite criticism over the years, persists to this day. Most recent "advances" in organization are either modifications of the basic concepts or isolated experiments within large scalar structures that continue much as originally described by Weber, Fayol, and Gulick.

But the reflective reader of both the "classical" and "scientific" literature of organization is struck by its didactic, polemical character. Each writer reached definite conclusions and set them down in no uncertain terms. Light had dawned, the puzzle was solved, and the administrator was handed a set of tenets, usually with few qualifications or modifications. Learn these principles and go forth and run an organization. Unfortunately the administrative life is not that clear and simple, as we will see after fitting Frederick Taylor and Scientific Management into the picture.

The Scientific Management School

Just about when the classical theorists were first promulgating their principles, a separate theme entered organization under the term "scientific management." This theme stressed operations, the details of production, whereas we have seen that the theoretical group stressed structure. One aimed at control, while this new effort aimed at efficiency.

Evidently both groups sought the prestige of the natural sciences that were blossoming in their time. The classical school referred to the "science" of administration and the time-and-motion study group to "scientific" management, although neither is a science if the term is given any exact meaning. What they do represent is a rational and systematic approach to what goes on in large-scale organizations.

Frederick Taylor founded the scientific management school.[6] His work was done prior to World War I, when a new factory system was emerging, to which he was a direct contributor. Trained as an engineer, he early sought out a job as a manual laborer in a steel company, going on from there to the position of chief engineer. Clearly a creative individual, he invented over 100 devices on which he gained patents.

Taylor systematically studied and measured shop operating procedures. Menial tasks came under his scrutiny, such as shoveling coal; he determined the optimum load for each heave, the best size of the shovel, and the most productive sequence of movements. Skilled operations such as lathe work also were analyzed. Particular attention was paid to the tools used.

Taylor maintained that there is one best way to do most tasks, and that the best way could be found by observation and measurement. The stop watch was one of his favored instruments. He established time standards, the amount of time required to complete a task if the most efficient procedures were used, and applied the standard to the worker on the job. With objectively established standards of performance in hand, he went on to the next logical step of differential piece rates as a basis for remuneration. Now a means of control had been devised for the individual employee, even as the classical theorists had devised a means for control of the group.

In 1910 scientific management gained national recognition in hearings on proposed increases in railroad rates. Louis Brandeis, later an eminent member of the Supreme Court, argued that increases could not be justified until scientific management was applied to all aspects of running a railroad, and he won his case. Would that the same principle were applied to a variety of public utilities today, before rate increases are granted.

Over the years the concept of measurement and time standards for production methods became increasingly precise. The therblig as a unit of work was invented, comparable to a pound of pressure or an ampere of current in the physical world. Rules were formulated for best use of the hands (a parallel circular motion of both hands is preferred) and of the feet (often to activate holding devices so that both hands remain free). The assembly line can be said to be an outgrowth of scientific management, as can later automation of production. What started as one man at a work station with a stop-watch can be traced through to present-day production robots.

Scientific management led to industrial engineering. Time-and-motion study became an exact discipline, operations analysis and job evaluation were developed, quality control was added. One of Taylor's leading disciples, Frank Gilbreth, established a consulting firm with his wife that specialized in the reduction of fatigue and waste motion in plant operation. Thus Frederick Taylor and those who followed revolutionized industrial production.

To a degree the scientific management concept spread to such non-industrial endeavors as farm management, hotel operations, airline functions, retail stores, and banks. Office clerical pools are organized according to the same principles. The Gilbreths applied this approach to work in the home, making for the efficient kitchen. But some fields, and particularly education in its various modes, have been relatively untouched. Teachers fundamentally perform today as in the past, and the same holds true for librarians.

Scientific management and industrial engineering were not

imposed without criticism. The charge is that Taylor and his later cohorts considered human beings as machines, which are to function in a certain way and at a certain speed. Physical factors are stressed: motion, strength, muscular coordination. A running battle has been waged between labor unions and management on this account. In our personal lives, we all have had the experience of continuing to do some tasks in a way that we recognize to be less than fully efficient, for the reason that we get more satisfaction out of the familiar procedure. Taylor had no room in his system for the satisfaction of the worker—after all, the purpose was production, not personal fulfillment.

Industrial engineers respond to such criticism with the claim that most workers feel better when their performance is at a high level; there is satisfaction in being efficient. Further, with performance standards established, the individual can exceed them and thus get additional reward for additional output. On a broader scale, all in the society benefit from greater production and a healthy economy. The scientific management movement must be given credit for shifting the focus from general principles to individual human beings. A half-century later this would blossom into a humanistic approach to organization and supervision.

Taylor himself comes through as a paradoxical figure. The official biography portrays a person of considerable creativity, personal integrity, and convincing powers of persuasion.[7] Later revisionist work pictures a more complex and controversial individual. Here is the judgment of a recent biographer with strong interest in the labor movement:

> Sensitive in the extreme to relations among businessmen, he was indifferent, often ruthless, in his relations with workers, particularly those workers who were least able to defend themselves. A man of uncompromising principles in dealings with his economic and social equals, he was a man of expediency in dealings with his social inferiors. A reformer in one sphere, he was a reactionary in others.[8]

Whatever the final judgment, Frederick W. Taylor was a

significant contributor to the emergence of the "new factory system" prior to World War I, a system marked by the rational organization of work and changes in the methods of foreman-ship. His legacy has extended over the years to our time in the form of analytical approaches to management.

So what does all this have to do with libraries? Librarians as professionals exercise judgment, and judgment is not subject to motion study and time standards. However, record-keeping, routine processing, and physical handling of multiple resources constitute sizeable portions of the work that goes on in libraries. The scientific management movement, so important not only to manufacturing concerns but also to various commercial and record-keeping activities, may well have application to libraries.

Revision of the Classical Concepts and Principles

In the last thirty-five years, a steady barrage of criticism has been leveled at the simple hierarchical structure and the proclaimed principles of organization. The counter-attack, like the original formulation, has come mainly from social scientists looking at industry, business, government and service enterprises as group organizations, i.e., assemblages of people gathered to pursue an organizational as distinct from a personal goal. Some of the most concentrated fire has come from Herbert Simon,[9] used by him to clear the ground for his examination of decision-making in group enterprises.

The criticisms tend to cluster around two main points:

1. Organization is far more complex than shown by the neat hierarchical structure and the official chain of command.
2. The so-called principles of organization assume pas-sive, obedient workers without individual goals or self-motivation, and therefore do not accord with the real world.

The second of these criticisms, having to do with the role

of individuals within organizations, predominates in current administrative theory, and will be developed at some length in a later section of this volume. For the moment, attention will be given to those several factors that affect and modify the classical model, challenging its neat formulation.

At least four sets of forces work on the basic hierarchical structure of an enterprise: an unofficial and informal organization that builds up outside the official hierarchy, compartmentalization into distinct jobs and departments, the influence of specialized and staff positions, and the pressure of external forces outside the enterprise. Each of these has an effect, sometimes reinforcing and sometimes working against the formal hierarchy and chain of command. What workers actually do, what standards they maintain, what happens to their morale, is determined by the combination of these several influences. Sensitive, flexible administrators are tuned into several wavelengths and not rigidly focused on the chain of command. Unless they have this sensitivity, they will miss or misunderstand an important part of what goes on in the enterprises for which they are responsible.

A final criticism directed against the classic concept is that it inhibits change and innovation. In the long run this could be the most serious shortcoming of the hierarchical principle. This judgment will be examined after a review of the effects of informal organization, of compartmentalization, of specialization, and of external relations.

The Informal Organization

To comprehend an organization, one must grasp both its authority structure, as reflected in its organization chart, and its power structure, as reflected in actual spheres of influence. The two may be the same, but this is not often the case. Authority naturally bestows a certain amount of power, but other nuclei of influence grow up in an organization.

Almost inevitably there are stronger and weaker points within an enterprise, either because of differences among incumbents in positions or because of differences in kinds of work done. One or another staff member or unit chief, presumably neither above nor below other individuals and unit heads in the scheme of things, comes to exercise more or less influence than equivalent colleagues. One or another group—a union, the professional association, department heads, specialists—may hold power beyond the numbers in their ranks. Influence may result from greater experience, or greater knowledge, or clearer judgment, or simple aggressiveness, or some combination of these. Power tends to migrate to certain types of assignments: those controlling finance, for example, or those at the nexus of communication lines, or those having to do with expanding rather than contracting aspects of an enterprise. Thus from several sides the formal organization is modified and even on occasion threatened or thwarted by informal relationships within the agency.

The most common cause of growth of a power structure separate from the hierarchy of authority is limitations or weaknesses of incumbents in management positions. Organizations have a tendency to adjust to shortcomings in management; someone or some group steps forward to get done what has to be done. Someone has got to have ideas, someone has got to accept responsibility, someone must lead if there is a vacuum in leadership.

Stepping forward, the individual may step out of role and rank. Some co-workers accept this because they know that the gap must be filled if the corporate goal is to be accomplished, and they are grateful when strong individuals pick up the mantle. But others are resentful, either because they are organization-minded and do not want to see the established order altered, or because they are jealous and wish that they had assumed the additional role. Informal power centers may get a moribund enterprise moving again, or may exacerbate latent hostilities. Those who assume the mantle are characterized as "moving spirits" by one faction and as "empire builders" by another.

There are occasions when one or more subordinates actually control their official superiors. This comes about, for instance, when a department head knows less about an operation than a worker on the line—the head of cataloging about the classification of government documents, or the head of the science department who is weak in part of the science spectrum and must depend on subordinates with graduate degrees in these fields. The reversal of roles may also result from personality differences, a compliant individual being in nominal control and a dominant individual in actual control. Library directors have been appointed to headships, particularly from the outside, only to discover that one or a combination of strong-minded individuals within the staff actually call the shots, and indeed were a factor in undermining the previous director. Even distance can modify the superior-subordinate relationship, with the branch librarian responding more to community or faculty pressures than to official dicta.

Superior position in the hierarchy gives the right to command, but it does not automatically bestow the capacity to command. Where this capacity is weak or lacking, decisions are not made, or if made are obeyed reluctantly if at all. This situation arises when managers are appointed who are not equal to the task. Libraries are not immune to this weakness; in fact, they are likely to get their full share of inadequate middle and senior managers because administrators are drawn from the professional ranks, which means from among those who have demonstrated service capacity but not necessarily management capacity.

Influence centers outside the formal hierarchy are not necessarily destructive. Under strong central leadership they can be controlled and used as constructive forces, giving direction and balance and vitality to an enterprise without constantly waiting on inspiration or directions from the front office. Individuals and units within the agency do not naturally plot to challenge established authority. On the contrary, when the enterprise is effective and individuals within it are recognized for their contributions, the tendency is for the informal affiliations to support the formal structure. The two together make the organization "go." But the unofficial power centers are there, ready to move in troubled times and/or when confidence in the administration declines. These deviations add to the complexity of organizations, and when allowed to get out of bounds can make for a house divided against itself.

It is easy to dismiss the separate groups as made up of dissident individuals who are against whatever authority exists and individuals on their own ego trips. In many cases this would be incorrect, for some of the most able and supportive staff members may be centers of power. It is only when such individuals go over and join with actual dissidents that a significant split occurs and parts of the organization start to work against each other.

Unions are sometimes a magnet for persons who feel left out and want to have a say in the enterprise. If their ranks include genuine power figures, or if they attract such in times of stress, the union groups may thus acquire a leadership that moves them into positions of influence. Without such figures, unions are only another portion of the informal hierarchy.

When a deep division does occur, with opposing factions forming and with established officials under open challenge, the conflict cannot be readily resolved. Positions once taken are often defended for their own sake. At a certain point reconciliation is most difficult to achieve. A power struggle ensues. The formal structure has authority on its side. The opposition within the staff has comradeship and a sense of injury or righteousness to sustain it. Which will prevail depends on who can hold out longest. In time, if the opposition holds out, management compromises or resigns. If management prevails, overt resistance subsides but may go underground. Or the established authority may grasp at or even create an issue or crisis that diverts attention and for a time subverts the opposition—political leaders have learned to use this tactic.

In libraries as elsewhere the informal power structure becomes more active in time of crisis, such as a severe cut in funds. Which way the informal influences go may determine how the agency weathers the storm. If officials and workers close ranks and join hands, suitable adjustments become possible. If they are antagonistic, the problem is compounded.

The worker within a library, as in other organizations, must come to identify unofficial influence centers. This takes a little effort, because the informal power structure is not neatly recorded, nor is it immediately evident to the newcomer. But experience teaches rapidly; co-workers are glad to give instructions. The employee soon learns who "knows," who "to see" to get something done, whose views carry weight beyond their formal status.

The depth of feeling of members about the functioning of an organization depends on the importance of that enterprise to the individual. Local service clubs, cultural groups, and political parties may not arouse much reaction as to who is in control from the rank and file of members even though it is a matter of deep concern to the minority most involved. Associations organized around special interests or around professional affiliations—the American Library Association, for example—may stimulate greater concern, for the individuals have more of a stake in their success. The strongest feelings are often directed to the workplace and the employing organization, for this determines the livelihood of individuals and occupies a large segment of their time. When both the livelihood and special interest of the individual are combined, as in employment of a professional in a library, the incumbent may be particularly sensitive to the power structure and emotionally concerned as to whether it is a positive or negative force. Most librarians, by virtue of working in an organization rather than on their own, are parties both to official centers and to influence centers within their agency.

The informal power hierarchy is only one source of outside and sometimes counter-influence on the established chain of command. The limited span of control advocated by the classical writers is another source. Holding to a span of control of five or six individuals or units, even a relatively small group of 200 or 300 workers requires four or five levels of command between the mechanic on the assembly line or the clerk at the library circulation desk and the top echelon. Workers feel distant and isolated, and are open to any information source or influence affiliation that promises to bring them closer to the center of decision. In other words, they are ready to enlist in the informal organization.

Communication and the Informal Organization

Communication plays a part in this process. The chain of command is also a chain of communication. Official information flows through the chain, as do formal directives. Theoretically this is a two-way deal, with ideas, problems, and complaints flowing upward as well as commands coming down. In the usual autocratic system, there are more orders flowing down than suggestions flowing up. The multi-level chain of command is a far less than perfect channel of communication. Information and orders flowing down can be distorted, delayed, or even lost. Intelligence flowing upward is subject to the same natural failings, but in addition may encounter actual sabotage, if any one of the transmitters in the line believes there is personal advantage in doing so. The suggestion from a worker may be changed to fit the transmitters' idea or the complaint may be buried because it reflects upon the stewardship of the superior officer. As we know from another volume in this series,[10] blocked or distorted communication is like failure or malfunction of an organ in the body. Results may vary from inconvenience to incapacity.

"Follow channels," the communicator is told, and an important observation may be lost. "The information didn't reach me," the staff member responds. Thus are misinformation and red tape nurtured, and the very control jeopardized which the hierarchy is designed to achieve.

Once again the individual worker or the unit head suffering from clogging in the official information channels may, under the circumstances, turn to unofficial channels. The informal organization expands, achieving a role not envisioned by the designers of the classic model. It is worth noting that this non-official influence comes about in most cases not because of saboteurs within the enterprise but because of responsible, concerned staff members seeking sincerely to get their job done and finding it hard to do so in the face of a rigid structure.

Compartmentalization of Workers

The classical school stressed the concept of division of work, with each category of staff member to be given a clear and distinct job, and with the various categories separate from each other. Each employee would go into a slot. There would be laborers, machine operators, engineers, tool maintenance staff, stockmen, clean-up crew, and others, even as in libraries there would be acquisition clerks, catalogers, bibliographers, reference personnel, circulation staff, maintenance crew, and so on. The range of tasks that in a very small factory (or library) are done by one or a few workers, each engaging in a variety of operations, is in the larger hierarchical structure divided into separate jobs. The rationale is that the individual performing one task can be selected specifically for that assignment, he or she will learn by repeated performance of the same function, and the work station and the necessary tools can be organized for efficiency.

As a result contemporary workers find themselves in compartments. They have a given task and are to repeat it as often as there is demand. Their orientation is to that assignment, not to other parts of the enterprise, nor to its end product or purpose. Workers often report isolation and boredom within the compartment. It is indicative that under participatory management, where workers themselves have input on how work should be organized, they often request a "team" structure with a group of employees working together as a more or less complete operation, each member engaging in all or several steps in the operation.

When enough workers engage in the same task, a department is established. According to the classical view, each department is to have a function clear and distinct from that of other departments. Now the worker is within an individual slot within a group component.

Communication within a department is likely to be easy and frequent. But between departments the story is different. Theoretically contact for official purposes is to be made through the heads of the respective departments, hopefully going on from there to all members. Unofficially, contact and communication across departmental lines tend to be sporadic and incomplete.

The result is that the scalar plan requires an extra measure of coordination. Meshing of operations may occur naturally between individual workers in a compartment, but not between departments. As one measure, ways must be found to promote communication across the lines. As another, division officers above the departments may be inserted (Head of Technical Services, Coordinator of Public Services), thus adding to the administrative overhead and increasing the distance between worker and the front office.

Compartmentalization may not adversely affect the unskilled or semi-skilled worker. The immediate task and immediate contacts, along with supervision, may satisfy both the practical and psychic needs of the job. But skilled workers, and particularly professionals, by training have a wider view and by inclination have a wider interest. They are the ones who sense the compartment walls and would like to know what is going on elsewhere. Indeed, they would be better able to make decisions if they had this knowledge.

If the purpose of organization is, as we have said, to assign and mobilize staff in pursuance of a common purpose or product, then the classical hierarchy structure has characteristics that work against this end, and that can be overcome only by a complex and expensive super-structure of coordination.

The point is not that the classical hierarchy has been discredited, but that it has serious limitations. It prevails widely to this day, but is under increasing stress. For some time social scientists have pointed to its shortcomings. More recently workers themselves have rebelled, seeking greater variety of work assignments, more freedom in judgment on the job, more participation in policy decisions. Large-scale organization—in industry, business, government, education, health care, and other fields—can be viewed as a conflict of traditional control on the one hand and of flexibility and freedom on the other. A balance is being sought between the goals of the organization and the goals of the workers within the organization.

Specialists and Staff Officers

Classical theory from the beginning has recognized and approved the role of specialists within organizations, and in particular has encouraged the use of staff officers. What the theory did not recognize was the possible inconsistency between this concept and the basic tenet of unity of command; in practice both highly technical staff (computer specialists in libraries, for example) and standard staff officers (personnel specialists, for example) can work against unified control.

Staff officers are official and approved components in the structure. Common examples are the finance officer, the personnel specialist, and the maintenance head. Those who account for money often play a role in its allocation, thus influencing the budget of units within the organization. The personnel office often recruits staff, controls or at least influences promotions and transfers, and affects salary scales, thus bearing directly on staff members. Even the building and maintenance division leaves its impress by completing or neglecting repairs, by thorough or shoddy cleaning.

Theoretically these various "staff" or "support" offices should be completely in step with the line divisions, and in fact in the textbooks are described as having "no authority" and only "advisory functions." But reality is often not the same as the ideal. Often the line officer must learn to dominate the support services or, failing this, will be dominated by them. While it would be a mistake to see the various divisions of an organization as self-centered and warring fiefdoms, many line administrators have felt that they had to protect their responsibilities from the enemy within the enterprise.

On the national scene, we note as an example, the strategic role of the Office of Management and Budget. While a staff rather than a line office, this agency not only watches over money allocations to operating departments but, beyond that, influences the financial policies on which the government bases its planning. Many a department head, theoretically responsible to the President within the concept of unity of command, has found it politic to listen closely to the Director of the OMB. The example, while exceptional in being at the level of national government, also illustrates a related point. For specialized staff positions, capable and strong individuals are naturally sought. The greater their expertise and the stronger their personalities, the more line officers find themselves not in a unity of command, or even a duality, but under a multiplicity of forces that determine what can and cannot be done.

Within libraries an instructive example is the position of Coordinator of Children's Service, which appears in many large public libraries. In the organization chart this is usually a "staff" position; that is, it carries no authority in service departments and branches. Yet, with a strong incumbent, its influence is pervasive. In fact, a half-dozen eminent children's coordinators have left their clear mark on the design of children's library service in the United States. Their power has been out of proportion to their position. In coming years, individuals responsible for computerized services are likely to have a similar influence throughout the libraries they serve.

The children's librarian in a branch or department has learned to serve two bosses. The branch or department head controls building and hours and operations. The central coordinator sets policies and service programs. Budget usually falls somewhere between the two. This violates Gulick's first principle, but it has resulted in a distinctive and successful part of public library service.

Specialists may appear who are more line than staff officers, yet whose influence extends well beyond their own department or formal domain. This can occur when the officer with special background is responsible for a part of the total enterprise that by policy is being stressed, and/or when that officer is responsible for a new and growing aspect of the endeavor. An example of the former is the Secretary of Defense in the national government at a time when military preparation is given priority. An example of the latter is the head of a computer unit in a library, at a time when computerization is just coming to apply in various parts of the agency. While such individuals may not issue direct orders to personnel in other departments, their internal decisions may have wide repercussions and their opinions may carry extra weight. For practical purposes both the "orders" of the supervisor and the counsel of the technical expert may prevail, assuming the two work together. If not, there is conflict in the chain of command, and this is as likely to be resolved in favor of the specialist as of the line officer. The specialist may be closer to where the agency is going, while the line officer may be tied to the past, seeking more to keep the enterprise on course than to chart new directions. In the ideal structure, the specialist is fully sensitive to the existing organization and the middle manager is open to fresh incentives, but this does not always hold in the real world.

Specialists in an organization increase the amount of communication that must be exchanged and they also increase its technical content. Theoretically the distribution of information from staff officers and technical specialists should "go up through channels," and then down again to the action point, flowing through the various levels of the hierarchy. With staff officers and technical experts the volume of communication increases, and we have seen that often the formal information channels in agencies already suffer from overload. It is obviously important in a library, as elsewhere, for information about finances or personnel or computerized processing to be delivered promptly, accurately, and thoroughly. Staff officers therefore tend to build up separate and direct means of communication, outside of established channels. A common form is the bulletin from the personnel office directly to individual workers.

Opening of unofficial channels also works the other way. Department heads or workers on the line need information or guidance on matters beyond their ken. The individual stops in at the personnel office to get the matter straightened out; the department head calls the subject expert or the cataloger or the head of rare books for guidance on how to proceed.

This is normal operation, in most cases to be encouraged. After all, it would take much longer to go through channels. For the most part no orders are being altered and it is only advice and not directives that are exchanged. Usually the effect is to widen the flow of information and facilitate the making of decisions. But the content of this informal communication may not be known by line officers who should be privy to it. On occasion the word from the personnel office may contradict what the line officer has understood, or the information from the subject specialist may go counter to standard practice. In any case, the informal channels, once opened, tend to be used with greater frequency.

The neat classical pattern is thus further expanded, modified, and even distended. All of this becomes part of the "real" organization and contributes to its success or failure. In the process the structure advocated by the classical school as a means of control of disparate parts is supplemented, diffused, and in some cases weakened.

External Relations

An aspect of organization not considered at all by Weber, Fayol, and Gulick is what might be called the corporate structure in the private sector and the structure of governance in the public sector. Attention early, and to a great extent to this day, has concentrated more on internal relations, those within the enterprise, and not on forces from the outside that have an effect on policy and organization. This is a kind of third dimension, added to the official hierarchy and the informal pattern of communication, information, and guidance.

Few organizations exist without some external pressures or controls. Those at the top of a business enterprise have stockholders, government, and customers with whom to contend. The public library director has a board of trustees, a municipal government, users, and the general public with whom to be concerned; the academic library director has the president of the institution, the faculty, the faculty senate, and the students with whom to work; the school librarian has the principal, the superintendent, the board of education, and the electorate; the special librarian is affected by the corporate structure.

So the apex of the internal pyramid is not really the top of the hierarchy. Some writers have suggested that an inverted pyramid be placed above the chief executive.[11] Here the director is at the bottom rather than at the top of the hierarchy. But in actual practice this diagram is as subject to modification as the internal organization chart, because all contacts from outside do not flow through the single director.

The external forces also extend to operations. The civil

service of a city determines various personnel practices; education decisions taken by the faculty senate may change selection and reserve practices within the college library; the procurement practices of the business concern may affect the book-ordering procedures of the special library. Although not usually considered part of "organization" as such, these external relations constitute a chain of control above them with which administrators have to work as surely as they work with the chain of control below them.

Not only the head librarian is subject to these external influences. Staff groups, for instance, have learned that trustee decisions affect their well-being and have frequently sought and obtained recognized representation at board meetings. In the academic setting, decisions made on faculty salaries, for example, may or may not also apply to library salaries. The control from the outside can intrude into regular contact with the public. A branch librarian may be the recipient of a protest by a local group against titles in the collection, which goes on to the director and in turn to the board, and eventually involves segments of the public, and even the courts. Just try to diagram such an issue in the standard hierarchical chart!

External influences extend into community relations, politics, law, and budgets, and are therefore beyond the scope of the present work. They are treated in other volumes in this series, on the legal basis of libraries, on planning, on public relations, and on finance.

Resistance to Change and Improvement

Perhaps the most telling criticism that has been leveled against the classical theory of organization is that it inhibits innovation and change.[12] The theory was formulated when an era of mass production was opening. Mass production called for large-scale industrial plants with many workers engaged in a multiplicity of tasks, and this in turn for means to bring the complex operation under control. The challenge had to be met and the scalar structure for control was adopted, right down to the assembly line. Few could see far into the revolutionary transformation that would mark the 20th century. New technology, rapid communication, the expanding role of government, changing concepts of individualism, were not anticipated. Weber, Fayol, and Gulick seldom refer to flexibility or reorganization, or even periodic review.

On the contrary, the very strength of the hierarchy concept is its favoring of continuity and the status quo. It is a means of control and of continuation. There was production to be achieved, and no time for variation, experimentation, and conflict. Workers knew their jobs, managers knew their responsibilities, and the goal was production and profits. Innovation was discouraged in the formal organization. The worker got along more comfortably and the manager avoided new problems if the enterprise was kept on track.

Resistance to change works both up and down the line in the typical hierarchy. Employees at production and service points perceive some needed adjustment in policy or method and seek to pass on the word to middle management. However, such ideas may be disruptive of the established order and, furthermore, may imply a criticism of the supervisors, so they are suppressed. If the proposals go on to central administration they may be disregarded there, for general as well as middle managers become entrenched. Conversely, the front office may seek change and direct or encourage adjustments down the line, only to meet resistance from supervisors and/or workers. In government the "bureaucracy" and in industry the labor unions have long been charged with obstruction of needed improvements.

Middle managers are a key link in maintaining the status quo. They are cast in the role of top sergeants or petty officers, carrying out prescribed operations by prescribed methods. The good department or branch head in a library learns to follow the party line. Creativity, initiative, variation are not expected of them, and indeed may bring raised eyebrows if not disciplinary action. "We can't have all our branches going off any way they want," says the branch supervisor. The prevalent hierarchical structure is better fitted for keeping an enterprise on course than for steering it in new directions.

From the individual staff member's standpoint, the middle

manager in this traditional conception is the boss or supervisor. Workers are taught by their supervisors what to do, when, and in what way. To the extent that they conform, they are not disturbed, they receive good performance ratings, and in time they are duly eligible for promotion. On the other hand, the professional at the reference station and the clerk at the circulation desk who raise questions about procedures, who experiment with new methods, who make suggestions that could disrupt established practice are often brought back into line by peer pressure or supervisory indifference.

It would of course be an exaggeration to maintain that such rigidity inevitably occurs, whether in libraries or other enterprises. Some workers are creative and some managers are flexible. But the point is that the system, the hierarchical structure on which we depend, by its nature resists change and inhibits innovation. Here again libraries are not immune; in a later section of this volume we will note that libraries have experienced relatively little basic change since the prevailing structure was adopted, almost a century ago, despite the fact that these same years have seen profound changes in the provision of the product which libraries purvey, recorded knowledge and information.

Both workers and management settle into a pattern in which they are comfortable, and the hierarchical structure encourages them to maintain that relationship. Indeed they usually are not conscious that they are resisting needed change, and would protest angrily if so accused. This can be observed on the one hand in a library even of limited size, and on the other in the colossus of the federal government, which every recent President has tried to reduce without success.

The source of our present distaste for bureaucracy is evident. Instead of meaning effective control toward a shared goal, as originally conceived by Weber, the term now indicates rigidity, perfunctory performance, and red tape, with the goal obscured or forgotten. We apply the derogatory term in particular to government, which is a paradox, because government as much as industry has had to be adjustable to cope with world war and international conflict, with economic depression and unemployment, with civil rights issues and special interests.

What happens within a unit of government is that the original purpose that brought the agency into existence no longer holds because of change of one kind or another, but the agency— which means the supervisors and workers who comprise it— has a tendency to continue as before. As the goal fades, prevailing methods become all the more important to the worker. After all, persons on the job need something to give point and purpose to their endeavors. But because the goal is lost, enthusiasm and dedication weaken. Those workers who sense what is happening and protest are squashed or ignored, and soon subside or leave. Ritual alone holds the organization together.

Preventing Stagnation

Every enterprise needs constant attention to guard against bureaucracy in this inhibitive sense. The seeds are there in the very organization that made the agency effective in the first place. Either self-scrutiny and renewal are exercised or it drifts and in time is bypassed by other services or is forced into traumatic reorganization. Earlier examples in the private sector are railroads and textiles; a more recent one is the automobile industry.

How is stagnation to be avoided? Is there some alternative to the bureaucratic structure? Not really, although participatory management is sometimes advanced as the solution. In a sense the bulk of this volume is devoted to means to keep an organization flexible and effective, while retaining the control and coordination provided by the "principles" of administration.

For the present, a positive element can be introduced by referring to the work of John Gardner on excellence and self-renewal. "Most ailing organizations have developed a functional blindness to their own defects, they are not suffering because they can't *solve* their problems but because they won't *see* their problems."[13] Listening at a national convention of librarians, as participants discuss refinement of procedures while a communication revolution mounts around them, leads one to suspect that this comment was really directed at librarians.

Gardner goes on to suggest various guidelines for keeping an organization vital:

1. Recruit and develop talent;
2. Provide career structure for advancement;
3. Make employees feel part of the organization;
4. Build in provision for self-criticism;
5. Maintain adequate internal communication;
6. Evaluate and eliminate unnecessary policies and procedures;
7. Combat vested interests on the part of groups;
8. Concentrate on what the enterprise is to become, not what it has been.

A new dilemma arises in the environment of the last decade, when retrenchment rather than expansion is confronted by various parts of both the private and the public sectors. The standard hierarchy had earlier proved to be adjustable to expansion along established lines. With more units of production to be fabricated, or more people to be served, one could readily add more divisions, thus widening the pyramid, or one could add levels, thus heightening the pyramid. These alterations were used in the growth of industry in the early part of the century, and again in the second great spurt during World War II. Libraries expanded by the same means, as they grew in size during the 1920s and again in the 1950s and 1960s.

But when large business and manufacturing concerns diversified after World War II, the basic structure did not prove flexible for producing or handling markedly different products or services. The hierarchy was disposed to go in a straight line. So the new and to some extent contrary concept of decentralization, which we will examine shortly, was adopted.

Then more recently, when both industry and service institutions (including libraries) faced the need for retrenchment (many of them for the first time in a century or more), the standard hierarchy again did not prove adaptable. What had served well for growth did not serve well for contraction.

Existing departments and branches resisted elimination or combination. Supervisors as well as subordinates sought to protect their positions. Special-interest groups demonstrated against any modification of their particular privileges. More than one contracting agency finds itself saddled with the expanded structure of the past, a house too big for the means of the present occupants.

How does one reorganize a steel company with its market cut in half, or a library with a 25 percent cut in budget? We have to learn how to cut back even as we had to learn how to add. Some of the contemporary concepts of organization may be of help.

References

1. Weber, Max. *The Theory of Social and Economic Organization.* New York, Free Press, 1947.

2. Fayol, Henri. *General and Industrial Management.* London, Pitman, 1967.

3. Gulick, Luther. *Papers on the Science of Administration.* Dublin, Institute of Public Administration, 1937.

4. *Ibid.*, p. 195.

5. Mooney, James D. and Reiley, Alan C. *The Principles of Organization.* New York, Harper, 1939.

6. Taylor, Frederick W. *Scientific Management.* New York, Harper, 1947.

7. Copley, Frank B. *Frederick W. Taylor: Father of Scientific Management.* New York, Taylor Society, 1923.

8. Nelson, Daniel. *Frederick W. Taylor and the Rise of Scientific Management.* Madison, University of Wisconsin Press, 1980, p. x.

9. Simon, Herbert A. "The Proverbs of Administration," *Public Administration Review*, Vol. 6, No. I (Winter 1946), p. 53–67.

10. Stevens, Norman D. *Communication Throughout Libraries*. Metuchen, N.J., Scarecrow Press, 1983.

11. Gross, Bertram M. *Organizations and Their Managing*. New York, Free Press, 1964, p. 223.

12. Thompson, Victor A. "Hierarchy, Specialization and Organizational Conflict," *Administrative Science Quarterly*, Vol. 5, No. 4 (March 1961), p. 482–521.

13. Gardner, John. "How to Prevent Organizational Dry Rot," *Harper's Magazine*, Vol. 231, No. 1385 (October 1965), p. 21.

III CONTEMPORARY CONCEPTS OF ORGANIZATION

THE PRECEDING SECTION traced the foundation of organizational theory. Most of the original work was done in the several decades between the turn of the century and the depression years. The theories were applied first during the period of industrial growth before and after World War I, then in the governmental expansion of the 1930s, again in the challenge of World War II, and most recently in the surge of commercial and service activities in the 1950s and 1960s.

During these latter years the functioning of organizations was continually examined and re-examined. The earlier pronouncements were not allowed to stand as a permanent credo without scrutiny. Some of the concepts were extended and refined. Criticisms of the classical school were advanced, some of which were reviewed in the preceding section. More positively, revisionist views were developed, based on research into operating enterprises and reflecting changing conditions and values. Attention must now be directed to this more recent work, which will bring us up to the present on organizational theory.

Decentralization

Earlier practice as well as earlier theory favored centralization. If an organization was a miscellaneous group of people working together for a common purpose, close central control was needed. Further, in that workers in manufacturing and business firms—it was assumed—had little interest in the success of the enterprise, being there solely for the weekly pay-check, it was necessary to watch, direct, cajole and if necessary discipline. The genius of the assembly line was that it controlled workers without requiring an excessive number of supervisors; it was not just a way of assembling a product efficiently but also a means for keeping workers in line without constantly issuing orders. No wonder that Charlie Chaplin developed a tic in the movie *Modern Times.*

In service and governmental enterprises, assembly lines could seldom be utilized. Instead rules and regulations were issued, and, once started, they proliferated. The worker would be kept in line with formalized orders, often set down in manuals. The clerk in the department store, the teller in the bank, the government employee in the tax office, all were expected to operate "by the book."

At the same time, in service activities the number of levels of supervision was increased, with unit heads and bureau chiefs and department officers, all to hold staff members to the central purpose and the approved procedures. See the pyramid grow and the structure become more bureaucratic! One has only to try to find one's way through the labyrinth of offices and functionaries in a large government department to note the result.

Centralization contributes to unity. At the same time, as we have seen, it also contributes to rigidity. It was the unifying aspect of bureaucracy that earlier impressed Max Weber; it is its rigidity that has brought bureaucracy into disrepute, and not only in government establishments. The problems are greater the higher the point in the hierarchy; the rigid, inflexible functionary is irritating, but the rigid, inflexible manager can sap the life blood from a whole department. As a means to enable enterprises to achieve their purposes in a changing world, centralization has significant shortcomings.

Interestingly enough, it was industry that first broke the pattern of centralization. Credit is given to Alfred P. Sloan at General Motors and Pierra S. DuPont at the DuPont conglomerate for leading the break in the 1920s. The new concept of decentralization came to the fore with assignment of responsibility for major parts of the firm to independent units, holding them accountable in terms of results rather than of methods or prescribed models. Control was financial and not operational. GM carried the idea to the point of making the decentralized units—Chevrolet, Pontiac, Oldsmobile, Buick—competitive with each other. In this case we actually find two units of the same corporation across the street from each other, competing for the same customer. This is a far cry from the textbook conception of the whole company cooperating and working together.

It is not only giant corporations that have adopted decentralization. Some book publishers, for example, have found that a sales force can be built up only to a certain level, after which sales remain on a plateau. But if another sales unit is established, under independent management, the volume of business can be increased even with no change in the product. Effective management requires a driving force, and this can be stultified under close central control. In smaller enterprises central executives must learn to balance control with freedom and responsibility in order to respond to variety of circumstance and to local opportunities.

Decentralization should be distinguished from delegation. Everyone is familiar with delegation, which occurs in most enterprises of any size. Delegation is a transfer of authority within closely-prescribed limits. In substance the subordinate is being told: "We have this job to do, your part is thus and so, carry it out and report back to me."

Decentralization assigns responsibility as well as authority, limited only by an agreed goal or purpose. Here the officer heading the decentralized unit is being told: "Your goal is as follows. You have the financial means to achieve it. Use whatever plan and methods you can devise. You will be judged by results."

Federal decentralization is the term usually applied to this organizational structure. It rests on the distribution of responsibility and authority to semi-autonomous units. Heads of the units are given wide discretion within the broad goals and policies of the activity. Each unit develops its own objectives and performance standards, and in business generates its own profits. The entrepreneur is rewarded more than the team-player. For the large enterprise this pattern has introduced vitality into what could become moribund structures.

Today many corporate firms apply the decentralization prin-ciple. Observers not familiar with the pattern are often confused to note that the corporation has not one but several "presi-dents"—actually heads of decentralized units. They may also be confused by the policy of some large firms, of encouraging subsidiaries to locate physically away from the corporate head-quarters, perhaps in another city, in order to put them on their own and promote independence.

The present author had to adjust to decentralization in transferring for a ten-year period from the library field to a large publishing firm. I was given a substantial sum of money and told to rebuild several existing encyclopedias and produce several new ones. After a few months I went to the President and said that I knew how I had to proceed, but that I lacked several kinds of personnel, various types of equipment, and adequate space. I said I was unsure of what authority I had in these matters. He looked at me in astonishment and in sub-stance said, "Don't come to me with these problems. You have the money, you know what you are to produce. You hire whoever you need, get what equipment is required, find space in this building or anywhere else. What we ask is that you make the books within the time and budget on which we have agreed—we hired you to decide how to do this. If we don't like what's going on, we'll tell you." He was a polite individual, but I knew he meant: if we don't like what's going on, we'll fire you. The encyclopedias were produced on schedule, with some of the work actually done in another city. There was regular control to see that I was staying within budget. I went out of the way to exhibit work in progress, and in the end the publications were accepted. That was the extent of central-ized control.

The application of decentralization can be seen more readily in large business firms, but the principle—and its advantages—apply in much smaller enterprises. Most universities are exam-ples of fairly decentralized organizations. The law school, the

English department, and the physics laboratory have different standards, practices and rewards. The undergraduate division is distinct from the graduate schools. There may be extension units at a distance, following their own aims and conducting their own programs. The institution is more effective under this pattern than if all divisions followed the same model. No doubt some university presidents would say that the other side of the coin is that it is next to impossible to get such disparate units to adopt common goals, uniform financial restraints, and joint academic ventures. Thus the lively administrative push and pull that characterizes most academic institutions—and thus the disparity in strength of academic departments in the same institution, with some preeminent and others weak.

Several advantages accrue from decentralization. The tendency toward a lockstep is averted. Flexibility and variety replace rigidity. The enterprise can serve different purposes and different markets or clienteles through its various independent divisions. The focus is on results rather than on regulations and common models. Leadership is encouraged, for the head of a semi-autonomous unit has freedom and incentive. This is a structure which nurtures and tests executives. Each unit, standing on its own feet, is more accountable because its output—whether of profits or services—is not intermixed with the results of other units and can therefore be more readily measured.

There are also benefits back in the central office. General executives, freed of operational control, can concentrate on policy, financing, and long-range planning. There would be no Standard Oil Company, General Electric Corporation or IBM as we know them today without utilization of this principle.

On the other hand, decentralization places great dependence on the heads of semi-autonomous units and on the wisdom of their selection by general officers. The wrong person given wide responsibility and authority can lead to dire results; more than one business firm has been severely damaged by the failure of one of its federated units. To make decentralization work there has to be freedom to dismiss managers who are not producing, and this in turn leads to frequent turnover in the top managerial ranks. Responsibility for a decentralized agency is more like riding a spirited bronco than a placid dray-horse.

We will see in a later section that libraries for the most part are centralized agencies; they have not taken advantage of decentralization. There are various reasons for this, including small size, the inherent nature of operations, and the usual functional basis of organization. As a result, libraries, as we will also note, display many of the characteristics of centralized enterprises. Branches of public libraries tend to be similar to each other, as though cast from the same mold, as do departmental units of academic libraries. The heads of departments in libraries normally do not exercise much initiative but concentrate more on keeping in line. In the front office, the library director is typically caught in operational matters and the meeting of small and large crises rather than having the time to evaluate the effectiveness of the agency and to plan for its next stages of development. Strong executive leadership is usually not nurtured among middle managers in libraries—hence the scarcity of promising candidates when top positions are to be filled. These characteristics of libraries will later be analyzed in some detail.

Every organization has its own balance of centralization and decentralization. A variety of factors affect this balance: the number of services provided or of products made, the mix of authoritarian management on the one side and participatory management on the other, the extent of specialization in job assignments, and geographic spread of the enterprise. Even the markedly authoritarian organization has a degree of decentralization, with department heads and individual workers making some decisions, while the decentralized enterprise often exercises close control within each of the semi-autonomous units. The task of all administrators, whether their enterprise be centralized or decentralized, is to be alert to the problems inherent in the type of organization that prevails and to detect and correct the shortcomings of that type before they become endemic. The alternative attitude, to defend the prevailing organization because it is established and familiar, leads toward trouble.

It would also be a mistake to believe that decentralization

applies only to huge industries. Smaller enterprises, including libraries, can exhibit rigidity, conformity, confusion in goals, and uncertain results. Decentralization might get moribund enterprises of modest size moving again, by injecting leadership at various levels rather than depending on direction solely from the top. But we will see that this approach has to be used with care in libraries because of the close relationship and mutual dependence of the various parts of this particular form of service enterprise; it is not easy to break off parts of a library and make them autonomous, but where it is feasible, some of the underlying problems of libraries would have some chance of being solved.

Conflict Within the Organization

Definitions of "organization" usually specify or at least imply cooperation, joint action, among participants; staff members are expected to work together. But as a structure composed of human beings, the organization can also be an arena for conflict.

A group enterprise pulls disparate individuals together. The bond between them may be no more than a shared interest in making a living. Other than that, their commitment to the agency may vary from hostility to indifference to respect to enthusiasm to undue dependence. These variations in attachment may themselves be cause for disagreement and conflict. The alienated worker looks on the company enthusiast as someone who has sold out to the establishment, while the dedicated worker sees others as "goofing off" and "going along for the ride." People come to the group with their own predispositions, expectations, and suspicions. Throw them together in the work environment and sparks can fly.

Over the years different attitudes towards conflict have evolved, from the classical view that it was a deterrent, to administrative theorists who welcome conflict as a possible source of renewal. The earlier emphasis on hierarchy was in part motivated by the desire to limit disagreement, whereas some contemporary writers seek to open up organization in order to encourage contrary views and resolve latent conflict before it becomes destructive.[1]

It would be a mistake to see conflict as inevitable. The very act of accepting employment implies enlistment in a common cause—if not, why not work elsewhere? The purposes of an enterprise typically have a unifying effect, the more so as those purposes are clear and manifest. That elusive quality called leadership arouses loyalties. Success in institutional performance—the downright fact of delivering service—spreads satisfaction through the organization. Even institutional reverses—a cut in funds, public criticism deemed unjustified, an accident to the physical plant—can bring staff members together, as troops in the army join forces under attack. More than one group has closed ranks in the face of adversity.

Many forces in an agency are positive, and the wise administrator cherishes and nourishes them. But complacency and dull uniformity must be guarded against. The concept of the "happy family" should be taken with a grain of salt, for it could be a euphemism for placidity. As Tolstoi had it, "All happy families resemble each other; each unhappy family is unhappy in its own way." Anthony Hope went further: "Good families are generally worse than any others." No matter how novelists see it, experienced administrators know that apparently cooperative workers can suddenly become recalcitrant when asked to change or to take on added responsibilities.

Differing perceptions and values can lead to conflict. The individual has goals other than those of the agency, the worker has expectations at odds with those of the managers, groups within the organization have different aspirations. The supervisor seeks productivity but the worker seeks self-fulfillment, the reference librarian wants instant information but the cataloger wants consistency, one librarian aims to promote use and another to protect against misuse.

Mary Follett[2] was one of the first to characterize conflict as not only likely but desirable. She was a political scientist who probed into the working of democracy. She championed a dynamic conception of group enterprise. As she saw it, it is only the passive, inert organization that is free of tension. Conflict is a challenge, an opportunity, a source of vitality.

Differences of opinion by definition bring out the fresh view, the new insight that can be lost when all is smooth and sedate. The clash of views can in the end lead to sounder policy, the challenging statement can lead to clarification, the opposing view may be the one that rescues an institution from stagnation. Of course, differences of opinion can also bring out questionable views and irresponsible proposals, but it is better to subject them to scrutiny than to have them continually working below the surface and gathering malcontents.

Follett posited three ways of resolving conflict: domination, compromise, and what she called "integration of desires." Domination is the method of dictatorial government and autocratic management; it suppresses the opposition and thus loses the possible benefit of contrary positions. Compromise is not much better, for it means that both parties must give up something, resulting in half measures and lukewarm support for the position reached. Her "constructive conflict," on the other hand, can lead to a new decision that meets the needs of both sides. One homely example she cites is of working in a room at Harvard University where one person wanted the window open and the other wanted it closed. By means of consultation the solution was found: open the window in the next room and also the connecting door between. She does not say what the "constructive" solution would be if there were no adjoining room or connecting door.

Mary Follett's lectures and essays in the 1930s and 1940s had an influence on business and government officials alike. She is cited by many of the subsequent theorists of the humanistic school. She signalled a shift in emphasis from control and order to concern about worker motivation and participation, and she was an eloquent spokesperson for the movement.

It has come to be recognized that the group process is not all sweet agreement, but involves exchange which can lead to greater common insight. At its best the dynamic enterprise is greater than any one individual within it—wiser, more responsive, more forceful, and therefore more effective. Conflict in the organization may have the same effect as moderate tension in the individual. In each case the deviation from complete equanimity can be stimulating, leading to effort that would otherwise be avoided.

Communication

Early organizational theory recognized the role of communication in directing, controlling, and coordinating the activities of an enterprise. In fact the need for communication was seen as one of the advantages of the hierarchy; it provided channels of information as well as levels of control. Simply put a directive or a piece of intelligence or an exhortation into the pipeline and it would in due time reach every member of the organization. Simply have the member put a suggestion or a complaint into the pipeline and it would eventually reach those who could take action. The trunk line had been established and would hold the enterprise together.

This proved to be a mechanical and simplistic view. It was comparable to depending on a telephone trunk line to carry all the information needed by individuals and families. No doubt useful and critical intelligence reaches recipients by telephone. But what about conversation over the dinner table, an exchange over the back fence or at the grocery store, a speech at a meeting? What about the content conveyed by newspapers, radio, television? There is even the understanding which individuals gain simply by observing, whether what they look at is their business or not. In private life few people depend exclusively on one formal channel for all they need to know or are curious to know.

Similarly an organization is a labyrinth of communication. Orders flow down "channels" and reports go back up. But a host of other information reaches the worker, by direct conversation, by rumor, by observation. The lunch table and water cooler as well as the office and conference room are settings for exchanges ranging from policy discussions to gossip. An organization is not just one nerve system of communication, but a combination of sub-systems, many of which are neither planned for nor sanctioned.

Management itself "violates" channels, by such common

devices as general notices, newsletters, and staff meetings, where information is distributed directly from the front office to the worker without moving through the echelons. Even a public pronouncement jumps channels. How many employees have said, "I didn't know what was going on in our firm until I saw it in the newspapers."

Every person and every unit in an organization seeks, receives, originates, transmits, stores, recalls, misplaces, and forgets information. Other than the specific task performed, participation in communication is perhaps the most frequent and important activity of the worker. The communication component of the job usually increases with the level of responsibility, and becomes a critical element for chief executives. One commentator tells of the administration consultant who "starts his studies in the mail room, for, by plotting the lines of actual communication, he can sometimes build a more accurate organization chart than hangs on the wall in the president's office."[3]

It is not just the quantity but also the quality of communication that is at stake. Ideally the information that comes through the pipelines should be clear, accurate, complete, balanced, and unbiased. In practice much of what flows through falls short of this ideal. It is possible to open the spigot and get a flood of misinformation.

Effective communication has become a cliché of administration. Everyone agrees with the need and every textbook on management stresses its importance. Most executives when questioned see themselves as good communicators, utilizing informal as well as formal channels.

Yet the hard, cold fact is that lack of adequate communication is found in study after study of organizations. The managers are convinced that they are spreading information far and wide, but individual workers see themselves as isolated, misinformed, and neglected. This has been the case in studies of libraries, as well as of other agencies.[4] Communication seems to break down further in time of crisis (sharp reductions in budget, for example), which is precisely when the group should be united in order to cope with adversity. Effective communication is agreed upon by all and achieved by few.

Recent national administrations have forcefully made the point. President Reagan, whatever the merits of his policies and programs, kept in touch with the people, and this sustained him in the face of economic stagnation and international turmoil. President Carter, on the other hand, was not a "Great Communicator" and this affected his standing and his programs, once again without regard to their merits. President Clinton is a paradox as a communicator: he is persuasive in speeches and in one-on-one contact, but both officials and the general public are often uncertain about his broad policies and principles.

An experienced executive, Chester Barnard, put the spotlight on communication 40 years ago.[5] He was first the President of the New Jersey Bell Telephone Company and then of the Rockefeller Foundation and, toward the end of a career devoted to large-scale administration, set down what he had learned. At times he describes communication as synonymous with organization, or at least its essential ingredient. He saw the hierarchical structure as more a network of information exchange than as a structure of control:

- An organization comes into being when there are persons able to communicate with each other.[6]
- In an exhaustive theory of organization, communication would occupy a central place, because the structure, extensiveness and scope of organization are almost entirely determined by communication techniques.[7]

Barnard was sensitive to the range of contacts outside the formal channels, and urged executives to identify and utilize this nerve system that animates every organization. In his view the administrator is primarily a communications officer, almost a switchboard operator. Barnard's whole ground-breaking book relates to communication—a sharp contrast with such standard library texts as Wheeler and Goldhor,[8] Wilson and Tauber,[9] and Lyle,[10] (even in the recent fifth edition) which do not even list communication in their indexes.

Communication within an organization can be viewed as the other side of the coin of coordination and supervision.

Workers who have the information they need do not need constant supervision. Where communication flows freely, fewer orders have to be issued to achieve coordination. The "tight ship," rather than being a model, is more likely a symptom of ineffective communication, or the constant control would not be necessary.

Even the grapevine has come into official approval. This informal channel may work at cross purposes with more formal sources, but this is not necessarily so. It can further the cause by translating management's formal orders into employee language. It can be used to correct as well as create misinformation. It can help to marshal the troops in the face of crisis. "Rumor and the grapevine are not the same . . . in normal business situations between 75 percent and 95 percent of grapevine information is correct, although most of the stories are incomplete in detail."[11]

Studies have been done on how the grapevine works. It is not a straight-line sequence, going from member A to member Z. Rather A tells a few selected colleagues. Only one or two of these pass on the information, and they are more likely to do so if it has to do with someone they know well. As the news becomes older, and less juicy, it gradually dies out. Periods of excitement and insecurity stimulate the grapevine; given the installation of a new computer the grapevine hums.

We all know how hard it is to achieve full and clear understanding even in a face-to-face exchange between two friends or two members of a family. Words are given different meanings, emphasis is placed on variant points, values lead to divergent interpretations. How much more difficult to achieve effective communication in an agency of ten, a hundred, or a thousand members. Some content never gets through. Some is distorted and some suppressed. Even if all goes well up to the point of reception, the communication may be perversely misunderstood or even rejected by the recipient because emotions get in the way. We hear what we want to hear. It is part of the task of administration to motivate workers to want to hear what is best for the organization—assuming that administrators know what that is.

In keeping with the central role of communication, a separate volume in this series is entirely devoted to the subject.[12]

Decision-Making

So much of organizational theory deals with keeping the enterprise on course and keeping it productive. It tells how to drive the train, but deals very little with determining where the train should go or how fast.

The classical position stressed structure and neglected dynamic internal forces. It was almost as though a neat hierarchy was somehow expected to generate its own purposes, direction, and energy. This assumption was consistent with the aim of keeping the established enterprise on course and producing. The hierarchical agency would presumably go forward on inertia and custom, with a minimum of policy revision and decision-making. For a period the very concept of planning was in disrepute.

The assumption proved justified so long as conditions remained routine and the aim continued to be more production of whatever product or service had been provided. But under pressure—of war, of depression, of new technology— such controlled structures proved to be rigid and inflexible. Procedures for decision-making had not been developed, particularly in the higher echelons. The ship stayed on course even though the previous destination was no longer relevant or valid. This may be an exaggerated characterization, but it fits some contemporary moribund organizations that seem unable to adjust or change.

Herbert Simon broke into the tidy pattern. His early work advanced telling criticisms of both the classical and the scientific positions of administrative theory.[13] He was clearing the way for a different focus, concentrated on what he saw as the critical point: deciding what is to be done rather than how to do it. For this latter work he was awarded a Nobel Prize.

Organization, to Simon, is ". . . the distribution and allocation of decision-making functions."[14] He saw decision-making as the force that moved enterprises, giving them purpose and impetus. This key step determines where the ship is going, what direction it will take, and how fast it will go. His interest was in the energizing force and not in the framework. It is decisions, both of wide import at the top and of immediate application at the bottom, that determine the effectiveness of an enterprise. Also, when new conditions prompt change, again it is the critical factor of judgment that sets a fresh course.

Having shifted attention from control to decision-making, Simon proceeded to examine this process in business and service concerns. What he found was by no means a logical and rational activity. Theoretically decisions represent a choice based on the collective wisdom of the enterprise. The pertinent data have been assembled, the experience of affected staff members has been canvassed, the views of specialists have been sought. All that remains, it would seem, is to reach a logical conclusion based on the evidence and on the counsel obtained.

But in reality the decision-making process and the established organization may be in conflict. The problem under consideration is deep in the structure and has not been clearly identified and defined. The organization has not given up all the pertinent facts. The information, experience, and counsel from members of the agency are subjective and may be slanted in self-interest. Past experiences rather than emerging prospects predominate. Personal values get in the way. We will continue making automobiles of a certain size even though the emerging demand is for a different size; we will continue to depend primarily on printed sources for data in the library even though computerized sources are more complete and up-to-date. It is almost as though the enterprise wants to remain as it is, even though this may be a death wish.

Decision-makers must depend on their organizations—after all, administrators are not omniscient—yet somehow rise above or separate themselves from the enterprise as it stands. Needless to say, this does not always occur. The decision is often made on the basis of precedent and not of opportunity, or on the basis of a general class and not of a particular case. What has been overshadows what can be; generality overshadows particularity.

Thus what is sometimes presented as a group conclusion comes down in the end to individual judgment. The buck has to stop somewhere, whether with the head of a small work unit or the President of the United States. Workers recognize this, and indeed are as quick to criticize indecisiveness in their superiors as they are to complain about lack of their own participation in policy determination. When decision-making falters at its prescribed place in the organization — that is, when it is unclear, postponed, or evaded — the committed worker seeks to circumvent channels and to get to someone prepared to reach a conclusion. The number of out-of-track demands of this type coming to general administrators is an index of the decisiveness or indecisiveness of middle management responsible to them.

With the shift in the end to individual action, one can more readily recognize the uncertainty that enters into decision-making. We are dealing with the frailty of human judgment and not with the group wisdom of an organization. Simon identifies what he calls "fact" and "value" in the process. It is the combination of the two that determines the outcome. Because fact may be incomplete, and value unclear and even unconscious, the judgment of the manager is usually less than the wisdom of Solomon. And, as one moves to the top of the hierarchy, the possibility of rationality declines, because the general manager deals with grosser and more intensely interpreted information.

What to do to improve decision-making? No clear prescription is offered. Emphasis is placed on the part of the equation over which the manager has a degree of control: full and clear information, the "fact" component stressed by Simon. Indirectly this is a boost for libraries, for they are conservators and distributors of information. On occasion in business libraries, when they are integrated into the decision-making process, one can observe their essential contribution, but too often the library is the collection apart, the storehouse to be ransacked when more immediate sources fail, and thus stands outside this motive force in enterprises.

Over the years a considerable literature on utilizing information in management has built-up. More and more this is presented as a logical skill. Techniques of mathematical analysis of information are presented.[15] According to this school, the figures will lead to the right conclusion.

But decision-making has not been reduced to a completely logical model; always Simon's other factor of value enters the equation. Administrators should go as far as they can with facts, thus widening the range where reason controls, but always recognizing that an element of uncertainty remains, where the value system of the decision-maker applies.

Group and Peer Pressures

One of the components of an organization is the existence of the groups that comprise it. This is self-evident, but what is not so obvious is the considerable influence that these clusters of individuals may exert, on purpose, on productivity, on standards and quality, on the total work environment.

Neither classical nor scientific theory gave much attention to internal groupings, even though Weber, Gulick, and others among the early pioneers had sociological background. They saw the enterprise as an entity which would inculcate common values and standards in employees. It was almost as though they advocated the hierarchy as a means to suppress and erase group preferences and differences.

Outside of the work environment, all recognize the role of groups within large entities. The body politic has its political parties, the community its different groups and interests, the library association its subdivisions by type of library, the country club its subgroups interested more in golf, or tennis, or parties. Further, we are familiar with the influence that peer groups may have on behavior and attitudes; the examples that come first to mind are children and young people, but adherence to group standards is by no means lacking among adults.

Small wonder then that similar pressures appear in the workplace. There are managers and workers, there are clerks and professionals and laborers, there are union members and nonunion members, there are supporters and dissidents. Even work units develop distinct identities, with buyers separate from clerks in the department store, pilots separate from flight attendants in an airline, doctors a group somewhat apart from the nurses in a hospital, catalogers on the one side and reference librarians on the other in a library.

Those various sub-units are not necessarily antithetical, working against each other. Nor are they necessarily opposed to management. But such contrary reactions can readily occur. Groups may oppose each other, one or another may oppose management, or several may join together to advocate alternative policies. Even when they do not, each group is likely to have certain norms of conduct and certain levels of production expected of its members. Positively, these standards can promote esprit de corps; negatively, they can work at cross purposes with the objectives of an enterprise.

It took the well-known Hawthorne experiments to document the influence of peer groups on the job.[16] Many people are familiar with this story, but it is worth repeating because it makes its point clearly.

The Hawthorne plant of Western Electric (near Chicago) commissioned a group of Harvard social scientists to study the work environment in the plant in the interest of maximum production. Emphasis originally was placed on physical factors, such as lighting, work space, equipment, arm movements—a kind of latter-day Frederick Taylor approach in a factory marked by precision of methods rather than by the handling of heavy loads.

The experiments started with lighting. The best known standards for intensity, reflection, glare, and other elements were applied to some of the workers assembling electrical panels. Production increased as compared with control groups for which no improvements had been made. All was going according to the textbook.

But some hard-headed investigators did not let it rest there. What would happen if lighting conditions were made worse for other worker groups, violating accepted standards? Intensity was systematically dropped. To the surprise of the researchers, production also increased under these adverse conditions, right up to the point when workers could no longer see the components clearly.

The employees were asked to explain this unexpected result. In essence they said: "We thought you people didn't know what you were doing about the lights. But you apparently were trying to help us. As long as you were working for our welfare, we wanted to show you what we could do, no matter what you did to the lights." In other words, a group response determined results much more than changes in working conditions; workers would produce as long as someone paid attention to them.

Similar experiments were tried with variations in rest periods, working hours, and other factors affecting the worker. In most cases the group conception and response proved more influential than the overt changes in working conditions. Management attention shifted from preoccupation with physical factors to concern about the human equation. To grasp the prevailing individual and group perceptions, Western Electric instituted an interviewing and consulting program and a more thorough means for handling complaints. The lesson is that employees constitute a human organization as well as a work force.

The administrator must be tuned in on and sensitive to not only individual subordinates but also to the various groups that have evolved. Identification of such affiliations is the first step. Beyond that the manager should seek to see the organization from the different perceptions of the various groups. This does not mean agreement with all, which would often be impossible because the groups themselves may oppose each other. But lining up the groups as allies on the one side (the staff association, the service-minded professionals) and enemies on the other (the labor union, the restless clerks) is to be avoided, because it invites internecine warfare. On the other hand, variations in group viewpoints need not be ignored or suppressed, for exchange among them can lead to Mary Follett's constructive conflict.

One important group is the labor union. Many individuals have automatic reactions to the idea of unions in libraries and elsewhere. Some look with skepticism or outright opposition on this development, seeing unions as self-seeking, restrictive, and even destructive. Other workers have a contrary reaction, welcoming the union as a means to gain employee representation and influence. In either case they are a fact of life in public as well as private enterprise.

If unions are recognized, and gain a contract, they become part of the formal structure. If we had adequate means to diagram the various dimensions of an organization, such unions would appear in a negotiating position that can influence decisions, a kind of third dimension in the chart. The recognized union must by agreement be brought into certain deliberations, ostensibly those having to do with personnel — and a very wide range of deliberations have implications for staff.

Often the union and managment are in adversarial positions, with agreement reached by negotiation and compromise. Administrators have accused unions of holding to practices that injure the business or agency. However, at a deeper level, unions often protect the enterprise as it exists, by defending existing jobs and also practices that they see as beneficial. Unions have worked with management to resist government encroachment. A few even have representation on boards of directors. At these points unions and management become one, the formal hierarchy and the workers joining hands. Unions that start out to challenge the establishment may in time become part of it or in fact assume ownership, as in the recent case of a major airline.

But even if not technically or legally recognized, unions may exert an influence by reason of their very existence and the fact that they represent some combination of employees, albeit not a majority. At times relatively small unions within libraries carry weight beyond their actual number of members. They speak with a single voice, which is not true of the rest of the staff. Directors and trustees keep a wary eye on such groups, seeking to limit their influence (and thus their membership). Officials may placate the union as it makes demands, hoping thereby to avoid a larger confrontation. Given this tendency, a small and formally unrecognized union group made up of only a minority of staff members can carry some weight, particularly if its officers are vocal and aggressive.

But groups, union or otherwise, form in every work force. Managers who ignore them do so at their own peril, for the plant neglected in the garden can come to dominate. A working enterprise is hardly a garden, but it needs to possess some of the variety and vigor of a good vegetable patch. There is nothing inherently wrong with interest groups within the staff, and they can be sources of peer pressures that further the aims of the enterprise.

Individuals in Organizations

In the contemporary era, the role and status of individuals tend to be defined by their place in organizations, and particularly in the organization from which they derive their livelihood. They are manager of the branch bank, secretary to the vice president, second baseman on the professional baseball team, or cataloger in the college library. Naming the position goes a long way toward characterizing the person. Each is expected to have certain skills and to perform in certain ways; an image automatically attaches to the job holder, whether high or low, whether justified or not. This is why one of our first questions to a new acquaintance is what do you "do." In the response the kind of organization is as descriptive as the work done, whether the individual is president of a business conglomerate or president of a junk yard, librarian in a great university or in a small village.

We depend on image and preconception in typifying people within organizations. The business executive is assured, decisive, people-oriented. The librarian is book-oriented, conservative, cautious. The difficulty is that on a moment's reflection we all remember business executives and librarians who are precisely the opposite.

Underlying much of recent organizational theory is concern for the individual worker. Where the classical and scientific schools stressed structure and the organization as a whole, the current preoccupation is with individuals within the organization, their role, their productivity, their satisfactions, their morale.

Partly this results from a humanistic outlook, a greater concern for people. Partly it results from a genuine period of individualism that has characterized recent decades, right up through the "me" generation. Even more it results from recognition that the well-being of the member determines the well-being of the enterprise. Evidence accumulates of factors other than close supervision and control affecting performance on the job. In the end it seems that the task of organization is not so much structure and order but the extent to which it fosters motivation and excellence in individual performance.

The former view was that workers were expected to fit into the organization as it stood. The enterprise had a purpose—profit, or productivity, or service, or entertainment, or education—and it had a structure to achieve that purpose. Here is your place as a staff member, the employee was told. Fit into place and all will go well. But we have seen how this neat pattern is broken in practice by decentralization, by conflict, by multiple communication, by group affiliation, by individual judgment in decisions. "Individuals do not divorce themselves from their own norms, attitudes, and personality needs simply because they join an organization."[17]

The reaction of people to any experience is predisposed by their expectations of that experience. If one has been told, for example, that a restaurant is of the highest quality, and then on a visit it proves to be only fairly good, the meal is registered as a disappointment. Conversely, the restaurant that turns out to be better than its reputation or its appearance is likely to get a high mark. So it is with what is anticipated in the workplace.

Formerly workers came to the job with modest expectations. They needed an income, and as long as salary was paid regularly and working conditions were tolerable, they expressed few complaints. But according to the behavioral school that has been in the ascendancy in recent decades, present-day workers look for additional rewards in employment. Working conditions must be not just tolerable but comfortable and even gracious. The work is to provide opportunity to exercise one's talents, thus contributing to personal fulfillment. For some staff members, such as librarians, the organization itself is to be perceived as successful, for the professional does not want to be part of an ineffective enterprise. Some expectations may not be within the power of the agency to provide: high prestige, for example, from a job that ranks low in the public mind, or opportunities for promotion when funds are restricted and staff turnover is low.

When an organization does not come up to expectation, dissatisfaction sets in. Where this is true of community groups or churches or special-interest associations, members simply drop out. In employment they do not have such a ready choice, so the reaction shows itself in grumbling, in criticism of management, in low morale, and in formation of adversary groups.

One of the unsolved questions of the day is how far the employing organization should go and can go in meeting personal expectations. Is the mission of an enterprise to achieve its formal goals or to provide self-fulfillment to its members? The reply is usually that the goals come first—they are the reason the organization exists—but that at the same time the legitimate aspirations of personnel must be met. All is fine when the two go along together, and indeed goals are more readily achieved when staff members derive personal satisfaction from the job. But what to do when agency and individual are not compatible—when the college library stresses support of undergraduate instruction while various staff members want to focus more on the research of faculty members, when some staff members want to emphasize outreach to non-users in a city whereas the appropriated funds barely maintain service to present users, when the high-school librarian seeks to instruct students in the use of resources in the face of a curriculum plan that places this responsibility on English teachers who tend to neglect it? One answer is for the individual to change jobs, if other employment opportunities are available. If not, dissatisfaction is bottled up and tension mounts.

To a degree enterprise goes on no matter how staffs react: automobiles are made, merchandise is sold, library books are dispensed. But reactions of individual workers, in turn, also affect organization. If employees are motivated, supervision can be relaxed. If they have confidence in their colleagues, coordination can be less formal. Conversely, the careless automobile worker necessitates more quality control on the assembly line, and the indifferent circulation desk clerk requires more immediate supervision.

Organization and worker are not discrete and separate.

There is a symbiosis between the two—an interaction, a stimulus, a tension. Individuals adapt within limits to the organization they join, some more and some less. We know that families and communities make an impress on members, and members in turn influence the larger group. The same holds between employee and employing organization.

Organizations on their side also must adapt, within limits. It is an economic marriage, which will work if the parties can find a fit that is mutually beneficial yet allows each its own values and style.

The administrator must come to see structure and worker as a living organism, a natural community. Rather than viewing the organization as predominant, with the individual in a neat box in a designated place in the hierarchy, it is worth recognizing the individual as the center of a complex of organizational influences. These associations for a librarian are pictured in Figure 1. It is notable that only one of the lines pictured there is reflected in the typical organization chart, that at the top representing official controls.

It follows that the effective organization is one that takes account of the individuals within it. The lesson for administrators is that they should understand what workers seek. This is easier said than done, in part because the perception of the organizer differs from that of the organized, and even more because the attitudes and expectations of different individuals are by no means the same. There are workers who say "up the organization" and want as little control and specialization as possible. But there are other workers—good, productive ones—who welcome the neatly-defined job and the clear chain of command. This is the "organization man."

The author remembers his first "administrative" job in a library, as "senior" book shelver with another shelver under him. I went out of my way to vary assignments and to explain the reasons for various practices, because this was what I liked on a job. I was brought up short when, after a few weeks, the junior shelver in substance said: "Don't worry about me. I am perfectly satisfied with regular shelving; these other jobs just throw me off."

In a sense, newer humanistic ideas of organization seek

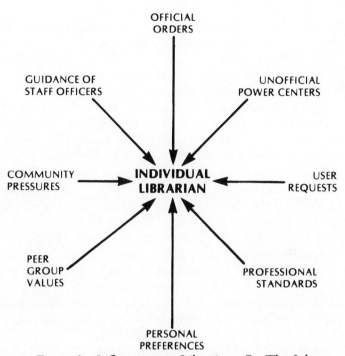

Figure 1 Influences on Librarians On-The-Job

to recapture in the contemporary workplace some of those incentives that characterized pre-industrial endeavor: the sharing of duties on the family farm, the satisfaction of craftsmanship in the small shop. Thus we come full circle, seeking older, small-scale values in large-scale and highly specialized enterprise.

But it would be overly sanguine to believe that all human values can be nourished in the workplace. The organization inevitably exerts influence on the individual, usually influence to conform. William Whyte[18] found the "organization man" being produced by subtle as well as overt pressures, and Robert Merton[19] noted the prevalence of the "bureaucratic personality" with little individuality. In the novelist's view, he wore a "gray flannel suit."

Thinking about organization should not start with structure and relationship, but with work and workers; i.e., with people and what they do. In architecture there is the principle that form follows function; in organization, structure follows work.

This does not mean that employees should "do their own thing" and that the organization must somehow accommodate their whims and desires. Joining and fitting into an established enterprise requires self-discipline and personal adjustment. The radical view pushes this further and maintains that organization necessarily begets alienation, but this applies only to the wrong worker in the wrong organization. For many workers, employment in a compatible organization—that is, one where individuals can use their abilities to produce a product they cannot produce themselves—presents an opportunity for accomplishment and satisfaction. This can apply to the worker in the steel mill, the member of a medical team, and the staff (non-professional as well as professional) in a library.

Further, the work environment provides social contacts and human associations that many people want and need. This does not mean that one necessarily loves all co-workers. Association even with colleagues about whom one is less than enthusiastic can fill a need for working along with others.

But these rewards of employment—sense of accomplishment, stimulating human associations—will be realized only if management takes account of the kinds of workers hired and the kinds of work they do. The agency does not have to adjust to the individual, but it has to work with the employee. Organization should follow people and not rest exclusively on product or efficiency or logic.

One of the subtle skills that the manager at any level must learn is to balance firm control on the one side with appreciation of individual variation and participation on the other. Many administrators err on one side or the other. There are the authoritarians who dominate. Some of the notable builders of the past fall into this classification—Henry Ford comes first to mind—but their style generates stiff opposition today. Then there are flexible and tolerant managers who never quite make up their minds, or who adopt a position and then readily shift ground under pressure. These also lose the respect and confidence of staff. Management is in part a balancing act, taking account both of united group action and of individual variation.

Psychological Factors in the Workplace

Once the spotlight shifted from overall structure to individual worker within the organization, social psychologists moved in and have produced insights that should be familiar to all administrators. One of the most influential has been Abraham Maslow, with his sequence of five levels of personal motivation.[20] Human beings first seek to meet physiological needs, those conditions of air, space, warmth, and protection against the weather that maintain life. Safety factors come next, involving freedom from accidents and from threats to health. Assuming these essential needs are met, the human being wants a sense of identification, of belonging, of being part of a group. This leads to the next level, of esteem or ego needs, the feeling people seek of having some degree of importance. At the top of the scale is the desire for self-fulfillment or self-actualization, the realization of the special attributes of the individual. Maslow observed this chain of personal goals in many aspects of life, including employment.

Experience has shown that satisfaction of needs at one level does not settle the problem of motivation and morale, but simply moves the concerns of workers to the next higher level. If physiological and safety needs are met, attention shifts to social and psychological aspirations. Many a management that provides standard salary scales and good working conditions has wondered why workers are still dissatisfied—they have dealt with the physical person but have neglected the human being.

Another psychologist presented a similar thesis in a different formulation. Hertzberg separates "hygiene factors" and "motivational factors."[21] The former include working conditions and salary, which must be at a reasonable level or morale will suffer. But these factors alone do not ensure commitment and enthusiasm on the part of workers; dollars cannot buy dedication. The second group of motivational factors includes sense of achievement, recognition for work well done, opportunity for advancement. These are the source of high morale and extra effort beyond the call of duty.

Still another social psychologist, Douglas McGregor,[22] challenged the traditional view of the relation of worker to organization. The older view he termed Theory X, with these characteristics:

* management is responsible for determining policy and organizing jobs;
* workers are assumed to lack ambition and to dislike responsibility;
* workers are to be directed and controlled by management.

In its place he offered Theory Y:

* management is responsible for organizing the means of production;
* workers have potential for seeking to produce and assuming responsibility;
* management's task is to facilitate the achievement which the worker seeks.

Theory X places primary reliance upon external control of human behavior, while Theory Y relies heavily on self-control and self-direction.

Supervisors who remember indifferent, lazy, and even hostile subordinates will question Theory Y. But most supervisors can also remember recruits who responded, pitched in, maintained standards, and accepted responsibility.

In the face of this human variability, what management style should the supervisor adopt? Close control and detailed regulation, thereby alienating motivated staff members, or a more facilitating style, hoping thereby to bring along at least some of the unmotivated? When one has a majority of performers and a minority of non-performers, should the managerial environment be calculated to control the latter or to encourage the former? External control of human behavior, or dependence on self-control and self-direction? Individual managers have to answer these questions based on the group under their jurisdiction, but first making sure that they are not carrying a baggage of assumptions that puts down rather than builds up participation.

The work of David Riesman also bears upon the role of individuals within organizations.[23] He postulated three different sets of drives and satisfactions in the makeup of what he called "character." There are tradition-directed persons who rely primarily on custom, myths, and taboos as the determining factors in personality and conduct. Then there are those who are inner-directed, acting on values and beliefs inculcated by immediate and long-term associations, starting with the family. Finally, other-directed individuals follow more the standards of peer groups, acting not so much in response to fixed beliefs as to the approval or disapproval of others. The last-named group, in Riesman's view, predominates in contempory American society. We have noted the direct influence of other-directedness in the Hawthorne experiments on group reaction to alterations in working conditions.

Rensis Likert has carried the emphasis upon the individual worker a step further.[24] He sees a positive, supportive relationship between organization and person based on motivation, sense of worth, and loyalty. He has proposed a series of measures to determine organizational well-being, using absenteeism, job turnover, and grievance rates for the purpose.

The contemporary interest in participatory management grows out of this background, and leads to Total Quality Management, which we will examine shortly. Staff involvement in planning and decision-making serves Maslow's higher psychological needs, capitalizes on MacGregor's Theory Y, and leads to the supportive relationship projected by Likert. But it is not a panacea. At this point we go beyond organization as such, and leave participatory management for treatment in another volume in this series.[25]

It would be unbalanced to leave this topic without noting that business has at times reacted against the motivational approach. *Fortune* magazine has been consistently critical of what it terms the "social engineers," seeing in the behaviorial school a challenge to "economic man" and the profit motive. One advocate of this view puts it as follows: "To say, in fact, that the American worker is not really or primarily interested in money contradicts, in a deep sense, the very motive power of the economic system. Why else would people submit themselves to such a work environment?"[26] In other words, get back to the basics of Theory X. Librarians might be tempted to challenge this hard-headed position, for many chose their profession knowing that the monetary rewards would not be high.

By and large the motivational school has prevailed, at least in the theory if not always in the practice of organization. Greater productivity, more attention to quality, it is now believed will result from giving employees greater freedom, and from stressing goals and cooperation rather than rigid structure. Optimistic assumptions about human nature lay back of this new approach. Workers, it is assumed, will exert both greater effort and better judgment if they share in the purposes of the organization, participate in decision-making, and have freedom to adjust methods. People on the job seek not just a pay check but also personal satisfaction, even a little sense of creativity. In a later section of this volume we will see how this conception applies to libraries.

Total Quality Management

The preceding pages have traced the evolution from hierarchical, authoritarian organization to a humanistic, behavioral foundation for getting work done—a change from top-down to bottom-up administration, a change from command to coordinated action. One essential ingredient in this development has been a shift in managerial attitude, from skepticism about the ability and contribution of workers to confidence in their potential commitment and even in their creativity. The other essential ingredient has been a parallel change in the attitude of workers from thinking of the job as just a job to employment as a source of satisfaction and self-expression. This combination opens new prospects in organization and administration, both as viewed from the director's office and from the employee's workplace.

The culmination of this trend is Total Quality Management,

TQM. Before analyzing the nature and process of TQM, it may be useful to cite a few examples where it has had a significant impact.

We will see that the Japanese first used this approach. Among the results are the Toyota and Honda automobiles, which invaded the American market. Then, in a counter-attack, quality management at Ford Motor Company produced the Taurus automobile, which proceeded to come out on top in sales.

The Japanese also applied quality management to computers and made strong inroads into the American market. Users found their products to be more functional and "user-friendly"—even though the fundamental research in developing computers had been done in America. The United States had the basic ideas and the technical know-how, but did not have workers on the production lines devoted to quality, nor designers in close contact with customers. There was a gap between the knowledge of the specialists and performance on the job; the link between product and individual worker had not been forged. Now America has made a come-back, with the skill and sophistication of our software designers.

Another example of TQM is the best of the mail-order companies with which we are all familiar. Many people now buy with confidence from clothing and other catalogs. Note in these catalogs the attention to the customer: attractive booklets, clear and full descriptions of merchandise, accurate illustrations, exact instructions on measurements, liberal return policies. This emphasis on customer needs and attitudes we will see is one important factor in TQM—and libraries also have customers (users).

Historically TQM goes back to the standards and pride of individual craftspeople before large enterprises put workers into narrow slots in the fabricating or service processes. The earlier craftsperson, on his or her own, produced a product that was right for the customer and suited to the intended use, and did so not solely to get more customers but because his or her personal motivation was to turn out a result of high standard.

Then, more recently, under authoritarian organization, in many enterprises the job became solely a means of earning a

paycheck. The motivation of the worker was personal livelihood, and as long as management made no undue demands
on individual performance, the worker did what was asked. In
fact, the worker who raised questions or tossed off suggestions
was frowned upon by management, criticized as a griper and
troublemaker, and considered to be an individual who did not
fit in. Most employees pulled back, did what they were told
and had little motivation for improvement. The result was
errors or weaknesses in the product. Too many American manufacturers and service organizations came to have a reputation
for lack of reliability. Some even built in "planned obsoles-
cence" so that the product did not last too long.

The manufacturer, seeking improvement, then had no ready
alternative except to set up and staff separate quality controls
either along the line or at the end. This added to time and
costs. More pervasive in its results, it took responsibility for
quality off the shoulders of the individual worker because
someone further on was watching for shortcomings. Quality
went down rather than up.

One would think that attention to quality would evolve
naturally, as enterprises sought to improve their products and
services. But this did not occur, particularly in larger companies. We have cited the automobile industry. Other examples
could be mentioned, from house construction to retail mer-
chandising to government services. In each instance quality
was not at the forefront and the potential contribution of
workers along the line was not utilized.

Enter W. Edwards Deming—in the United States in the
1980s, at a fairly advanced age.[27] In his rambunctious way, he
preached his "14 points." These points or principles cover
everything from clarity and constancy of purpose to statistical
evaluation of the end product but their emphasis is upon
improvement of process and upon commitment to quality from
top to bottom. Included is an extra measure of training and
re-training of both managers and workers; if any enterprise is
not constantly engaged in training, trouble is not far off.

Deming did his work in Japan in the 1950s and 1960s, and
it took a decade to realize the benefits. He did his work in the
United States in the 1970s and 1980s and it took a decade to

produce the Taurus automobile. Florida Power and Light went into Quality Control in the early 1980s and won the much-sought Japanese-sponsored Deming Prize in 1989, with reduced errors in reading meters and with fewer "scams" (shutdowns of power plants). It takes time to create a new "culture."

Deming was called upon by other American companies, and sometimes the seed germinated and produced fruit. Other consultants on quality management entered the scene— Joseph Juran, Walter Shewhart and Philip Crosby among others. If the chief officer pushed the fresh ideas persistently, progress was made. But at the outset the whole concept was seldom adopted. Parts of TQM might be utilized but an enterprise-wide culture was not achieved. We will see that libraries by and large fit into this limbo, with some quality efforts but few wholesale and thorough adoptions.

One of the early responses in business and industry was "quality circles." A half-dozen workers would be designated to study identified problem areas, and would meet weekly for an hour or so and hopefully came up with suggested solutions to the problem before them. Management might or might not adopt the proposals, depending on the degree of commitment at the top. Quality circles came and went, produced for a time and then became sterile, involved some workers but not others, and after a period tended to fade. They lacked the Total in Total Quality Management.

TQM as a whole has not spread as rapidly as its advocates have wished because it flies in the face of beliefs built deep into managerial attitudes. Every enterprise has some workers who do as little as possible, some employees who become completely set in their ways and resist any change, and any experienced supervisor knows this. For TQM he or she is being asked to believe that all or most workers will respond to fresh and more demanding goals and that these same workers have ideas which will improve the enterprise. Adjustment of long-term and deeply-held attitudes does not occur easily.

Deming and others developed a variety of statistical and graphical techniques to analyze what was going on in an organization. These are aimed not so much at specific errors which occur repeatedly and which can be readily spotted, but more at variations from normal procedure and endemic shortcomings which can be removed. The techniques include indices of variation, scatter diagrams, histograms, Pareto distribution analysis, and complex graphical presentations, all gathered under the heading of "Statistical Process Control," also known as SPC. Outsiders coming fresh to a formal quality analysis can be confused and repelled by the esoteric nature of the presentation.

The various statistical analyses are aimed not so much at the finished product but at the separate operations that step-by-step determine what comes out at the end. Various treatments of Total Quality Management present details of the procedures involved.[28] In recent years the whole approach has been re-interpreted and systematized.[29]

The essential ingredient in TQM is not the various techniques it utilizes—statistical and otherwise—but commitment from top to bottom, from director to individual employee. Motivation all along the line is what produces the reliable product and the satisfactory service. At its best, Total Quality Management produces a new environment in the workplace. We will later see to what extent this has occurred or could occur in libraries.

Given its complexity, why then has TQM endured and to some degree gained acceptance? Because from the administrator's standpoint the human contribution proves greater and more consistent than expected, and because the individual worker gets a sense of importance and accomplishment in participation. This combination from above and from below has promising potential.

A fresh productive work culture can happen, as demonstrated by the several examples cited. An extreme example is the way many people, in and out ot the armed forces, gather round and exert their best effort in time of war. Many people not in uniform work overtime as well as take up nursing and factory jobs. There is a goal and there is dedication. Whether these same qualities can be mobilized in peacetime is a question before the United States—whether manager and worker will really join hands, and whether the work ethic will be retained.

Another question about Total Quality Management is whether this new organizational culture can foster adjustment to change—fundamental, mission-altering change—or whether it is primarily suited to improving what already exists. Will it only improve automobiles or will it also produce new modes of transportation? The Information Age will be the test. We will analyze the question in a later section (Chapter XI) on the present and prospective response of libraries to Total Quality Management.

Conclusion

There have been the various "schools" of administrative theory. But which is "best," which body of principle should the manager learn and apply? Are the recent behavioral views to be preferred because they are more "modern" and more "human"?

Who can say? We are not dealing with a body of verified and tested principles; in the end there really is no existing science of administration. Is Total Quality Management the panacea? Even TQM has been dropped by some agencies that went into it with anticipation. Others are now focussing their attention on Reengineering the Corporation.[30] The manager should consider each theory, but with skepticism. The manager should apply any one where it fits, but with caution.

Clearly the earlier theories had shortcomings. Later commentators have been deadly in locating the weaknesses. But what new body of principle have they set up in place of the earlier doctrine? The answer is, precious little; the previous neat structure has been pulled down but a new one has not been built.

What we have is a variety of overlapping and sometimes contradictory theories. No less than thirteen different approaches are identified by one critical observer of the field.[31] The perceptive article by Koontz seeks to give some order to what he calls the "management theory jungle."

It is now recognized that no one form of organization or body of precepts applies in all situations. It may be, for example, that libraries, by reason of their particular mix of purpose, function, staff, and clientele, need not adhere to the criteria derived either from industry or government. In designing our own house we may well benefit from the floor plans of others, but in the end must decide on the arrangement appropriate to our life style.

A cynical view is that we have moved up the hill and then down again in our understanding of the management of organizations, and are left where we started—except that the number, size, and complexity of business, fabricating, and service enterprises have increased in the interval. But one can benefit from the precepts set forth fifty or more years ago and from the revisionists' analysis of them in the last several decades. Even though we are far from an exact body of knowledge about administration in general and organization in particular, managers have much to learn from efforts to date to understand how people do and do not work together.

Changes over the years in thinking about administrative organization reflect changes in Western society, and particularly changes in the conception of the individual. At the beginning of the 20th century, when large-scale enterprises appeared first in industry and later in government, a theory of organization grew up which emphasized structure and control. This approach was solidified in military administration in two World Wars. In recent years the spotlight has swung to the individual within the organization, with special attention to motivation and to cooperation.

In neither period was the dominant theory applied directly to libraries. Rather, the concepts prevailing in industry and government trickled down to libraries, usually in diluted form and after some delay of time. Forty years after a "science" of administration was advanced by Weber, Fayol, and others, those interested in library administration began to study their organization charts and to apply specialization of tasks. This was after World War II, when academic, public, and governmental libraries grew rapidly in size, and library directors sought to cope with their burgeoning enterprises. Ironically, just about that time the prevailing theories of organization were being challenged by a new generation of social psychologists, but libraries did not heed the challenge even though they had the publications of the challengers on their shelves. Finally today, after the social upheavals of the 1960s and the budget constraints of the 1980s, library directors and supervisors are catching up with the new school, just when they lack the wherewithal to satisfy staff aspirations which are belatedly recognized.

Neither the earlier structural school nor the current motivational school have found the panacea for assuring performance and satisfaction among disparate individuals in complex organizations. Management that is less than effective is prevalent in the automobile factory, the department store, the government bureau, and the university, and is by no means absent in libraries. The library administrator would do well to absorb both approaches to organization, and their various modifications and permutations, and then apply them or adapt them or reject them in the special context of library service.

By way of summarizing the two predominant views—centralized and authoritarian on the one side and decentralized and democratic on the other—parallel and contrary precepts of the two are presented in Figure 2. One is the model of the traditional industrial organization (a bottle factory, for example) and the other the model of a contemporary service enterprise (a university in this case). One can compare the two by reading across for each of the characteristics listed.

Contemporary views of management have come to see organization as a social institution rather than a bureaucratic structure, and its functioning as a group process and not a job-task hierarchy. From this viewpoint new approaches to efficiency and control and new conceptions of motivation and morale have emerged. The literature is replete with pronouncements about democratic work environment and participatory management. This is the visible and popular part of the contemporary view, but the concept infuses most present-day management theory.

Much less attention has been given recently to such old-fashioned ideas as leadership and control. But these ingredients are still needed in the mix. Without them one may have a

Model of Centralized Authoritarian Organization (a bottle factory, for example)	*Model of Decentralized, Democratic Organization* (a university, for example)
Non-public Board	Public Board
Board has great policy control	Board powers limited
Chief administrator a management specialist	Chief administrator up from ranks of professors
Authority exercised by command	Leadership by persuasion
Chief officer highly compensated	Compensation does not show great gap
Centralized policy determination	Educational policy in hands of faculty
Employees lack tenure	Faculty has tenure
Little discretion for worker on job	Relatively wide discretion in teaching and research methods
Imposed standards of performance	Self-motivation
Dissatisfaction of workers: boredom, absenteeism, gold-bricking	Relative satisfaction
Organization adapts to change	Resistance to change

Figure 2 Contrasting Organizational Patterns

"happy family" that is on a kind of holiday, a placid enterprise that is adrift.

Library administrators will want to take advantage of the insights of the more recent behavioral school, but equally they can benefit from the earlier conceptions that contributed so much to American productivity. The two views are not mutually exclusive. On the contrary, the administrator who goes overboard for one or the other—close control on the one side or group participation on the other—is in trouble. Effective contemporary administration combines leadership with human concern.

References

1. Gross, Bertram M. *Organizations and their Managing.* New York, Free Press, 1964.

2. Metcalf, Henry C. and Urwick, L. *Dynamic Administration; the Collected Papers of Mary Parker Follett.* New York, Harper, 1941.

3. Redfield, Charles. *Communication in Management.* Chicago, University of Chicago Press, 1953, p. 7.

4. See, for example, Martin, Lowell A., *The Free Library and the Revitalization of Philadelphia,* 1981, p. 68, and A *Plan for the Development of the San Francisco Public Library,* 1982, p. 59.

5. Barnard, Chester I. *The Functions of the Executive.* Cambridge, MA., Harvard University Press, 1966.

6. *Ibid.,* p. 82.

7. *Ibid.,* p. 91.

8. Wheeler, Joseph L. and Goldhor, Herbert. *Practical Administration of Public Libraries.* New York, Harper and Row, 1962. "Completely Revised" by Carlton Rochell in a 1981 edition.

9. Wilson, Louis R. and Tauber, Maurice F. *The University Library; The Organization, Administration and Functions of Academic Libraries.* New York, Columbia University Press, 1951.

10. Coughlin, Caroline M. and Gertzog, Alice. *Lyle's Administration of the College Library.* 5th ed. Metuchen, N.J., Scarecrow Press, 1992.

11. Davis, Keith, "The Care and Cultivation of the Corporate Grapevine," *Management Review.* Vol. 62, No. 10 (October, 1973), p. 53–55.

12. Stevens, Norman D. *Communication Throughout Libraries*. Metuchen, N. J., Scarecrow Press, 1983.

13. Simon, Herbert A. "The Proverbs of Administration," *Public Administration Review*. Vol. 6, No. 1 (Winter 1946), p. 53–67.

14. Simon, Herbert A. *Administrative Behavior*. New York, Free Press, 1976, p. 220.

15. See, for example, Braverman, Jerome D. *Management Decision Making*. New York, Amacom, 1980.

16. Roethlisberger, Fritz I. and Dickson, William J. *Management and the Worker*. Cambridge, MA., Harvard University Press, 1939.

17. Pfiffner, John M. and Sherwood, Frank P. *Administrative Organization*. Englewood, N.J., Prentice-Hall, 1960, p. 34.

18. Whyte, William. *The Organization Man*. New York, Simon and Schuster, 1952.

19. Merton, Robert. "Bureaucratic Structure and Personality," *Social Forces*. Vol. 18, No. 4 (May, 1940), p. 560–568.

20. Maslow, Abraham. *Motivation and Personality*. New York, Harper and Row, 1970, p. 35–58.

21. Hertzberg, Frederick. *The Motivation to Work*. New York, Wiley, 1959.

22. McGregor, Douglas M. "The Human Side of Enterprise," in *Leadership and Motivation*. Cambridge, MA., MIT Press, 1966, p. 3–20.

23. Riesman, David. *The Lonely Crowd*. New Haven, Yale University Press, 1950.

24. Likert, Rensis. *The Human Organization; Its Management and Value*. New York, McGraw-Hill, 1967.

25. Sager, Donald J. *Participatory Management in Libraries.* Metuchen, N.J., Scarecrow Press, 1982.

26. Bell, Daniel. *Work and Its Discontents.* Boston, Beacon Press, 1965, p. 29.

27. Gabor, Andrea. *The Man Who Discovered Quality.* New York, Random House, 1990.

28. Walton, Mary. *The Deming Management Method.* New York, Dodd, Mead, 1986.

29. Crosby, Philip B. *Completeness: Quality for the 21st Century* and Creech, Bill. *The Five Pillars of TQM.* New York, Dutton, 1994.

30. Hammer, Michael and Champy, James. *Reengineering the Corporation: A Manifesto for Business Revolution.* New York: Harper Business. 1993.

31. Koontz, Harold. "The Management Theory Jungle Revisited," *Academy of Management Review.* Vol. 5, No. 2 (April 1980), p. 175–187.

IV ORGANIZATION OF LIBRARY SERVICE

MOST OF THE LATER PAGES in this volume are devoted to the internal organization of single libraries, what might be called the microcosm as distinct from a wider organization or macrocosm of service. The managerial structure of individual libraries, their organization into positions and departments, coordination among the several parts, the place of workers within the structure, and the flexibility of libraries in meeting change will all be focal points in later chapters.

Before proceeding to that internal analysis, the several kinds of libraries and relations among libraries will be examined, first the traditional pattern (or lack of pattern) of library service, then the informal "systems" that individual users work out, and finally the emerging formal system and networks. Thus the theme for the present will be the organization of service as seen by the library user, as distinct from internal organization as seen by the library manager.

The Grand Plan of Service

At the outset it may provide perspective to stand back and examine the broad pattern of library *service*, the way in which various types of resource needs are met and how different types of agencies share the burden. This is the macrocosm. With the spectrum of types of libraries before us, we can then move on to relations among the types, or coordination if the managerial term is used, noting the networks that have emerged in recent years.

Much of this review of types of libraries and relations among them will be familiar to librarians, in a sense too familiar in that it is usually assumed that the present pattern is the only possible or at least the most logical structure, a design that is sanctified by time and tradition. What we will see is the gradual trend toward a new pattern, a kind of federated national library system.

A *Single Library Authority*

An iconoclastic question can be raised here at the beginning as to why there need be the many different kinds of libraries — why not one system to meet the various needs of a locality or region? Metropolitan areas and even whole states have, for example, a single transportation system or one telephone utility or a single source for gas and electricity. Why not a central library facility, a single authority for this utility?

Think of a unified, encompassing facility, with one board, one set of policies, and one director. The central collection — *the* Library — would be a foundation of considerable scope and depth. There would be branches or outlets in towns and neighborhoods, in the schools and the colleges, and in other public institutions — working resources for immediate use. A computerized record would show holdings in all agencies, with access to this record in each agency by means of terminals. All users would have equal access to the central collection as needed and to all component "branches" — not "reciprocal" borrowing but universal borrowing from what the user would view as a single system. Publications would be exchanged freely among the units — intra-library rather than inter-library loan. To the extent that a central processing division would be desirable and efficient, such would be maintained for all types of libraries. Personnel could be transferred and promoted as needed, thus strengthening staffs and opening additional career opportunities for librarians. Financing would be from one source, either an existing governmental jurisdiction which encompasses the total territory served or a library district established for the purpose.

The advantage would be unity and built-in coordination, as against the vagaries and disjunctions of voluntary cooperation among academic and public and school and research and special libraries. Planning and policy-making would be done overall, with total needs in balance. Budget allocations would be in accord with area-wide purposes and priorities. If and when financial restrictions hit, cutbacks would be shared rather than affecting one or another sector disproportionately.

This fanciful unified system for a region or state becomes more conceivable with the advance in rapid electronic communication. It is communication that holds a system together. Think of immediate transmission of text as well as factual data from a central source, which may be the direction in which library service is moving. One way or another, we are likely to see larger units of service in the next seven years.

Library managers will throw up their hands in horror at this prospect. They don't want to be part of a vast conglomerate. They don't want to take orders from a central authority or follow uniform policies. All they want to do is to impose central authority and uniform policies on the city or institution for which they are responsible, even though the city is composed of markedly different neighborhoods and the university of markedly different departments. Central control over my subordinates but not over me.

The single facility is a grand and neat plan. It is not likely to occur administratively but it is evolving as we move step by step toward the "virtual" library, which will be examined in Chapter XII. To understand the overall organization of library service one must think both of the many separate independent libraries and also of the networks and super-networks which already exist: structure as seen by the library administrator and structure as seen by the library user.

Prevailing Decentralized Structure

As against a single library authority, the pattern that actually exists grew more by chance as need and opportunity were

perceived. Libraries are a historical growth, reflecting perceptions of the time when they were established, and that time
was before the 20th-century flood of print and the current
overload of information. The interdependence of resources
was not foreseen.

It is interesting that at an earlier stage total library provision
was somewhat more unified. In many cities the first school
service came from classroom collections provided by public
libraries and from library rooms administered and staffed by
the municipal agency. At that earlier stage many commercial
firms, even large ones, depended entirely on business branches
of the public library. In these locations, when separate school
libraries and business libraries appeared, they were in a sense
spin-offs from the single, general municipal facility. Another
way to express this is to say that the public library, having
given birth to robust offspring, was unable to sustain them and
they set up their own homes.

Today the various units stand distinct and separate. Rather
than consolidation, over the years proliferation of libraries has
occurred. The public library has its resources and policies and
problems, as do the school libraries, and the colleges, and in
some localities one or more university libraries. Then there
are the collections in the hospital and the art museum and
the historical society. From the librarians' standpoint these are
separate agencies, albeit coordinated to a limited degree in
one or more cooperative schemes.

The division into various types of libraries, the fragmentation
of service, is an example of the principle of decentralization
in organization that was discussed earlier. For all the theoretical
advantages of an overall unified system, stronger forces
prompted the appearance of separate collections in various
settings and agencies. The single system might well be more
efficient and would permit truly coordinated planning; that is,
it would have the strength of hierarchical organization. But
the stronger force that brought the present pattern into existence was the desire of each establishment to have its own
resources over which it has complete autonomy. With such
decentralized control, the particular circumstances and needs
of each constituency can better be met, with decisions made

within the agency and not by a central library authority. The college librarian does not want to follow the same policies as the school librarian, nor the university librarian to maintain the same program as the public librarian. Each seeks to "do his own thing," even though to the user the separate units may look as much alike as the Chevrolet, the Pontiac, the Oldsmobile, and the Buick (there are few Cadillacs among libraries).

Recently, with educational funds constricted, an ironical twist has appeared in the pattern. School service, as we have said, was earlier provided by public libraries in various cities. Then school authorities took over the function, maintaining their own facilities. Now that educational funds are short, some school systems, in substance, seek to reverse the process. School libraries have been cut back significantly in some cities, and library personnel reduced (one professional for a group of schools, for example). Students have no choice except to turn to the public library. School authorities know that the community agency is there and, while seldom admitting so, have subconsciously adopted a policy of shifting the burden of providing materials in support of the curriculum back to the general agency. Earlier the schools took library service to themselves; now some would like to give it back. The pattern is coming full circle.

Public library officials, on their side, find themselves caught. They have long since given up the function of providing curricular reading for students as part of their collection-building policies, they too are short of money, but there are the students at the librarian's desk asking for help. It is the students who are the victims of unilateral retrenchment, and the public or general library that feels the pressure when other parts of the informal network cut back.

A parallel sequence can be traced for the academic library. As municipal funds become constricted, both public and school libraries cut back on acquisitions. As a consequence, the high-school student and the community resident turn to the local college or university collection, just at a time when the latter is also experiencing reductions in funds. Even as users tend to look on all types of libraries as parts of a single macrocosm in time of expansion, so the same view prevails in a time of contraction. If seekers cannot get what they need in one kind of agency they naturally turn to another.

The User-Designed "System"

From the users' standpoint the many kinds of libraries are all part of the "public" resources which they may use or would like to use. The youngster starts to consult an encyclopedia article in the school at two o'clock and finishes the assignment at four o'clock in the neighborhood branch library. College students can't get a recommended reading on campus during the day so they go to the central public library in the evening. Business persons consult some marketing data in the company library during the morning and then locate additional sources in the public library on the lunch-hour, and perhaps even more material in the map or documents division of the university library.

In the broad social sense, all readers and seekers of information have a constellation of resources to which they can turn. Material is there, in scattered locations and jurisdictions, for the persistent searcher. There being no unified macrocosm, individuals fashion their own "system," piecing it together from whatever kind or size of library or other source that gives promise of having what they need.

It is worth noting the full spectrum that is available for different categories of seekers.

For *General Readers* seeking written commentary about the world in which they live:

    Public libraries

    Newsstands, magazine and paperback racks

    Bookstores

    College and university libraries in the area

    Company library (if one exists where individual works)

    Materials from friends and acquaintances

For *School Students* seeking study material:

    Classroom collection

    School library

Public library
Home library
Bookstores
Friends and classmates
For *Academic Faculty Members* pursuing a research topic:
Faculty office collection
Subject and professional journals received
Departmental library
Central college or university library
Bookstores
Public library

One of the more easily perceptible of these personal systems is that fashioned by faculty members. Almost invariably there are resources in the individual office containing the professor's working tools. As another convenient source, every faculty member decides which journals to subscribe to and which to consult in the library. The library most frequently used is likely to be the departmental unit within the university complex. The central university library is turned to at intervals, and perhaps the public library on occasion. For special projects faculty members may resort to other research collections, some at a considerable distance. Which of these is the professor's library? The answer is all of them, as faculty members call on one or another unit in their personal library systems.

Any single library, from the users' standpoint, is part of a matrix. Their immediate library does not exist in isolation. Resources sought may be obtained from other than the collection down the street or across the campus, and indeed it may at times be easier to get at the "other source."

By no means do all seekers find the full range of resources that they might use. Some with strong motivation take advantage of the whole panoply. Others with less special needs turn to one or a few collections convenient to them and do not persist beyond that point. Still others with only occasional curiosity will use an outlet if one is near them, and if none such exists will do without.

Seekers work out their own designs. Some are quite ingenious in the process. I recall the high-school student, doing a senior paper, and wanting to use a nearby university collection

that required identification at the door: she put on an incon-
spicuous outfit, combed her hair to look a little older, took a
package lunch, waited near the library entrance until a group
of college students entered, slipped in among them, and spent
the day in the stacks. Even as some young people become
"street smart," others become "library smart."

Or a different kind of example. A friend asked where he
could get some earlier and also some recent demographic
information about our community, and was sent to the small
local public library, which proved to have very little of what
was needed. However, he was referred for the earlier material
to the local historian, who had the resources in her home.
For a time he thought he would not be able to locate the
recent material but by chance mentioned this at a service-
club meeting to the school superintendent, who said the school
library gathered the information. What had started as a standard trip to the public library ended up as a period in an easy
chair in the historian's home and two hours at a table in the
school library among groups of rambunctious teen-agers. Both
the high-school student with a paper and a local searcher for
information had worked out their own systems, and neither
primarily involved the library that had ostensibly been set up
to serve them.

Even in the librarian's office unexpected patterns appear. I
am struck by the number of times I have asked public-library
and also academic-library directors where they turn for their
personal reading of current publications on which there is
heavy patron demand, and they say, "I buy the titles." Right
within the agency maintained to provide a service, officials
turn to alternative sources.

The library organizer would do well to stand back and
consider the macrocosm. Libraries do not exist in a vacuum,
nor is any one library the only or even the primary source for
its users. Library managers must be knowledgeable not only
about other libraries their readers may use, but also about
commercial and personal sources to which they may turn.
Think total resources available, not "my collection" alone.

Planning for any library should proceed in the context of
the constellation, the macrocosm of sources. The constellation

exists; there is no point in disregarding it. The public library need not try to provide what is furnished by the newsstand; the school library need not duplicate what is in the classroom; the university library need not provide what is already in the public library. Most librarians would agree with this in theory but it is not applied consistently in practice, and because it is not, at any given moment we have the same resources standing unused on the shelves of several libraries within a short distance of each other.

Categories of Libraries

Libraries therefore exist within a larger system for the provision of publications and information. Turning from but not forgetting that larger system, one can note the several types of libraries as component parts of the macrocosm.

We will first fit these separate types into the larger scheme, identifying the niche that each occupies, before proceeding to inter-connections among them. The professional literature often exalts the roles of the several types of libraries—the public library as the "people's university," the academic library as the "scholar's workshop"—claiming more of a contribution than is actually delivered. This may reinforce the self-image of the librarian but it does not make for an accurate description of the macrocosm of library service. The attempt in the following brief characterizations is to retain balance, noting both achievements and shortcomings that add to or detract from the total service organization.

Libraries are usually divided into four categories: public, academic, school, and special. Actually each of these includes a considerable range of sub-types, some of which contrast sharply with each other within the same category.

Public Libraries

Two characteristics identify the public library: support from government and free access to users (the "public"). On this basis the category encompasses, on the one side, the small village library open a few afternoons a week, and on the other, the Library of Congress, with the largest collection in the world. One is the agency for the local citizen and the other the agency for what can be called the national or international citizen.

Actually there are a variety of public libraries for national citizens and also for state-wide citizens. At the national level, besides the Library of Congress, the National Library of Medicine and the National Agricultural Library come first to mind, and there are many others. These contain notable collections, with definite research capacity, and many play a strategic role in maintaining a national bibliography and systems of service that extend across the country. They are supported by the public and provided for the public, and therefore by our definition are "public" libraries.

State libraries, also "public" under the general definition, equally occupy key positions in the general service organization. Their collections in some instances are distinctive, particularly in regional history. They directly serve the representatives of the public, in the legislatures and state offices. They (or a parallel state extension agency) function as the cornerstone for whatever degree of cooperative and coordinated service has been built up throughout the state. While the average citizen and general reader may not personally use the national or state resources (although they would not be prevented from doing so), the existence of these public agencies greatly strengthens the knowledge resources available to the society, and also reinforces the local outlet to which the local citizen does turn.

Public libraries in the narrow sense—i.e., local, free, tax-supported agencies—also display great variety in size, content, and function. There is the village library, typically with an accumulation of little-used older books acquired over the years, plus a modest selection of current publications. On a wider geographic scale, but with a range from minimal to substantial, are county and regional agencies. Suburban libraries may have a stronger position, focusing as they can on the less specialized needs of their patrons, leaving the provision of more extensive resources to large city collections to which suburbanites often have access but which they do not support financially.

Public libraries first appeared in larger cities and for many years flourished in that setting. They have become the unofficial "central" collections for whole metropolitan regions. Suburbanites from over the area have access to the central facilities without charge for in-house use and even for circulation purposes if they work in the city. In a few locations ways have been found to share the cost of the central facilities over all or parts of the metropolitan region (Rochester, N.Y. and Atlanta, Ga. are examples), but in most cases hard-pressed cities find themselves maintaining a large collection used by out-of-city residents, who get a free ride. In a few instances (Maryland and New York, for example), the state has recognized the situation and provides money to support the city facility, but in most centers the beleaguered city carries the burden alone. In many cases city libraries have had to cut hours and book funds, with a consequent weakening of the unofficial structure that emerged earlier. When this occurs to the city library, suburban as well as urban residents suffer a loss. The informal relationship between the city and its environs deteriorates at the core.

City libraries are multi-purpose agencies. They provide subject resources of considerable scope, they are adult education agencies, they stimulate and guide the reading of children, they serve students, they provide popular reading for recreational purposes, they maintain information services. Some have research resources (rare book rooms, special collections, local history departments). Some maintain out-reach programs to low-income neighborhoods, and others serve as community centers with meeting rooms, programs, and local projects. Subject library, research center, free bookstore, children's library, information center, community center—the public library is all of these to some extent, no one of them preeminently; all things to all people.

From time to time the public library tries to focus its energies on one or another of its missions. One example is the periodic effort to re-kindle the adult education flame that got the institution started a century ago. For a period in the 1920s and

1930s readers' advisers were common, providing individual counseling on what to read. Then the emphasis shifted to group programs, often only loosely connected with reading. There was a period of "outreach" to adults with limited formal education, and recently there has been a flurry of attention to the problem of functional illiteracy. The flame glows, sputters, and then is re-kindled.

A recent example is the concern about "independent learners." "The concept was that the library, functioning as a vital learning resource center, could be an active agent in orienting the unaffiliated adult students to the process of learning, helping them to recognize how their own jig-saw pieces of experiential, often short-termed, and seemingly unrelated episodes fitted into an organized whole."[1] In other words, the aim was to make adult readers into sustained and persistent learners, to help them get their acts together. The catch is that adults must do this for themselves, and if they cannot or do not do so, it is doubtful if a librarian can help them very much. The library and the independent learner had its day in the 1970s and early 1980s, and is now fading from the scene.

The very scope of the public library's purposes and offerings, combined currently with constrained financial support, prevent it from concentrating on and carrying through with any one mission or group of functions. Again and again the agency has sought to focus its energies on some clear target, only to fall back in time for lack of capacity to sustain the effort.

Of the several types of libraries, the public library is the least sure of purpose and least clear on clientele needs. The other types each have fairly clear objectives and have continuous contact with individual users. Public librarians come to know only a handful of users with any intimacy, while school librarians work regularly with a circumscribed group of students, academic librarians with faculty whom they know personally in terms of resource needs, the special librarian with a small group of company users or agency staff members. Without intimate user contact and understanding, the public librarian lacks a basis for deciding on objectives with certainty, and ends up responding to any expressed demand, which is the policy of a commercial enterprise rather than of a public agency established for a social purpose.

The public library, which started as a cultural-educational extension of the schools with a fairly clear mission, now finds itself to be an umbrella agency, picking up where a variety of other knowledge-materials resources leave off. Thus the "all things to all people" character of community library service programs, each carried out to a limited extent. Thus also the residual nature of the agency's "publics": consumers of popular publications who for economic reasons do not utilize bookstores and paperback racks, students who cannot get what they need in their school or college libraries, information seekers who do not find what they want in the newspaper, on television, or among their home or office resources. For most patrons the agency is a second choice, turned to after more convenient sources are exhausted. Many recent studies have proposed a setting of priorities[2] — "concentrate and strengthen" has been a recurring theme — but this proves difficult in practice because both staff and residual user groups resist change.

Because of the wide diversity in size and scope of public libraries, they play markedly different roles in the macrocosm. In some cases the local school collection is actually stronger than the village collection, with more of the classics and more introductory works in subject fields, and extending to audiovisual resources almost completely absent from the community agency. A nearby academic library may, in other locations, hold the preeminent resources in the area. On the other hand, some of the large city libraries loom head and shoulders over the other installations of the region. It is the wide variety in capacity of public libraries that makes for the inequality of access to resources that marks the American library scene.

Despite its disparities, its uncertain objectives, and its dispersed program, the public library has retained a considerable measure of public esteem, based on a general faith in reading and information sources. In the overall organization of library service, it plays in metropolitan regions a role of back-up resource for diverse publics and a role of primary source for a small minority. It fills in the holes left by other collections, public and private; while it is not preeminent in any one service—whether research or subject collections or adult education or student materials or diversional materials or information service—without it there would be distinct gaps in the macrocosm.

School Libraries

The other very large group of libraries consists of installations in schools. Practically all secondary schools have such a resource, but the picture is considerably less complete at the elementary level, particularly if private and parochial institutions are included in the count.

School libraries range from attended stockrooms to educational centers functioning in step with the classroom and reaching out to individuals. On the one side they simply house materials needed for study purposes, with the librarian serving as organizer and custodian of the stock—a storeroom, a reservoir, a study hall with books. On the other end of the spectrum, some school libraries stimulate and guide media use, working hand in hand with the teacher, and contributing directly to individual learning.

The goal was presented in an earlier basic text on school libraries in such phrases as: "provide boys and girls with the library materials and services most meaningful in their growth and development as individuals"—"stimulate and guide pupils in all phases of their reading"—"provide an opportunity for boys and girls to develop helpful interests, make satisfactory personal adjustments, and to acquire desirable social attitudes."[3] These noble objectives continue in the most recent statement of school-library standards, issued under the hopeful title of "Information Power."[4] The aim over the years has been to bring the library media center into a partnership with the essential teaching function of the school. Most school libraries fall somewhere short of these goals, providing supplies of supplementary material and with the librarian providing some instruction in the use of resources.

Thus in the macrocosm most young people have experience with one or more school libraries in the course of their basic education, and this applies to reluctant as well as enthusiastic readers. They may or may not also have access to other materials in the classroom, the home, and the community. They may or may not turn to the public library, but they can hardly avoid the media center in the school. It is logical to assume that the experience in the school influences later library use, whether for better or worse.

For those who continue into higher education the progression is clear and direct; it is the library-wise who tend to go on to college. For others all studies show a sharp falling off in library use on graduation. Not often does library use in school inculcate a life-long library habit, a natural turning to other collections, and this holds for readers as well as non-readers. It would be unjustified to blame this turning away on school media centers, for other forces are at work on the individual, but the school library cannot be termed the entry portal to the larger macrocosm for the majority of young people. Too often the school media center is not a door to a larger world but a room which students must enter even as they must go into the classroom, and a room to which they shut the door when they leave.

In the overall organization of library service the media centers in schools each stand as small and isolated units. School librarians may not have contact with any other librarian in the course of a regular work week or month. Their orientation is inward, toward teaching and the classroom, not to resource provision in the community at-large. Ask either the school librarian or the nearby public librarian when they last had a professional conference about their mutual responsibility to young people, and the answer often is that such an exchange has not occurred for several years if it has occurred at all.

We will shortly see that school libraries have been the last to be drawn into regional networks. This insularity adversely affects both librarian and student. The former lacks the stimulus of periodic contact with colleagues facing the same problems and trying similar experiments. The student perceives library to be a resource for getting school work done, not as a stepping stone to a vast world beyond. One objective indicator of this isolated position is the small number of interlibrary loans sought by most school libraries. They have limited resources, but do not regularly participate in exchanges with other collections. The school library is the most isolated of the agencies in the service macrocosm.

The number and quality of school libraries increased decade by decade, up into the 1970s. For a period a significant amount of federal money went directly into their collections. The better installations gained strength not only in books but also in other media, and came to be called media centers. Whether this development will continue through the 1990s is problematical. The federal money is uncertain and as local funds have become constricted the school library often takes a disproportionate cut. With limited money available, school authorities frequently put up to the electorate the question of whether to cut athletics and/or the library, and in many an instance football is voted in and library books out.

In the macrocosm the school library can be considered as part of the foundation, in the sense that it reaches most youngsters, whereas the clienteles of other libraries are distinct minorities within their population groups. But the foundation has not been planned in relation to the rest of the overall structure.

Media centers no doubt help to get some lifelong readers started. On the other hand there are individuals who use school libraries as students but no other organized collection for the rest of their lives. At this point we are driven beyond the province of this volume to the question of human aspiration and motivation, which directs individuals toward or away from the record of knowledge. Certainly it would be no more justified to ascribe the shortcomings of adults to the school library than it would be to ascribe the ills of the world to the school.

Academic Libraries

Here the contrasts within the category are rather sharp, although not at the extreme found in public libraries. The college units have primarily an instructional orientation and the university libraries are focused more toward research. Some of the latter include distinct college units within the university library complex, while the bulk of the collection is pointed toward graduate and professional study.

College libraries can in part be thought of as extensions of high-school libraries. This applies in particular to the many community colleges that have grown up in the last two decades. There is the collection of circumscribed scope, the familiar bibliographic apparatus, the general reference and circulation desks, a continuation of earlier instruction in library resources and use. They often have the utilitarian appearance of the typical high-school library. In other cases, college collections, usually in older liberal-arts institutions, have substantial depth in the traditional academic subjects, sufficient to sustain honors and advanced project work. Some have the ambiance of a club and place emphasis on individual study locations. These definitely broaden the resources available in the districts where they are located, and many have liberal provisions for use by local residents.

Essentially the college library is a supply agency, albeit in some cases a fairly sophisticated one. Books are acquired to support the courses offered, and beyond that titles are ordered which faculty members recommend. Once acquired, the resources are fitted into an organized collection, usually following the order determined elsewhere as conveyed in OCLC (Online Computer Library Center) or other remote-source entries. To control use, reserve sections are maintained. Orientation is given in the use of the library, and occasionally more advanced bibliographic instruction. For the many institutions which promote individualized study and maintain honors programs, the collection is a primary source of supply.

Over the years there have been experiments in making the campus library more of a direct teaching force.[5] Individual study programs have been built around the collections. Adjacent physical locations have been used, with classrooms and faculty offices located around the library. Librarians have joined with faculty in the classroom. For a period such approaches were espoused under the term the Library-College.

Relatively few of the experiments to orient college instruction around the library have taken root and grown over a period of time. Most have been discontinued or diluted, with collegiate instruction returning to the customary base in classroom lectures and discussion, backed up by a textbook, and supplemented by library resources. Most of the stimulus to use resources, and guidance in their use, emanates from the classroom and the faculty office. For the most part the supportive function of the college library has remained central; the academic librarian is more accurately referred to as "the keeper of the book," although the professional literature likes to refer to the college library as "the heart of the institution."

University libraries differ not only in scope but also in function. Some are among the largest collections in the world; in the United States, after the Library of Congress, the next half-dozen collections in size are in universities (Harvard, Yale, Illinois, Columbia, Michigan, California). The purpose is graduate study, research, and professional preparation. While few of these libraries would claim to be complete in their areas of specialization, this is not for lack of trying; they strive for self-sufficiency, although even the largest never quite make the grade. We will later note the internal organization of university libraries into subject departments in an effort to deal with the flood of documents and the variety of users.

For those individuals who go on to higher education—now over half of high-school graduates—the college and university library comes to play a strategic role in their educational experience and their preparation for a career. It is conceivable that a high-school student can get through the secondary institution without darkening the door of the school library, but this is most unlikely for a college or university enrollee. At least for a period, the library is essential for them. They are thus potential lifetime users of the whole macrocosm of library resources, and one test of the total organization of library service is whether college and university graduates continue over their adult years to have access to the record of knowledge they need.

Both college and university collections have impact beyond the immediate campus. The publicly supported institutions are usually open by policy to all residents of the taxing jurisdiction. Private colleges often accept and even welcome off-campus use (at least those in "college towns"), as part of their integration into the community. Even those private universities that restrict and monitor use will usually grant permission to a serious scholar who has no other source. Despite the open or partially-open door, the amount of community use of academic libraries is modest. In fact, a public library may be maintained across town with many of the same titles as on campus.

Whether the library experience of students in higher education leads them to lifelong use of the record of knowledge, of course, differs from individual to individual and differs depending on the vocation entered. Most come of necessity to learn how to use their college or university libraries. In some cases these are compact collections that are not too hard to grasp, and even when collections are large and dispersed, students find their part of the total by repeated trial and error. Then they graduate, leave the campus, and enter a less organized environment of resource provision. There is the limited office or company collection, beyond that the uneven public library, perhaps occasional contacts back on campus. Even with the academic experience, libraries are not easy to use. The college graduate and the advanced-degree holder often come to depend on a few resources needed in their careers, but beyond that are little more likely than the high-school graduate to fit libraries into their regular round of activity. The vagaries of the commercial sources come to replace the neat order of the academic library.

Because of their super-status, the strongest university libraries tend to stand apart in the macrocosm of service. Their very strength isolates them from lesser collections in the area, whether in schools, colleges, or public libraries. Examples of larger public libraries and university libraries working closely together are rare. For joint action the research-level libraries tend to work with other similar institutions in other states and other regions of the country. This distinction and peer affiliation is likely to continue as networking develops further.

Most types of academic institutions have moved from a long period of quantitative growth (in students, faculties, budgets) to a current stabilization or reduction in enrollment. This poses the problem of maintaining quality with declining income. Some institutions are consciously planning for reduced enrollments. The number of students will be cut and faculty will be reduced as retirements occur, in order to bring the enterprise into a new balance. College librarians are attempting to meet these changes with a revised statement of standards. Will the library also be reduced in size? Not directly, but indirectly by means of budget restrictions and pressures to squeeze every ounce of gain from cooperative ventures. In academic library administration, this is a time not for the builder but for the conservator.

Special Libraries

This really is a catch-all category, encompassing collections that do not fit readily into the public, school and academic classifications. Here are the great research institutions (Morgan, Folger, Crerar, Newberry, and Huntington libraries), and also the small working collections in banks, insurance companies, publishing houses, and a host of other commercial firms. Here also are the collections that support professional and cultural endeavor. Legal and medical and scientific collections may have some considerable depth, while the "library" in a small research enterprise may consist mostly of runs of technical journals. Organizations devoted to special fields—history, conservation, the arts, religious interests, the sciences—have their special collections. City administrations maintain their resources (municipal reference libraries), as do many state legislatures (legislative reference services).

The *Directory of Special Libraries and Information Centers* lists 1200 collections in New York City alone, and the listing is incomplete. From the kinds of special libraries one can discern the different characteristics of cities: historical collections in Philadelphia, technological collections in Rochester, collections relating to the entertainment world in Los Angeles. Expanding cities such as Houston, Denver, and Atlanta add special libraries year by year.

In the macrocosm of total resources, special libraries fill two quite different roles. One is that of the immediate working collection, established for convenient access. Such collections seldom contain resources unique to their regions, but are composed of frequently-used duplicates brought close to hand. The other function of a smaller number of special libraries is to search out, house, organize, and preserve very specialized and unique materials. The latter constitute additions to overall resources, a filling in of gaps or extending of depth.

The purposes of special libraries are usually quite clear and their clienteles quite specific. Typically they are staffed by personnel well versed in the subject area or special character of the collection, and typically they work quite closely with users. Some special librarians, for example, are in regular contact in person and by phone with a relatively small number of frequent inquirers. Definiteness of purpose usually enables the special units to concentrate and to achieve their objectives.

However, when they are part of business-industrial enterprises, they can be orphans in the organization, attached to divisions or placed under corporate officers to which they are not intrinsically related. Perhaps for this reason special librarians, particularly those in business libraries, often maintain active professional groups in metropolitan areas, thereby gaining associations that they lack in their separate enterprises.

The question of user access applies less to the working collections, which by definition are there for affiliated individuals who need them, but user access can be a problem in the case of the unique collections. Specialists in various endeavors may desire access to them, yet for the most part they are privately financed and established for company personnel or designated groups of scholars. It takes a little doing for the unconnected searcher to be admitted in New York City, for example, to the collection of the Metropolitan Museum, the Grolier Club, or even the Spencer or Arents Collections of the New York Public Library, and substantially more negotiation to get into such corporate libraries as those of *Newsweek* magazine, the Manufacturers Hanover Trust Co., or the Advertising Research Foundation, to name only a few examples. Some specialized users have learned that they can sometimes get around barriers by leaving the restricted-access library entirely, returning to their customary agency, and requesting items through interlibrary loan.

The smaller special libraries, as working collections, often turn regularly to larger libraries for materials not on their own shelves, most often to the public library. They may limit their acquisitions as a matter of policy because of this connection. A few companies recognize and acknowledge this dependence and go out of their way to support fund drives on the part of the larger resource, but many simply take the relationship for granted and are surprised when asked to contribute to a publicly-supported agency that is contributing directly to their private profit-making activity.

Larger special libraries are often valuable parts of the total resources available in population centers. At the same time, because of their independent nature, they are also slow to enter into coordinated networks and thus for practical purposes may not be an integral part of available resources. When reference is made to opening the full range of national resources to any seeker needing them, the gaining of access to the total macrocosm, it is often major special libraries that are meant, but in reality many of these libraries remain closed to the unaffiliated seeker.

Growth of Library Cooperation

Library development in the United States and Canada has been marked over the years by cooperative effort, joint action for and among libraries. As the volume of publication increased, and the quantity of recorded information multiplied, it became increasingly evident that few if any libraries could handle the flood alone. Keyes Metcalf, one-time Director of the Harvard University Libraries, was fond of saying that unless alternative policies were adopted, library demands would so eat into the university budget that several faculty positions would have to be sacrificed each year, and at an accelerating rate, to the point where the institution would be all library, with no faculty for instruction and research.

Progressive steps in library cooperation have occurred since the turn of the century. This can be thought of as an effort aimed eventually at organizing a single, coordinated library service system—a national service system—out of more than

100,000 libraries. The goal has been to make material as needed available to readers no matter where they are located, and no matter where the material is held. We will note to what extent this objective has been achieved and the structure that has been built up in the process.

Virtually all libraries are being drawn into the coordinative process. This affects not only the service that each library unit can render, but also internal organization for selection and acquisition of materials, for bibliographic control, and for public service. Increasingly in the next years the organization *among* libraries will be as important as the organization *within* libraries, and administrators will find themselves spending as much time relating to other institutions as relating divisions within their own agency.

The many cooperative efforts can be grouped under three broad purposes, which are interrelated and reinforce each other:

> *Joint Projects to Aid Individual Libraries*
>   Centralized cataloging
>   Central processing centers
>   Storage centers
> *Building of Bibliographic Records:*
>   Periodical indexes
>   Union catalogs
>   Union lists
>   Descriptions of resources
> *Sharing of Resources:*
>   Interlibrary Loan
>   Specialization of fields of acquisition

The first group is designed for individual libraries, to help get their work done. Of primary importance is centralized cataloging, now used by the vast majority of libraries, thus tying them into a national recording system. Cards prepared and distributed by the Library of Congress opened up this whole prospect. Commercial suppliers later got into the act, and in recent decades automated sources have gained wide acceptance, the largest being OCLC (Online Computer Library Center). The result is a product of uniform and high quality, obtained without expensive duplication of cataloging by each library. From the user's standpoint, the searcher can go to almost any collection and consult a recognized and familiar form of record. And from the standpoint of a national library system, the central computerized record facilitates both cooperative acquisition and interlibrary loan.

OCLC has cut out a place as a library cooperative utility since its establishment in 1967 as a state consortium. It broke through with the first on-line shared cataloging system in 1971, which is now used by thousands of libraries over the country, and has built up a huge data base of holdings records. In 1979 an automated interlibrary loan sub-system was added, and automated acquisition programs are now in place. Nor is OCLC resting on its laurels: experimentation is under way with an on-line data base for home computers.

With great expansion has come criticism of the OCLC system, on the grounds that it is a monopoly, and that the product best serves a middle range of agencies but not those with special missions. It is most difficult, from one source, to serve effectively the whole range and variety of libraries described earlier in this chapter. A recent controversy was over OCLC's application for copyright of the bibliographic data base it maintains; opponents argue that the data base is not owned by OCLC, nor is it an original work. In 1991 promising consultation between OCLC and the Research Library Group (RLG), designed to move toward a single national database of holdings, was broken off. But other efforts with this same goal will no doubt occur, perhaps starting with the Library of Congress.

We commented earlier on the tendency of large research libraries to go their own way in cooperative ventures. This separation is demonstrated again in the case of a bibliographical utility. The Research Library Group (composed of several major research libraries) in 1978 sponsored RLIN (Research Libraries Information Network), based on resources that had been built up at Stanford University. It has developed into an advanced service with a high-quality data base providing authority control and powerful subject research capacities.

RLIN has picked up clients, but is not as yet as well established financially as OCLC.

Cooperative ventures for processing and storage have not gained as wide acceptance. Commercial processing centers, which deliver books ready for circulation, are used in some cases. Several central storage facilities have appeared, to hold lesser-used items from member libraries; what started as the Midwest Inter-Library Center has developed into the national Center for Research Libraries, and has added an acquisition program to its storage function.

Even earlier than centralized cataloging for individual libraries was the analysis and listing of the contents of periodicals, thus starting to build a national bibliographic record. The 19th-century model here is Poole's *Index to Periodical Literature*. Today there are literally hundreds of index and abstract records of journal publication.

For books, the early and continuing models are the National Union Catalogs of the Library of Congress and the National Library of Canada, the aim in these cases being a virtually complete register of important books held in the two countries. Another sizable part of the record is made up of bibliographies in subject fields, to the point where there are bibliographies of bibliographies. Then there are union lists for location purposes, the most notable being the *Union List of Serials in Libraries of the United States and Canada*. Finally, among cooperative location sources, are general descriptions of the holdings of libraries in a region or in a subject field, several thousands of these being listed in *American Library Resources; a Bibliographical Guide.*[6] What started as guides to publications have themselves become so numerous and varied that only the most skilled of searchers can find their way among them. Note the steady effort toward a coordinated macrocosm of library resources.

The third and prevailing stage of library cooperation can be characterized as opening of access to and sharing of resources. Actually this has been the objective of joint effort since the beginning. Interlibrary loan came into the picture early, but was long impeded by lack of information about location, lack of a uniform code for lending, undue concentration of demand on a small number of very visible libraries, and in some instances a reluctance to share. Considerable progress has been made against each of these impediments, so that large quantities of publications are exchanged each year, but it would be overly sanguine to conclude that the pipeline is entirely clear.

The beginning of wisdom is recognition that few of the present network structures are final or permanent. Library cooperation is still evolving. The library administrator should not seek the ultimate panacea, for it does not exist, but must be prepared to adjust as network patterns change and technology develops further.

The proliferation of cooperative ventures is now being met by the standard administrative response, that of adding coordinating levels to the pyramid.

Most states have introduced some form of system or network. The two terms, incidentally, are often used interchangeably, but a useful distinction to keep in mind is that "system" usually refers to combinations of one type of library (most often public libraries), while "network" refers to joint effort among different types of libraries (usually with academic and research libraries in a prominent role).

New York Structure as an Example

The state plans vary from rudimentary to quite elaborate. New York State has one of the most developed coordinative set-ups and it is worth describing as an advanced example.

The public libraries of the State are organized into 22 systems, a few of these "consolidated" (member libraries as branches of a main library), some "federated" (created by one or more county governments but with member agencies governed by their own boards), and the larger number "cooperative" (formed by autonomous libraries without action by a governmental entity). Almost without exception the 700-plus public libraries in the State are members of systems. The systems headquarters maintain a long list of services for their members, of an administrative character, in technical services, and in facilitation of public services. Each system contains one or more "central" libraries with stronger than average collections open to all residents of the district, and in some cases to all residents of the State.

The 64 academic libraries in state institutions are grouped in the SUNY (State University of New York) system. Recently the final group, school libraries, has been pulled together in 43 systems. All these coordinated groups are statutory under state law.

The several kinds of libraries—including all academic institutions, special collections, and the various systems—work through nine Reference and Research Library Resources Councils (3 R's). The key element is inclusion of the several types of libraries within regional networks, with primary attention to ". . . the information needs of library users ranging from professional researchers to high-school students."[7]

Activities include inter-library loans, delivery facilities, union lists and indexing, cooperative collection development, and continuing education programs for member staffs. The Councils also openly share access to OCLC and to Internet to small libraries that cannot afford them.

The whole structure is related to the New York State Library and indeed has been stimulated and guided by this agency at all stages. Over $80,000,000 of state funds (in addition to the appropriation for the State Library) go annually to the maintenance of this multi-system structure, in excess of $4.00 per capita. The various components of the network are authorized in state legislation.

A notable feature of the whole plan is that it works without centralized control as espoused by earlier theoreticians of organization. No doubt a form of control exists in the major dependence on state money, and the broad pattern is set in state legislation. But the State Library has avoided autocratic dictation of projects and service structures, the 3R's Councils function on a cooperative basis, and individual libraries retain autonomy. It is a structure that looks as though it would not work, because of its complexity and lack of central control, but in practice it functions with relatively little friction and with perceptible results. Cooperative action day-by-day has become a way of life. All this is in contrast with the earlier conception of "larger units," which sought to combine libraries into new legal entities but which made only limited progress.

The basic goal is user access to existing resources. This has real meaning to the readers in small towns, as they receive material from their central public-library systems and beyond, and equally to the researchers in larger centers who gain access through their 3R's Councils to specialized resources anywhere in the region and beyond. A coordinating structure, maintained by state money, has released the potential of joint action.

At the same time, all this has not been accomplished without some disagreement on how state money should be used. Local libraries challenge some of the cooperative ventures, preferring to get money directly to put books on their own shelves. Some public-library systems question the allocation of funds to projects that benefit primarily a small and specialized group of users.

But overall the statewide plan delivers. The New York network illustrates several characteristics of this type of development:

- where strong enough, the state constitutes a viable base for integrating library resources and services;
- money from outside of localities—i.e., state or federal money—is usually needed to stimulate and sustain network development;
- coordination among libraries can elicit interest and support on the part of the state and federal legislators and officials;
- the separate types of libraries tend to enter first into their own systems before becoming part of a larger integrated network;
- cooperative structures, to endure, must be built from the bottom up, responding to the needs of individual libraries;
- materials in substantial numbers flow through the cooperative links and get to readers;
- the users helped most are at the two ends of the spectrum, those with very limited local resources and those seeking quite advanced materials;

- in time networks build up elaborate coordinating structures, which can exhibit bureaucratic characteristics of their own.

Regional Networks

Most regions in the United States have developed inter-state library networks, which now number over twenty in the country. Examples are NELINET (New England), SOLINET (Southeast), AMIGOS (Southwest), and WLN (Northwest). Once again the basic purposes are to assist member libraries by joint effort and to open access to resources on the part of users. The regional networks act as brokers to national services (such as OCLC), sponsor bibliographic projects needed within regions, promote interlibrary loan and further sharing of resources. Essentially they are bibliographic utilities.

At this level the cooperative effort applies to only a small portion of library use, that for highly specialized materials not available within states. This does not negate the need for regional resource sharing, because the demands served are highly important even though they may be limited in number. As one moves up the network ladder, the focus is on a smaller and smaller number of seekers of the record of knowledge.

One issue that remains is whether some libraries—those that are already the strongest—will be more able to participate in and benefit from networks, while many smaller libraries will be outside the fold, weak and isolated. Formerly it was the small agency that benefited from interlibrary loan, drawing strength from the larger collections; now it is often the larger and stronger agency that benefits from regional networks. Emphasis in the library movement has shifted from reaching persons of limited background, which got it started in the 19th century, to serving those with heightened needs, reflecting the complex civilization of the 20th century.

At both state and regional levels, new technology comes into prominent play. Computer capacity and electronic communication make possible many of the network functions. To this point they have been used to further the traditional library mission of providing access to materials that have been gathered into collections. Access has been the keyword.

As technology develops further, the emphasis will shift to distribution and dissemination, with the user/materials interface occurring at a distance, in home/office/classroom/laboratory, wherever the information or the document is needed. The transfer will occur without involving a visit to a library. This will involve a fundamental change in the delivery system.

To this point automation and new means of communication have been used largely to do better and more rapidly what libraries have always done. Further development of this technology will open the prospect of a small number of central data banks with contact provided over wide areas. Dissemination rather than access will become the keyword.

Whether networks will lead the way into this new organization of service remains to be seen. They are less encumbered than individual libraries by a collection in place and by staff protected by civil service and other tenure provisions. Networks should be more amenable to change. On the other hand, their roots are in the existing local structure, and this may prevent them from moving with the times.

Certainly the inter-state networks are not free of problems. Fragmentation and competition have appeared. Financial pressures are endemic. The relation of state to inter-state systems is unclear. OCLC is being challenged by more specialized vendors. Networks constitute an open marketplace in which customers must beware.

Such problems aside, networks large and small operate at the cutting edge of coordinated service among libraries, forging an organized macrocosm from many thousands of separate units. What improvement comes in library service in the next years is likely to be brought about by state and regional networks.

A National Library System

Who will coordinate the coordinators? Some voices have been

raised for a single, unified, national network, headed up in the Library of Congress or some other national center. The concept is appealing, for it would bring order to complexity.

Some years ago an eminent library administrator postulated that ". . . . one (or a very few) national pools for the acquisition of current serial and monographic resources on as comprehensive a basis as possible. . . ."[8] would be the most cost-effective approach to acquisition and access problems. As to the alternative of cooperative acquisitions, Fussler concludes that this would ". . . be more costly in aggregate expenditures, less stable, less reliable, less comprehensive, and a slower system of access for contemporary and future acquisitions than a centralized pool approach."[9]

There are a few models of unified systems. A single national structure exists for medical information and literature, with a legal base in federal legislation, a national collection at the apex, the Medlars/Medline data base, and regional medical libraries across the country. A parallel national structure exists for agricultural materials. A long established nationwide system provides materials for the blind and physically handicapped, again with a regional structure. In each of these cases a specific purpose and user group are served, in causes that engender support on the part of the U.S. Congress. Now we move into a new phase in the federal relation to information and library service, with the interest at the national level in an "Information Highway" system. Do we have the strength—the national economic base, the unity of purpose, the coordinated political action—necessary for a new infrastructure at least as complex as the National Highway System needed in order to build the new highway?

A single, over-branching structure for all libraries and all users does not have the same clarity and appeal, either to legislators or to library practitioners. Both have learned to be skeptical of grand plans. As another factor, diversity has long characterized many aspects of American life and institutions, including libraries. The individual seeks to hold to community roots, even as the user holds to localized libraries. Managers look suspiciously at monolithic structures, and administrative theoreticians caution against them. Much of the disillusion with national service programs results not from rejection of their purposes but from dissatisfaction with their performance, the problems that seem inevitable in vast-scale government enterprises. The same concern was reflected in the recent debate about a national health system.

The view contrary to a single national system is expressed by another university librarian: ". . . there is a role and market for a number of general, special and regional networks. A single monolithic national network embracing all libraries and providing all types of services is neither a realistic expectation nor a desirable goal. . . ."[10]

Another librarian pushes the criticism further: "A critical issue that we must face is the tendency to consider existing networks as interlopers that have usurped the rightful roles of some unspecified federal agency, and our tacit assumption that a federally-managed national library network is in our best interest. Some of us have got to begin to say to the national planners that the Emperor has no clothes."[11]

However, advances in technology—both in computerized recording of text and in electronic communication—could settle the argument. The Library of Congress has recently proposed creation of a National Digital Library.[12] The impact of such a development will be considered in the final chapter on "The Electronic Library."

The goal remains, partially achieved: to meld library collections into voluntary systems and networks that will open access to all resources held in the society. Formerly this was attempted without much structure. Then, before and after World War II, consolidation was the theme, outright combination of libraries, but it did not get very far. In the last two decades a multiplicity of voluntary organizations has appeared for the purpose. While the internal structure of libraries has remained much the same over the years, the structure among libraries has steadily evolved.

A single, coordinated library service system has not been achieved, and may never be. But progress has been made. Diversified microcosms are in process of being fashioned into a loose macrocosm. There may well be two distinct systems, one for the local resident and student (public, school, and college libraries) and one for the cosmopolitan scholar and researcher (university and research libraries), with occasional linkages between.

References

1. Brooks, Jean S. and Reich, David L. *The Public Library in Non-Traditional Education.* Homewood, Illinois, ETC Publications, 1974, p. 4.

2. Palmour, Vemon E. *A Planning Process for Public Libraries.* Chicago, American Library Association, 1980.

3. Fargo, Lucille F. *The Library in the School.* Chicago, American Library Association, 1947, pp. 8–9.

4. American Asociation of School Libraries. *Information Power; Guidelines for School Library Media Centers.* Chicago, American Library Association, 1988.

5. See Branscomb, Harvie, *Teaching with Books* (Chicago, American Library Association, 1940); Johnson, Byron Lamar. *The Librarian and the Teacher in General Education* (Chicago, American Library Association, 1948); Knapp, Patricia B. *The Monteith College Library Experiment* (Metuchen, N.J., Scarecrow Press, 1966); and Shores, Louis. *Library-College U.S.A.* (Tallahassee, FL., South Press, 1970).

6. Downs, Robert B. *American Library Resources; A Bibliographical Guide.* Chicago, American Library Association, 1951.

7. Welch, Janet M. "Reference and Research Library Systems in New York State," In *The Bookmark* of the New York State Library, Spring, 1980, p. 384.

8. Fussler, Herman H. *Research Libraries and Technology; A Report to the Sloan Foundation.* Chicago, University of Chicago Press, 1973, p. 76.

9. *Ibid.,* p. 77–78.

10. De Gennaro, Richard. "From Monopoly to Competition; The Changing Library Network Scene," *Library Journal*, Vol. 104, No. 11 (June 1, 1979), p. 1217.

11. Markuson, Barbara Evans, "Revolution and Evolution; Critical Issues in Library Network Development," In Markuson, Barbara Evans and Woolls, Blanche. *Networks for Networkers; Critical Issues in Cooperative Library Development*. New York, Neal-Schuman, 1979, p. 16.

12. *New York Times*, September 12, 1994, p. A10.

V THE LIBRARIAN'S VIEW OF ORGANIZATION

ALTHOUGH ALL LIBRARIANS work within an agency structure of some kind, they are not particularly concerned about organization as such. Most have been attracted to librarianship by the lure of books and the prospect of service, the chance to work with the recorded knowledge of humankind and with those consulting this record. Their view is from the inside, from the service desk, and they see structure only as it impinges on service performance and judge structure by how much it facilitates or blocks such performance. Service is central in this view; organization is auxiliary.

There is merit in this emphasis on results, on resources and help to users rather than on some preconceived model to which an agency is expected to conform. In the process, however, those who look at libraries from the service desk may accept uncritically a framework that works against the goals of the agency and their own standards. It is remarkable how most libraries have a similar organizational structure, despite the wide variation of purposes and clienteles, which raises the question of whether librarians unconsciously have a standard model which they apply in all situations without much reflection.

Yet librarians, of all professionals, have a stake in organization. Many others—doctors, dentists, lawyers, clergymen, scientists—may elect to work primarily within their own offices, hanging out their own shingles. For the most part they make their own organization, which can be kept small and simple if they so prefer. While they relate at one time or another to

127

group structures—the hospital, the courts, the congregation, the laboratory—essentially they are on their own, unencumbered by a pre-existing framework. Not so librarians, who must perforce work within an organization called the library. This structure will define their positions, outline their careers, determine their clienteles, facilitate or frustrate their professional endeavors, and establish both their public and their self-image. Decisions made before they joined the organization, and decisions currently made at other points within it, set the scope and limits of their endeavors. As sailors should know their ship, librarians should know the agency for which they work and how it functions.

The librarian's view of organization contrasts with that of those who aspire to a career in administration, say a graduate of the Harvard Business School. A librarian looks at a library and thinks collections and readers. Those who are administration-oriented look at a library or any other enterprise and think of command and functions and relationships. A librarian evaluating a library is likely to propose better collection building and improvements in staff training; the manager is more likely to propose reorganization and improvements in communication and decision-making. The difference can be seen in the contrasting emphases in survey reports of libraries, depending on whether they are done by librarians or by management firms.

A gulf can develop between the two viewpoints, with the professional seeing organization as secondary and those who are preoccupied with it as theoreticians, while the administrator looks on the professional as provincial and lacking in understanding of the working of the whole enterprise.

Neither of these one-sided attitudes is to be commended. Librarians should perforce look carefully at structure because it directly affects service and their own careers, and the manager should evaluate organization not by abstract principles but by the criterion of the end product being produced. Librarians would be wise to hold to their personal performance standards, but at the same time should be cognizant of good and bad organization. The bottom line is performance; organization is one important contributor to that goal.

Literature of Library Administration

Until recently the literature of library management reflected the same anti-organization bias. Says one author whose book in the field has gone through several editions:

> The longer one serves in college librarianship the more one becomes convinced that organization charts and techniques of management are less important in successful administration than personal qualities of character and intelligence.[1]

The emphasis on such old-fashioned virtues as character and intelligence is to be applauded. But to set these in opposition to organization and management is to create a pseudo-contrast. The fact is that organization and management exist—whether there are organization charts or not, whether there are character and intelligence or not—and, for better or worse, require attention.

The same author continues:

> In the small college library either there appears to be no need for organization or else the library has automatically organized its work around the particular skills of a few staff members.[2]

But every library has an organization, even if we say it is "disorganized." Even the one-person agency has some grouping of duties, some distinct locations where the one staff member performs different functions, some schedule for disposing of different kinds of work.

To speak of "no" organization is to fail to recognize relationships which exist as surely as there are books on the shelves. In the sense that the term is used in this volume, every library is "organized," whether anybody so wills or not, whether organized well or poorly, and whether managed by individuals of high or low character and intelligence.

Lyle is correct in pointing out that ". . . organization in the small college library, and occasionally in the medium-sized or large one, becomes a matter of adaption to individual capabilities rather than of assigning related activities to a particular position or department."[3] However, building structure around individuals still does not mean that organization has been abandoned. A decision, for example, to have a reference librarian also engage in cataloging is still a decision about structure, even though it may not follow orthodox lines. And once such an arrangement is established, it raises organizational questions that should be watched by the library director: are the capabilities of the individual equal to both functions, does one activity tend to take precedence over the other, does the combination facilitate coordination between the two? The very decision to fashion structure around individuals leads to more rather than less attention to organization.

Even when social scientists examined libraries—as for example in the Public Library Inquiry[4] of the late 1940s—relatively little stress was placed on organization. The Inquiry group included political scientists, sociologists, and psychologists, but no management experts. One turned to the series of volumes for an appraisal of the social purposes of libraries and of the impact of their service programs, but not for critical review of their structure and management. It would be hard to imagine a review of a city or a university or a business firm that did not give attention to how it is organized.

Standard Works in the Field

The early standard works on library administration, appearing in the 1940s and after, emanated from the library director's office, not from the management firm or the proponents of managerial principles. Few showed an acquaintance with or appreciation for the body of organizational theory that had emerged in the early decades of the century. Until very recently the literature has not forged a bridge between libraries and what was learned about administration in other fields.

One of the earlier comprehensive works on the administration of a type of library was the recognized volume on school libraries by Fargo.[5] Not long after came the earlier standard work on university libraries by Wilson and Tauber, which appeared in the 1950s.[6] Another substantial volume appeared in the early 1960s, this one on public libraries by Wheeler and Goldhor.[7]

Each of these was a breakthrough. They pulled together prevailing experience in the direction of the several types of libraries. Seasoned managers set down their experience and insight, what they found worked in the circumstances they faced. Essentially this constituted a coding of the folklore of library management. In this sense they were parochial, despite their depth of professionalism.

The same approach prevailed until fairly recently. The 1971 Rogers and Weber volume on university libraries, which has come to replace Wilson and Tauber, is frankly stated by the authors to be a "personal document,"[8] based on their observations and experiences. The systematic revision of the Wheeler and Goldhor treatise by Carlton Rochell adds this practitioner's insights to the earlier compilation.[9]

The various standard works follow a common pattern. At the outset there is general description of the purposes and functions of the type of library being treated, with little questioning of the institution as it exists nor much attention to review and planning. The responsibilities of the director are discussed, with consideration of relations to trustees and institutional officers. The topics emphasized in the volumes are collection building, personnel, and finance, certainly essential ingredients in the provision of service. Organization is dealt with to the extent that an unsolved problem exists in one or another kind of library—for example, departmental libraries within the university complex—but not as a factor that brings the various functions together to achieve a common purpose. It is indicative that "communication," which welds separate staff members and departments into a unified enterprise, does not appear in the index of Wilson and Tauber, nor Fargo, nor Wheeler and Goldhor.

In the second edition of Wilson and Tauber (1956), a brief section of the work of Fayol, Gulick, and Urwick was inserted. The latest of the group, the revision of Wheeler and Goldhor by Rochell (1981), has a few paragraphs on the Human Relations School and refers to the work of Rensis Likert. A body of principles which had long resided on the library's own shelves is starting to be applied in its own operation.

This modest infusion of theory did not readily carry over into library-school curricula and instruction. Depending as the courses did on the available literature within the profession, library-school courses on administration long continued to emphasize descriptions of how it is done in libraries—a passing on of the folklore—with little criticism or consideration of alternatives. At the advanced level, doctoral dissertations in library schools have seldom been devoted to administration. The topic is too diffuse to lend itself readily to a compact research design, nor can variables be readily controlled in the field, so doctoral candidates turn to more tractable topics.

Later Works on Library Management

The aspect of administrative theory that first received sustained attention from within library ranks was scientific management and its later applications and extensions. Ralph Shaw was an early advocate of this approach.[10] In his library-school courses at Rutgers University he liked to start off a new class by asking a student to come forward and file one hundred catalog cards, after which scientific-management principles would be applied to the filing task and the time usually cut in half. In time systems analysis of library service and operations, and sophisticated application of probability statistics, led to fresh library-based concepts (the Poisson distribution, for example).[11] One aspect of the administrative theory of the turn of the century was finally coming to libraries.

Then, in the 1970s and since, there belatedly appeared a connection with the administrative theory that had long existed. The Association of Research Libraries established its Office of Library Management Studies, leading to a fresh look at the libraries of Columbia University and other systems.[12] A spate of articles and books built around the long-existing principles has been published in the library field in the last 15 years. The light was finally perceived. All at once it was recognized that a gulf or vacuum had opened, between pragmatic administration of libraries on the one side and evolving management theories on the other, and various authors and publishers rushed to fill the vacuum.

An early example is the compilation of articles by Wasserman and Bundy, which included pieces by such management theorists as Herbert Simon, Chester Barnard and Peter Drucker;[13] the emphasis in this case was on the application of behavioral disciplines. A series edited in Britain applied theories of organization to libraries, starting with an essay on "The Study of Organizations" in the first volume in 1972,[14] and continuing at intervals in six successive volumes appearing up to 1982; those few American library administrators who follow British literature in the field received an early introduction to management theory in this series. By the mid-1970s the flood-gates were open. In close succession there appeared works by Evans,[15] Hicks,[16] Rizzo,[17] and McClure.[18]

Beyond these titles, typical of the new breed, what was termed a "primer" in library administration has a basic chapter on "mechanistic" and "organizmic" approaches to management, drawing on the early structural school and the later behavioral school.[19] In 1981 a college librarian and a public librarian collaborated on a volume that has many of the earmarks of similar texts being issued for administration in business and in public-service institutions.[20] Where the student of library management earlier sought in vain for treatments that recognized that libraries shared problems with other enterprises, now the question is which of many similar publications to study. It is indicative that the fifth edition of the standard Lyle text—the one where he originally deprecated organization as such—now has a section devoted to the topic, replete with organization charts [21]. Another recent addition in the field has chapters devoted to organization, both internal and external.[22]

Several common characteristics of these compendiums of the last fifteen years can be noted. Most treat administration of the several types of libraries together, rather than devoting separate publications to public, academic, school, and special libraries. Emphasis is usually placed on planning and on evaluation; MBO (Management by Objectives), PERT (Program Evaluation and Review Technique), and PPBS (Planning Programming Budgeting System) are sure to be covered. Maslow and Likert and Theory Y are likely to be there. Decision-making is given some attention, because it has been a focal point in recent management research. The new library administration texts are a mirror image of what has occurred in the study of business and government.

Impact of the Recent Literature

No easy measures exist by which to determine the effect of the recent stream of administration texts. Reviews of them have shown respect for their wider base in theory but are usually noncommittal on what has been contributed to the substance of management competence. No doubt students in library schools are exposed to them but they have seldom changed the substance of administration courses. Management theory is not evident in discussion of administrative problems at meetings of librarians, nor has it infused the bulk of journal articles on the topic.

The practical impact appears to be limited: very little has changed in the director's office. Reasons can be found both in the orientation of librarians and in the limitations of the new administration treatments.

One significant factor has already been mentioned, that librarians as a group have not been administration-minded. Nonetheless, all library managers, whether directors of a large enterprise or supervisors of small departments, operate according to some guidelines, whatever their source. Every situation is not considered ad hoc, but is settled at least in part on the basis of values or prior experience or professional standards that the individual decision-maker accepts without thinking of them as "principles." One practical reason for acting on the basis of theory is that it would simply take too long to consider every problem without reference to what has been learned earlier or what has worked elsewhere. Library directors who claim they do not act on theory may be surprised to discover that they have been talking prose all the time.

Then, too, most libraries are not large in size, and it is only in larger work groups that organization presses for review. This, however, cannot be a sole and conclusive reason for lack of attention to management theory, for some libraries grew rapidly after World War II, becoming million-dollar enterprises with hundreds of staff members, and some librarians actually made careers of organizing and reorganizing libraries, moving from one to another location for the purpose.

Libraries, furthermore, are usually auxiliary parts of larger structures—municipalities, schools, colleges, business concerns. What management scrutiny they experience may come when the "parent" organization is analyzed. In this case the library director may be more a spectator than a prime mover of the broader study, with results imposed from the outside rather than generated from within. There may well be more of these inclusive examinations in the coming years as governments and educational institutions are increasingly pressed for funds and look about for ways to reorganize and economize.

But part of the limited impact of the new view of library administration comes back to the recent publications themselves. The first limitation that strikes the working library manager is that the newer treatments lack that wealth of day-to-day know-how that distinguished the earlier texts on which the authors themselves were raised (Wilson and Tauber, Rogers and Weber, Wheeler and Goldhor). One looks in vain for the feel and reality of the director's office. The fine new theories often seem to be more products of the study than of the conference table. Zero-base budgeting, MBO, PERT and PPBS are seldom organically connected to libraries in the recent literature. The two worlds of practical management of libraries and general administrative theory still for the most part stand separate and apart.

Pragmatic operators simply do not see how the new theory will help them meet the problems on the desk and still stay within a constricted budget. As expressed by one university library administrator:

> The real danger with ... management systems is that they offer mechanistic formulas for dealing with complex realities

and keep us from thinking about and solving our management problems in practical, realistic and common sense ways.[23]

If the task is to hold the library together, not much time or thought can be given to long-range planning, to reorganization, to priorities—yet this is precisely the time when consideration of basics is most needed.

It is worth remembering these several factors and attitudes playing upon libraries as we go on to examine library organization and the extent to which it has adhered to and departed from accepted theory.

References

1. Lyle, Guy, R. *The Administration of the College Library*. 4th ed. New York, H. W. Wilson, 1974, pp. 49–50.

2. *Ibid.*, p. 41.

3. *Ibid.*, p. 41.

4. Leigh, Robert D. *The Public Library in the United States; The General Report of the Public Library Inquiry*. New York, Columbia University Press, 1950.

5. Fargo, Lucille F. *The Library in the School*. Chicago, American Library Association, 1947.

6. Wilson, Louis R. and Tauber, Maurice F. *The University Library: the Organization, Administration and Functions of Academic Libraries*. New York, Columbia University Press, 1951.

7. Wheeler, Joseph L. and Goldhor, Herbert. *Practical Administration of Public Libraries*. New York, Harper and Row, 1962.

8. Rogers, Rutherford D. and Weber, David C. *University Library Administration*. New York, H. W. Wilson, 1971, p. vii.

9. Wheeler, Joseph L. and Goldhor, Herbert, *op. cit.* Revised by Carlton Rochell, 1981.

10. Shaw, Ralph, ed, "Scientific Management," in *Library Trends,* Vol. 2, No. 3 (1954), pp. 359–483.

11. Morse, Philip M. *Library Effectiveness; a Systems Approach.* Cambridge, MA., MIT Press, 1968.

12. Booz, Allen and Hamilton, Inc. *Organization and Staffing of the Libraries of Columbia University; a Case Study.* New York, Redgrave Information Resource Corporation, 1973.

13. Wasserman, Paul and Bundy, Mary Lee., eds. *Reader in Library Administration.* Washington, D.C., Microcard Editions, 1968.

14. Holroyd, Gileon. *Studies in Library Management.* London, Linnet Books and Clive Bingley, 1974.

15. Evans, G. Edward. *Management Techniques for Libraries.* New York, Academic Press, 1976.

16. Hicks, Warren B. and Tillin, Alma M. *Managing Multimedia Libraries.* New York, Bowker, 1977.

17. Rizzo, John B. *Management for Librarians; Fundamentals and Issues.* Westport, CT., Greenwood Press, 1980.

18. McClure, Charles R. and Samuels, Alan R., *Strategies for Library Administration; Concepts and Approaches.* Littleton, CO., Libraries Unlimited, 1982.

19. Boaz, Martha, ed. *Current Concepts in Library Management.* Littleton, CO., Libraries Unlimited, 1979.

20. Stueart, Robert D. and Moran, Barbara B. *Library and Information Center Management.* 4th ed. Littleton, CO., Libraries Unlimited, 1993.

21. Lyle, Guy R. *The Administration of the College Library.* 5th ed. New York, H. W. Wilson, 1986.

22. Gertzog, Alice and Beckerman, Edwin. *Administration of the Public Library.* Metuchen, N.J., Scarecrow Press, 1994.

23. De Gennaro, Richard. "Library Administration and New Management Systems," *Library Journal*, Vol. 103, No. 22 (December 15, 1978), p. 2482.

VI EXTERNAL ORGANIZATION OF LIBRARIES

WHEN ORGANIZATION IS MENTIONED, one usually thinks of the internal structure of an enterprise, the officers and departments and positions within the agency; this internal structure is the subject of later sections. The present chapter deals with external organization, the relationships from the library out into the larger world.

A library is not only an organization in its own right, but also an enterprise or division within an organization. Practically every library is a part of a larger structure: a governmental unit, an academic institution, a school, a business firm, a professional or subject association. Where and how the library fits into this larger structure is fundamental to its nature and development, in the way that the family is fundamental to the development of the individual, and the community in turn is fundamental to the family.

Even as children and families react differently to their wider associations—some close and others distant, some flourishing and others frustrated—so libraries respond according to the nature of their administrations and staffs. Some prosper, some languish, and some hide. There are public-library directors who build and cherish close relations with city hall, while others consciously establish distance between their agency and the political arena. Some academic-library directors have weekly and even daily contact with presidents and deans, while others mix only at formal meetings. And no matter how frequent the contacts, the nature of those interchanges—whether supportive or adversary—go a long way to determine whether the library flourishes or suffers, to say nothing of whether the library director rests easy in his/her sleep.

Internal organization is often pictured as a pyramid, with the director at the apex. But above the executive officer a host of relationships should also be pictured. This can be done in the form of an inverted pyramid, with the director at the bottom instead of the top (see Figure 3). Just as relations widen out within an agency, through middle managers to individual staff members, so also external relations widen out through legal and formal controls to users and the general public.

From the director's office looking down, the key concept is control: from the same spot looking upward, the key concept is being controlled. This is true no matter how polite or indirect or subtle the external pressures may be. How managers connect and balance the two—forces from the outside and forces with-

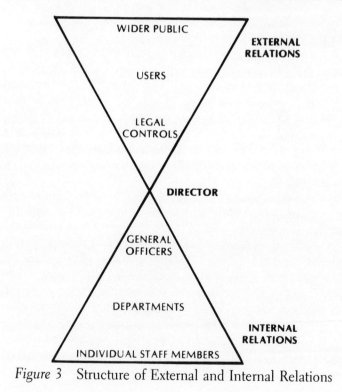

Figure 3   Structure of External and Internal Relations

in — goes a long way toward determining their success or failure. Here as elsewhere there are variations in administrative style. Some directors are equally surefooted in each domain, in the meeting in the mayor's or university president's office and also in the meeting with library staff. But there are those who are strongest in relations with the board and city hall or with the president's office and the university senate, and others who are effective within the library building but less so outside. Individual managers know which they do best, and so do their staff members.

Because of dissimilarities and contrasts in the external relations of the several types of libraries, each type will be discussed separately. Then the common elements in the relations of libraries with the larger world will be noted.

Public Libraries

The public library should be seen as the center of a host of outside and lay forces. It perforce is a "social" and a "political" agency, whether it so wills or not. This fact of life was noted in the Public Library Inquiry over 45 years ago, and it applies even more today. The library operates ". . . within a matrix of political forces . . . it is of paramount importance . . . that public librarians understand and appreciate more clearly the political world."[1] The theme of Garceau's treatise was that many public libraries act as though they are not part of local government.

The congeries of lay and outside influences working on the public library is pictured in Figure 4. The closest association is with the Library Board, and then influences extend outward through various local and state government offices, and on to the general public in several configurations. Library systems and networks add a further dimension. All of these take time and attention and sometimes manipulation. Small wonder that library directors sometimes wonder when they can be done with these "extraneous" relationships in order to get back to the bottom line of maintaining and improving service to users.

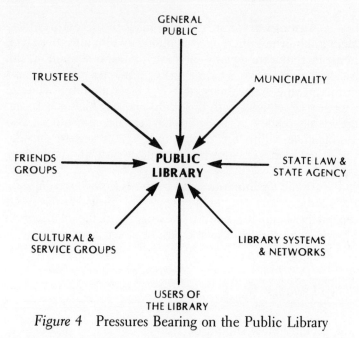

Figure 4 Pressures Bearing on the Public Library

The Trustee Form of Government

The Board of Trustees, composed of lay appointees, is not so much an "external relation" as the legal and policy heart of the agency. Here, by state law, is the authority for the public library, and the ultimate responsibility for performance. Director and staff are creatures of this body. New trustee appointees are often surprised at the power of the Board. They thought they would be asked for advice on library matters and, beyond that, bask in the prestige of serving on the board of a respected cultural institution. They find that in actuality they are responsible for funding, for financial control, for policy, for personnel, even for the books selected.

The formal designation of the responsibilities of library trustees in state statutes is something of a legal fiction. According to the detailed New Jersey law, "The board shall . . . purchase books, pamphlets, documents, papers and other reading matter, hire librarians and other necessary personnel, and fix their compensation."[2] There is no mention of an executive officer or director. "The public library shall be managed by a board of library trustees," says the California Code,[3] and the Arizona Statutes repeat the prescription that the trustees shall ". . . purchase necessary books, journals, publications and other personal property."[4] Many other examples could be cited from across the country. Most of the laws do not say that boards shall set policies for these operations, or supervise their performance, or delegate them to hired staff, but simply that the board will act. One could conclude that most trustees must arrive at the library promptly at 9:00 a.m. and proceed through the day to exercise their many management functions, having a few staff members available to carry out their orders.

In reality, of course, board members typically turn up for monthly meetings and often little beyond that. The chief librarian or library director selects and hires personnel, evaluates and orders books, and directs the various other operations of the agency. In substance, the board delegates the responsibilities specified in law. This is sometimes spelled out in the library's bylaws. However, in many cases this delegation is not made explicit, so that the library director proceeds without any clear basis in law or regulation, and could theoretically be challenged for usurpation of powers.

This odd situation came about because, when state statutes were adopted for public libraries, conscious effort was exercised to set the agency apart, free of direct government intervention and free of improper political influence. In the early years, trustees sometimes had to be active in the administration of the library, particularly when the staff lacked professional qualifications. Over a period of time the professional director came to the fore, and trustees fell back either into their policy-making or their rubber-stamp roles, depending upon the library and the individuals.

The law says one thing; practice follows a contrary pattern. Everyone accepts the contradiction and proceeds to get the work of the library done. In practice a working relationship evolves. The head librarian is expected to manage the agency. The trustees are to be involved in larger financial and policy questions. A rule-of-thumb applies, which usually suffices but which at times leads to confusion and friction.

In some instances the ambiguity is removed, either in laws of the governing body or in bylaws within the library. The San Francisco charter states: "The librarian shall be the chief executive of the department. He shall appoint, and at his pleasure may discipline and remove, all employees of the library department."[5] Similar statements appear occasionally in library bylaws, but are not common. Other libraries would be wise to define and set down the respective authority and responsibility of the board and of the executive officer, and in the process would be forced to clarify just what each is supposed to do.

The fiction of detailed Board review is preserved by the common practice of having trustees go through the routine of approving book requisitions (sometimes after the titles are ordered and received), and having the trustees approve all staff hirings and separations (sometimes after the employees are already on or already off the job). This charade reduces board deliberations to a routine and tends to de-emphasize the really significant functions of policy review, community representation, and procuring of funds. Dealing with details, trustees neglect the essentials.

Then there is the other side of the picture, individual trustees who go way beyond the figurehead role and become directly involved in library affairs, in the process interfering in internal administration. Usually one or another particular aspect of library service catches their attention. They become familiar with it, and push for change in their pet interest. Some library directors learn how to deal with such individuals, holding them at arm's length; others become dominated by persistent trustees pursuing personal interests.

It is a rare appointee who becomes a trustee statesman or stateswoman, taking the lead in policy-making and in broad development of the library. The case for lay library boards rests with such exceptions.

Of course, it must be admitted that part of the failure of boards to take hold of policy matters is the fault of library directors. Some consciously hold back from presenting such matters to the trustees; this might raise questions and open avenues of inquiry that the director believes are best left alone. Others fail to present policy questions clearly and fully, so that board members feel that they have little to grasp and inadequate information on which to base decisions.

When technical matters come before a lay board, various reactions that are not helpful are entirely possible. Individuals may suggest doubtful solutions without much sense of responsibility—after all, they won't have to carry them out. A few individuals may dominate and distort the discussion. Others may hold undue influence by virtue of social position or political connections or even wealth.

In basic policy matters, the give and take of this kind of exchange between lay people and professionals may in the long run lead to the best conclusions. But when fairly routine management matters are subjected to this kind of review, much time can be wasted and the proposed solution actually weakened. What the executive officer could decide effectively in a few minutes may be decided less effectively after several hours of group discussion by people not fully informed about the matter under examination.

Then why a lay board at all? Why have amateurs "hiring" personnel whose qualifications they do not know and authorizing purchases of books they have never examined? Why not move away from administrative boards, towards advisory and friends groups to maintain library-community relations?

When the question is raised, most librarians come down on the side of retaining the administrative board form of library government. This was true in the classic study some years ago by Carleton Joeckel,[6] and he had evidence from 310 libraries on which to base his judgment. It is also the view of most practicing library administrators today. They have learned to live with and to use the board. The hope is that the board represents the community in policy decisions, that it promotes the cause of the library in government circles, that it stands firm with the librarian in resisting efforts to censor additions to the collection.

A case can also be made from the societal standpoint. The two public agencies that provide recorded knowledge to the community are the school and the library. This is a solemn trust; if it were misused, society would suffer. Lay boards controlling policy in these two key agencies are the best device yet found for furthering democratic values and reaching decisions based on the values of the community.

If the board form is to be retained, what relation should exist between trustees and the executive officer? The usual response is that the board sets policy, which the executive then carries out. According to the recognized manual in the field, "Policies drawn by the library board delineate the conditions of library operation; the librarian chosen by the board carries out these policies."[7] Like other pat distinctions in administration, this is an overly-simple formulation. To begin with, the difference between policy and execution is not always clear or easy to define. One reacts upon the other, with policy questions often arising in the daily give-and-take of operations. Further, trustees are seldom in a position to take the initiative on policy; they are not that much involved, nor that much informed. The raising of a basic question usually originates with the director; it is this individual and his/her aides who gather the relevant facts, and usually this individual also who makes a recommendation on the matter. Policy is customarily not "drawn" by the trustees; what the board does is to accept or reject or occasionally modify.

Nonetheless, the distinction between policy and operation provides a guideline. The board can properly respond to, and in due time adopt a book-selection policy, but this does not mean that trustees will "select" titles. The board can properly consider and in due time approve hiring and promotion standards, but this does not mean selecting personnel (other than selection of the director). And when a budget crunch comes, trustees as representatives of the people can help decide what should be kept and what dropped. There are areas where responsibility can be shared—public relations, for example:

> Management is responsible for developing a public relations program, but trustees play both a direct and an indirect role in shaping and executing it.[8]

A few boards, concerned about what is going on in their

libraries, have tried to come up with evaluative criteria for judging performance both of the agency and of their executive. When this takes the form of precise standards of management conduct—how much time the director spends on the job, for example, or frequency of contact with city officials, or number of staff meetings—it is questionable. Administrative styles differ widely, and should be given free play, not fitted into a formula. Yet trustees, to carry out their responsibilities, must have some idea of what is being accomplished. The sound approach is for board and director to adopt together a set of clear and concise objectives, with a reasonable timetable attached, and then review the extent of progress at intervals along the way and at the end of the period specified. Performance in relation to agreed goals should be the measure.

Personal relations enter into the equation. Directors may develop an affinity with some trustees and an antipathy towards others, and such relations work both ways. Factions can open within the board, with the librarian caught somewhere between. The ideal, of course, is an easy relationship based on mutual respect, with a little social distance maintained so that an additional dimension does not enter. Given all these variations and permutations, it is small wonder that many head librarians find their work with the board to be one of their most sensitive and uncertain external relations.

A small percentage of public libraries function without lay boards. The library director in these cases is usually responsible directly to a city or county manager or other officer, an arrangement found in a number of cities and counties in California, and which appears also in Texas. There is little evidence that the agency fares either better or worse under this arrangement. Put differently, as far as any objective evidence can be marshaled, the lay board form of library government has yet to prove itself.

Friends of the Library

There is some tendency in the literature to dismiss or deprecate Friends organizations in public libraries. Wheeler and Goldhor observed (without approval) that "Some trustees fear that the Friends will get so influential and active that they will tell the trustees how to run the library."[9] An equal fear is that the group may be so inactive as to be hardly visible. A relatively small number of users band together, make some effort at recruiting supporters, raise modest funds, sponsor a lecture or other event once a year. The effect on service or on financial support can hardly be discerned.

Yet the device of a non-administrative organization can be beneficial. There is latent good will toward the library in the community at large. A segment of the people—both library users and others who believe in the institution—want to have an effective library, and are ready to devote at least a little time and money to the cause. But they are unorganized and individually powerless. The Friends group is a rallying point for such individuals.

These organizations tend to fall into one of three types. Too often they are simply cultural clubs, providing a focal point for individuals who appreciate the library and who gather at infrequent intervals to sing its praises. Then there are Friends groups—not very many, it must be admitted—that venture into the political arena, pushing the cause of the library, using the connections of their well-placed members for the purpose. Finally there is the group that raises money and engages in projects which develop library service.

The Friends of the San Francisco Public Library provides an example of the latter. Its membership of 2,000 and its $10.00 annual membership fee give it a start. A full-time executive director position is maintained. Various projects are carried out—for instance, each year a series of lectures by authors which nets over $25,000. The Friends seek and obtain grant money from foundations and private sources, using the funds to get agreed programs started in the library, such as computerized information service. Volunteers who are members of the group staff an information desk at the entrance of the Main Library. As in any organization, it is effective because a few individuals are dedicated, forceful, and hard-working.

The politically inclined Friends depend on the prestige and position of members. A luncheon with the Mayor, arranged by several business leaders who are Friends, can have an impact at budget time. A session with council members, arranged by local community leaders who are Friends, can further a plan for branch library development. The very fact that these are neither members of the Library Board nor members of the hired staff, but simply concerned citizens, adds to their influence.

Support groups have been used to good effect by other community agencies. Parent-teacher associations have a mixed record, but some contribute equipment needed in the school and a few have influenced educational policy. Volunteer and auxiliary groups for hospitals make a distinct contribution, and many hospitals have a staff member to organize and train the volunteers. It is not unusual to have volunteers staffing the reception desks, handling the gift shop, and helping nurses in the wards. Libraries for some reason have not capitalized on such volunteers. They report that volunteers are not reliable and require too much time for training and supervision. Could it be that there is also concern that intelligent and motivated volunteers might handle some tasks as well as trained staff?

The Friends constitute one more external relation that the library director must nurture. Some of these groups need encouragement. Others are free-wheeling and need control. All tax the skill of the administrator, not in library principles but in human relations.

Connections with City Hall and State House

Beyond the trustees and the Friends stand the various offices of local government. Formerly the relations were infrequent and formal; currently they are growing closer. Often an adversarial relationship develops. The budget office seeks to limit appropriations, the personnel office seeks to impose uniform staff standards, the purchasing office wants to control acquisitions. Mayors seldom have the library high on their list of priorities. When the present author conducted studies in three major city libraries, in two the Mayors hardly knew of the existence of the study, but in the third the incumbent became actively involved—and it was in this last that the greatest advance was made in library support.

Libraries compete with other government services for funds. Particularly in the larger cities they compete for scarce resources, as metropolitan decentralization continues, draining jobs and ratables from the center, while physical deterioration and crime persist. Currently, the same conditions appear in the older, established suburbs.

The minorities that increasingly occupy the central cities are gaining political power and electing members of their own group to high office. This could strike at the automatic public faith that in the past has sustained libraries, the assumption that books and reading are worthwhile—not that minorities are against reading and learning, but that they take a hard look at existing institutions to evaluate their contribution to the people they represent. The public library has been more effective in serving an educated, established majority than in reaching under-educated minorities. The changing demographic composition and political climate of metropolitan areas—where most public libraries exist—must increasingly be reflected in deliberations in the library board room, or the institution will be perceived as a carryover from the past that has only marginal value in the tough job of maintaining the urban complex today.

The library director has little choice except to get into the political arena. This does not necessarily mean party politics and party deals. There is more than one game played in the arena. Regular businesslike relations with the various heads of the city administration are a starting point, and should be sought out rather than avoided. Instead of hiding behind the board, it is wise to go out of the way to communicate with and get reports to the various municipal officers. They will note that the library executive has taken the initiative in functioning as part of the urban family, despite the existence of an administrative board. In some cases where head librarians have pushed long-range planning in their agency or adjusted the branch configuration to conform with changing demographic patterns, they have been held up as models to other department heads.

Librarians should also seek out opportunities to appear before the legislative body—city council or town board or county supervisors—in order to keep the library to the fore. Legislators, rather than dismissing the agency as unimportant, may take up the cause, in the process recognizing the library as an asset in building and preserving the quality of economic and community life. Elected representatives, particularly those newly elected to office, often look for an issue that they can adopt and champion. The library is a candidate for their sponsorship, being non-controversial, not requiring huge amounts of money, and reaching more residents (voters) than many other government services.

One entry point to city government is the young assistants who tend to appear around the Mayor soon after election. Sensing the complexity of problems, Mayors often gather help outside the bureaucracy—ostensibly to do research or write speeches, actually to extend the brain power of the newly-elected official and to do so in a tight little group that the Mayor can control. The assistants may not have fancy titles but they are approachable, they have ideas, and some have influence. They are more likely than city department heads to be regular library users, or they have young children who use the agency, and this provides a point of contact. As new incumbents they seek connections with agencies but are often held at arm's length by bureaucrats who want no interference. The library director who cultivates them may well open a conduit of information and advice to the Mayor and back again. It is not unusual for one of these to be designated as liaison with the library, opening regular library-government relations that are too often lacking.

In large cities the budget office enters prominently into relations, particularly if funds are limited. Many a mayor has this office out front in cutting requests, watching the results and stepping in at critical points. Citizen pressure is not as effective on the budget officer, an appointed official, but it does register on the Mayor. With the budget office, a good strategy is to go out of the way in preparing justification for the request, with evidence of the amount and kind of use of services, with unit costs, with trends in expenditures, and where helpful, with comparisons with other libraries. Budget officers naturally have respect for a well-made budget and on the basis of that respect are more inclined to discuss what funds are needed. Of course, to present such documents library directors must first put their own house in order, being sure of what they want and how much it costs.

The city planning office also deserves special attention. At the least it will be a source of data useful in the library's own planning. More valuable is the sense of the city or county "to be" that can be gained, the future community and constituency on which the library's own planning should be based. Most valuable in the long run is inclusion of the library in developmental plans for the area. The pay-off may not be as immediate as with the budget office, but can be constructive as municipalities develop.

It is a jungle out there in the corridors and offices of city hall. Every service would eat the others if it could. Every politician counts the votes. Influence is rampant and dollars are scarce. The librarian comes in without great visibility and usually without an organized constituency. But equally, the librarian comes in with a certain aura of respectability; few in government actually oppose books and reading. If the librarian can demonstrate how library service relates to the problems of the city, to its economic and community life, at least a hearing will be granted. And it turns out that the librarian is not asking for huge sums of money, perhaps an increase from one percent to one-and-one-half percent of municipal expenditures. At a certain point the two connect—the value of the agency and its modest cost—and advance can occur even under prevailing adverse circumstances. It has happened, and will happen again, where relations with city hall are open and positive.

Besides existing under state law, public libraries have other connections at the state level. Certification of professional staff applies in some form in more than half the states. Most states provide some financial aid to local libraries, and with this go regulations and in a few instances standards that are to be maintained to qualify for aid. Annual reports of finances and activities are usually required.

A characteristic of the past 30 years has been the development of statewide systems of library service, which puts one more outside influence on the individual agency. The local library stands to gain in these systems, but usually is called on to participate and make some contribution. Providing borrowing privileges to residents beyond local boundaries is one example, and another is participation in interlibrary loan arrangements, furnishing as well as receiving books that are requested. State planners and state authorities have for the most part respected local autonomy, and participation in systems is usually voluntary. For all the light hand exercised, some local agencies have held back; even in New York State, which offers substantial service and monetary inducement for participation in systems, there are still a few hold-outs.

Relations with states and state offices are usually minimal and cordial. State agencies, whether the State Library or an Extension Division, typically seek to lead or guide and have little authority over local boards. A recent trend has been toward larger public libraries being designated as statewide resources, which leads to additional state money and closer relations. Where this close coordination of state and local responsibilities has not occurred, rivalry and even antagonism have sometimes appeared between the State Library and the larger city libraries.

Whether cordial or not, relations with both local and state government are facts of library life. Enter the political arena, library director, and take your place among the elected and appointed officials. You may even find that you have some political skills in the best sense, using the complex and cumbersome democratic process to further the service for which you are responsible.

Participation in Cultural and Service Groups

One definition of the public library is that it is an agency for the dissemination of contemporary culture. It collects the cultural heritage, much of which has been recorded in print, in picture, in sound, and on film. Users coming to it may not say, "I want to get some culture," but when they seek history or art or music or current affairs or biography or technology or crafts, even when they seek fiction, they are absorbing the present-day world of ideas, expression, and values, which is the sociological definition of culture. When the library puts on group events—film showings or art exhibits, meetings on literary topics or current problems—once again it is dispensing culture.

This suggests that the library ought to have lines out to all the cultural groups and organizations in its area. The number is likely to be large, including not just the major music and art organizations but also drama groups and dance groups and literary clubs and the local history society and many more. Here is where external relations can be divided among the staff. Subject librarians naturally gravitate to some of them, and may be members on their own. Even if the library is not organized by subject, individual librarians have interests and talents which should draw them to one or another group.

Then there are the service organizations such as Kiwanis, Rotary, Business and Professional Women, and others. Some individuals, including librarians, tend to dismiss such groups as cover-ups for aggrandizement by local business people. However, their membership extends well beyond overtly commercial ranks to professionals, government officials, technical specialists and retired people; such groups are among the few community organizations that doctors and clergymen join. They are partly social groups, and partly service clubs which engage in community projects, sponsor scholarships, and help in local events. One could go a long way before finding other organizations in which librarians could get better exposure.

Several benefits can result from working with cultural and service groups. Librarians, with their knowledge of publications and access to information, are a resource for the organizations. Conversely, librarians can learn at first hand of interests and impending demands, and they can pick up current information that is useful at the reference desk. And there is a public relations dividend for the library in such participation.

Yet too often the connections are not made. It is surprising to find that professionals who have elected to devote their lives to the world of ideas and expression often participate so little in community groups devoted to the same interests. In one sense the library is the center of culture in the community; in another sense it often stands separate and aloof. When library directors and department heads are asked about the limited outside participation by staff they are likely to point to constricted budgets, the load of duties, and the lack of time.

A nice administrative question is whether staff should be expected to participate on their own time. Who are the members of the various groups? Other professionals and business people and residents of many backgrounds who attend on their own. Yes, the librarian may reply, but they are there because of their business or their professional practice—they just want to get customers. Well, if a mercenary reason is to be used, it applies to librarians as well, because their business benefits from exposure and from additional users. But reasons for cultural and service relations go deeper, and affect the very role of the library in the community. For some reason it is only teachers and librarians who hold back, and expect extra pay or compensatory time if they engage in community affairs, when one would think they would be among the first to engage in the life around because of both their personal inclinations and their vocation in community educational agencies.

The place that library directors make for themselves in the organized group life of their constituencies is one significant piece in the public image that is formed of the library. At this level it would be inaccurate to say that librarians do not participate, for directors are likely to belong to service clubs and perhaps to cultural groups. Here the question is whether participation means only dutiful attendance or whether they become active, contributing members. It is not often that the library director becomes one of the "boys" or "girls" at city hall, part of the group that gathers in a local watering place when the day's work is done, but some have been accepted in intellectual and artistic circles and can be found lunching with compatriots when not having to eat with a possible donor or a visiting fireman.

It would be useful to have some infra-red or laser device showing the relation of the library to the cultural and intellectual life around it. Lines would be evident going into the building, representing the dependence of alert and active residents on the collections. But too often there would be relatively few lines going out, representing the participation of staff in the life for which they maintain a primary resource.

Academic Libraries

The classic Wilson and Tauber volume lists no less than 35 groups, agencies, and individuals in the university complex with which the library has contact, from trustees to the bookstore, from buildings and grounds to the university press, and of course including students, faculty, alumni, and community residents.[10] The fact that many academic libraries are a step or more removed from the political process—that is, not directly connected with an elected governmental body—does not eliminate or minimize external relations. Campus politics can play the same role as city politics. Once again we have a situation where the financial support of the library, and the parameters of its development, depend on contacts outside the library itself.

Two organizational questions have dominated the placement of the library in the academic hierarchy from early on. One is the relation of the library director to the president and the other the relation of the staff to the faculty, and particularly the matter of faculty status. Neither problem has been completely settled to this day.

Paradoxically, both matters loomed less large in the earlier years of the 19th century, before professional administrators took over the library. In one arrangement the college president kept the library under his wing, with a custodian directly responsible to him in charge. Or an established faculty member took on the duties of library director, often on a part-time basis. There was no question of access to the president, nor any question of faculty status.[11]

Joint faculty-librarian appointments continued in the latter part of the century. When this was not the case, the custodian-librarian was often listed in the institutional catalog with the registrar and other second-level managers. Organizational access and control were achieved by subordination.

Then the period of eminent scholar-librarians appeared. Prominent among these were Justin Winsor, William Warner Bishop, Andrew Keogh and Theodore Koch. After 1900, with the appearance of several library schools, academic librarians came more from these professional training centers. By the time the Graduate Library School of the University of Chicago arrived on the scene in the 1930s and 1940s, with its doctoral program in librarianship, a considerable number of academic library directors were recruited from this source. The School not only awarded the Ph.D. degree, but also imbued its graduates with an inquiring and research turn of mind, both of which were assets in the academic community.

The Library in the Academic Structure

The typical organizational pattern placed the library director in a senior administrative position, directly under the president, and usually with faculty status. The arrangement was comparable to that of a dean, although formal designation as such was uncommon. While this did not necessarily ensure full access and adequate financial support, it was as direct a relationship as could be devised. For some decades the association between president and librarian posed no special problems.

Then, in the 1950s and 1960s, many institutions of higher education grew rapidly, and the role of college and university presidents changed. Their external relations increased; they found themselves spending more and more time raising funds, conferring with government officials, dealing with alumni. As a solution to the increased outside load, the position of provost appeared in the academic structure. Typically the incumbent was a respected inside manager, moved up from the ranks of the faculty or from among the deans, and given broad supervision of both the educational and the business programs. An intervening echelon was thus established between the head librarian and the president.

But reorganization did not stop there. As growth continued,

a series of vice-presidents replaced the single provost in some cases: one for academic affairs, another for finance and business, still another for planning and development. Not only was an intervening echelon re-inforced; now it was split up into several segments.

For library directors in the larger institutions it has become a different ballgame. They lack direct access to the center of decision, and those to whom they report each have responsibility over only part of the concerns of the library. By its nature the library is institutionwide, and thus by definition is beyond the ken of a general officer with responsibility for only part of the university.

Looked at from the other side of the desk, to each of the vice-presidents the library is something of an odd man out, being neither an instructional unit nor a non-educational support unit. The library has no close counterpart in the university, either in function or size or cost. To the academic vice-president the library is a division apart, not a teaching or research department but an auxiliary unit with standards and problems with which the officer is likely to be unfamiliar; there may be little disposition to promote this outsized oddity in the academic family. To the financial vice-president the library is even more of a problem. It is a division that grows and grows, needing more books, more journals, more non-print resources, more shelf space, more expensive automated equipment, all without direct reference either to enrollment or to educational output. The library becomes a ready target for the curtailment of funds.

At a few institution—Columbia University, the University of Texas, and the University of Utah—this situation has been met by designating the Library Director as a Vice-President. Theoretically this restores direct access to the President. But such an adjustment is unusual; most academic libraries are seeking to establish and protect their place a step or two down in the institutional hierarchy.

Faculty contact and support may or may not be an asset in this situation. Naturally both the teaching and research staff want the resources that they need, so they would be inclined to favor more money for the library. But with the flood of publication of recent decades and the appearance of new disciplines and departments, the library is hard-pressed to keep up with demands. Faculty discontent and complaints appear, and the image and status of the library are eroded. Some directors are able to use this criticism as a lever for getting more funds, but many find a negative faculty attitude to be one more obstruction on an already bumpy road.

Both these factors—an intervening echelon of vice-presidents and rising faculty expectations of the resources that they feel should be made available to them—were cited by McAnally and Downs for the unusually high turnover in library directorships which they found in the early 1970s.[12] In a three-year period half the directors in the 78 largest university libraries changed, four of them twice. Additional factors in the turnover were growth of enrollment, the pressures of inflation, and frequent changes in the presidency itself.

In the last decade, pressures have if anything mounted further. Inflation pressed relentlessly in the 1970s, academic disciplines and demands increased, federal funds were constricted, automation became a necessity. As the relationship of the library director to the president and other general officers goes, so goes the library. The head librarian is less librarian and more adventurer in the academic bureaucracy.

The Library and the Faculty

Academic institutions must be understood as having a dual hierarchy, one an administrative relationship up through the president and on to the trustees, the other an educational relationship through the faculty and up to the Faculty Senate or Council. Educational policy and standards are determined by the faculty; this is a long-standing example not only of participatory management but of actual policy control by the staff of an organization. Will there be a curriculum in black culture, what will the requirements be for a degree in environmental studies, will greater emphasis be given to vocational training, to courses for older adults, to extension work off-campus? These and other questions are decided not by the President but by the Faculty or its elected Senate (this is the most common term, and it is appropriate because its functions are legislative). Within an individual department or school, will an assistant professor be given promotion and tenure, will certain courses be dropped or added? Here again the faculty makes the basic decision, not the Dean or department head.

Not that the division between educational and other policy is always that clear and simple. Administration and policy-making, as we noted previously, are intertwined. A forceful president leads the institution, an innovative dean can affect a subject department or a professional school. The financial control lodged in the front office affects what goes on in the classroom. Faculties may have the deciding vote on who will be promoted, but this amounts to little if a freeze has been declared on promotions. This interplay between administration (president, dean) and policy (faculty) can be found on every campus.

The library stands somewhere in the middle. Its line responsibility is to administration, its clientele is the faculty and their students—and the faculty controls educational policy. The library director must work with both sides, and sometimes this constitutes a delicate balancing act.

Chief librarians should hold faculty appointments and thus be part of the group served. They should be members of the Faculty Senate and thus of the educational legislature. They should be involved in discussions within individual faculties that have to do with resources for study and research. In actuality many directors have worked out these several relationships, but this does not necessarily mean that they have been fully accepted as part of the teaching-research staff. Once again one notes the ambiguous position of the library, being neither an instructional division nor a non-educational support unit.

Most academic institutions have a faculty library committee in some form. This may be designated (usually by the President) from the total institution, or it may be a standing committee of the Faculty Senate. The Coe College by-laws succinctly and positively state the function of such a group:

The Library Committee studies library needs in view of the academic program and advises the librarian on matters of general library policy, the development of library resources, and upon means which may best integrate the library program with other academic activities of the College. The Committee serves as a liaison group between the Faculty and the Librarian.

Not many of these groups actually "study library needs," but they do react to proposals from the librarian, and can be a grievance channel if there is widespread dissatisfaction with service. Their role, as noted in this instance, is advisory and not administrative. They are likely to be involved when a new director is selected, and they can advise on materials selection policies, budget priorities, allocation of book funds among subjects or departments, practices on circulation and on hours of opening, and at the time of a building program.

The Library Committee of the Faculty is usually an asset to the Director. Library-minded faculty members tend to be appointed. They become familiar with library needs and problems, and the Librarian would be wise to help them in this process. They can speak for the library, and if necessary defend it. There are exceptions, committees that become critics of the library or of its Director, but in many such cases the opposition is justified and may lead to action favorable for the institution even if not for the librarian involved.

Some committees include student members, and in a few institutions separate student library committees exist. Such representation is desirable, both to bring in fresh viewpoints and suggestions and for promoting the cause of the library. A basic task of the Director is to tell the library story, to get across the role that it does play, and all faculty and student contacts can be useful for the purpose.

The library staff as well as the Director would be well advised to reach out. They have something to contribute to educational review and planning in the institution, with their knowledge of resources, their contact with students and faculty, their bibliographic skills. If staff members stand up and volunteer they will be drawn in, for committee groups are always looking for workers. (The amount of committee time in colleges and universities is a standard complaint of faculty members; one of the repeated academic stories is of the distinguished

professor who was asked to continue beyond his usual retire-
ment year, and said he would do so only if he were released
from all committee assignments.) From the library staff members' standpoint, such participation would be advantageous,
for they often feel isolated in the institution, not a part of the
faculty and its affairs.

Faculty status not just for library directors but also for professional staff members increased steadily before and after World
War II. The case was made that the librarian building a collection, giving research guidance at the reference desk, and alert-
ing classroom instructors to new resources in their fields was
performing an educational function. Faculty designation
affected salaries, career structure, and benefits, although few
service librarians achieved full professorships. Such designation may also have enhanced the status of the librarian in
the institution, although seldom enough to break down the
scholarly and social barriers with which subject specialists
surround themselves.

The gain did not come without some cost. Academic librarians seeking faculty status sometimes faced the need for extra
graduate study and degrees, requirements that might not be
pertinent to their service performance, and those seeking to
protect that status sometimes faced pressures to "publish or
perish." The professorial career ladder could impose a relatively
low ceiling; most librarians with faculty status are at the level
of assistant professors. And many still feel like second-class
citizens in the academic pecking order.

In the last decade the push for faculty status has slowed
down somewhat. Institutions watching the dollars now and in
the future hesitate to make commitments that may involve
lifetime tenure. Librarians, on their side, have sometimes been
uncomfortable with the professional standards imposed on
them. Some have proposed a distinct sequence of career steps,
parallel to the professorial sequence but built on requirements
and standards that apply more to the service desk than to
the classroom, and hopefully opening up a higher level of
advancement for those who display scholarly competence on
the job. The concept is that librarians, rather than being pressed
into a mold developed for the teaching staff, should have

recognition in their own right. No standard structure has emerged for this purpose. Part of the problem is that it is not easy to answer, to the satisfaction of academic administrators and subject faculties, such questions as what exactly is the special knowledge of librarians, just what do they contribute to the academic endeavor, and how does this equate with traditional scholarship, teaching skill, and research production.

We have said that external relations determine the fate of the library. They also determine the status and the rewards of the individual librarian.

The outside demands and pressures may be most evident on the university librarian, but they apply to the college library director and staff member as well. The liberal arts college may not have expanded as much in size as the "multi-versity," but it has been subject to many of the same educational demands: library readings replacing textbooks, honors courses, independent study, to say nothing of research by faculty members seeking academic advancement. The liberal arts college and the technical institute do not have as many levels in the central bureaucracy, nor as many departments clamoring for resources, nor as many original researchers. But the institutions are subject to the same proliferation of publication, the same information explosion, the same fragmentation of disciplines. And the resulting demand must be met with a smaller collection and a smaller staff. Trying to do more with less, the college librarian looks throughout the institution, and beyond the institution, for all the help possible.

Liberal arts colleges in particular will be under financial pressures in these next years. Those with large endowments have an anchor to windward. But many see enrollments turning down while demands for other, often vocational, curricula increase. The library inevitably comes under review. The demand will grow for college libraries to hustle to find funds to maintain collection and staff. In this situation, college library directors who have come out of their building to work with administration and mingle with faculty will find themselves further afield, in alumni meetings, in corporate offices in which graduates are employed, in consultation with foundation officials.

At this point both college and university librarians increasingly fall back on the networks that can help them do what they cannot do themselves. Another set of external relations comes into play. What network will really buttress service and relieve the budget? And then the management questions: how to fund the joint ventures from limited budgets, how to extract enough from the networks to justify what is put into them, how to orient faculty and researchers to an off-campus regional or national system?

Put differently, accountability in one form or another has caught up with academic libraries. As was the case with public libraries, in the past a faith in the provision of the record of knowledge sustained them; this was symbolized in the phrase of "the library is the heart of the institution." But how now to demonstrate the educational value of adding another 10,000 or 25,000 books? Indeed, the very aspirations of the academic library are called into question. Is it really possible and feasible to provide all or most of the materials needed by faculty and students? Is it really possible and feasible for a library staff to judge critically and fully utilize resources in a host of subject disciplines? Is it really possible and feasible for librarians in their brief contacts with users to function in a continuing educational relationship? Or are these aspirations to be claimed in the literature but seldom realized on the job? So far as these and similar questions are considered at all by either the library staff on the one side or the general academic administration on the other, the two groups are likely to reach different conclusions.

School Libraries

The organizational relations of school libraries or school media centers are mostly external, a reversal of the usual situation. The library itself may have only one staff position, so that internal relations—organization in the usual sense—involves only some student assistants and perhaps some adult volunteers. Paradoxically, given this elementary internal structure, school librarians themselves must be particularly "organized" if they are to discharge the full range of their responsibilities.

But relations between the library and the school it serves are constant and critical. If they are not maintained the agency becomes little more than a stockroom for books and related materials that students and teachers need from time to time, and not even a very good stockroom because the stock-keeper has no way of knowing what should stand on the shelves. The essential requirement for a school librarian is the ability to "relate."

At its best, the school library is integral with the classroom. Relations become so close that there is little distinction in purpose and results between the media center and the rest of the school. Under these ideal circumstances, the library is not only auxiliary, providing resources needed in the educational process, but also imparts learning in its own right, teaching the skill of locating and using recorded knowledge.

This skill is often overlooked in public concern about education. Some years ago a national study of schools was issued under the title, "A Nation at Risk,"[13] which spoke of "a rising tide of mediocrity." The criticism has continued in the last decade. "A Nation at Risk" stressed not only the ability to read but, beyond that, the use of this skill to lead to a "Learning Society" which is to provide "the opportunity to stretch . . . minds to full capacity from early childhood through adulthood."

Few would disagree with this sentiment, but the next questions are: to read what, obtained from what sources? The reports say little about sources of reading and about skills for locating resources. Are the well-educated students of the future to read only their school texts and then later the newspaper and their job instructions? Or is reading a means to a more important end, the lifelong development of the full mental and cultural and civic and emotional capacity of every individual? This, of course, is why reading is stressed. But how is the individual to find the factual sources and the written material needed for this development? The answer is in inculcating skill in locating and using recorded knowledge. Failure to develop this competence, along with reading, is like giving a person driving instruction and a driving license but no vehicle to drive.

Needless to say, the concept of the library as a teaching arm of the school is not universally applied. Because it is not, the school library often stands separate. External relations atrophy. Educational goals are set elsewhere in the school, lesson plans are made, children motivated and taught, with only occasional involvement of the library and the librarian. What could be a media center becomes a stockroom and a study hall.

Relations with the principal are critical. If there is mutual confidence and a shared educational goal, the library is promoted as an additional dimension of instruction. While some teachers hold to the text and the classroom exercise, others welcome this new resource. The interchange between librarian and instructors opens the way to fresh teaching materials and to nurturing library skills as a natural part of learning about the world and oneself. Even without support from the principal, some teachers reach out and use the library, to the benefit of their students, but many do not make the connection. Fortunately, some exceptional students learn to capitalize on the collection in their midst even though they get little encouragement or guidance in the process.

While relations with the superintendent of schools and the board of education are usually infrequent, they can at times become crucial. This is obviously true at budget time. In some localities the allocation for library materials is actually voted on as a separate item in the school election; or if a budget proposal is turned down, library materials may be one item put forward for the voters (in a second election) to confirm or eliminate. There are instances where library materials are voted out and athletic equipment kept in.

In such circumstances, the electorate is acting on the basis of its conception of the value of the library in the school. Most people have very little idea of what the media center has or does. The challenge to the school librarian is to demonstrate its value. But how? Some parts of the school program have a natural visibility: athletics of course, and computer classes, and the drama and music groups. One possibility is simply a

"Library Day," when parents and others can come and see the range of materials in the collection, and also see the way that students use it.

Some school libraries have gained allies through the parent-teacher association. This education-minded group provides a forum for showing what the library does, and beyond that the media center can furnish material useful in the work and projects of the association itself. Some PTA members volunteer for service in the library and thus come to join the cause.

The school librarian is often isolated from other librarians. He/she may be the only library professional within the school. For some reason relations with the local public library are often quite tenuous, even though the same students and teachers use both agencies. Here the simple device of a monthly luncheon meeting would improve external relations on both sides. School librarians have been the last to be drawn into regional networks, although there have been experiments along this line, as in New York State.

So the school librarian, who at first glance seems to be off in a separate enclave, really has external connections with teachers, with students, with the principal, with the superintendent and the board, with the PTA, with the voting public, and potentially with other libraries. May the ties be strong, for without them the school library is a target at the time of a budget crunch.

Common Elements in External Organization

The external relations of all types of libraries have certain common characteristics. They call on and test attributes of librarians that are not stressed in administration classes and that are not developed in the usual rise though the middle management ranks within libraries. Some librarians gain in confidence as they take on added responsibilities in providing service, finding that they can get things done, only to feel uncertain and ineffectual before the variety of outside relations that go with the top job; others blossom in this wider world.

Constricted budgets usually pull the library director deeper into the world beyond the office door, and this applies to all types of libraries. It was one thing in former years (the "golden" age of the 1950s and 1960s) to cite the growing flood of publications and the increasing load of users, and on this basis to get more funds from city or school or academic authorities without much contact or cross-examination. The need was evident and the money was there. Now the case must be made, particularly to hard-nosed budget officers. In recent years, facing a cut in funds, there is no choice for the library director except to wade into the arena and fight.

This is a task carried mainly by library directors alone; they are the ones "out front." Although the performance of all staff members affects the outside perception and evaluation of libraries, making the case for the agency cannot be readily delegated. Staff members are not only isolated from contacts with boards and presidents and government in most cases, they are also quick to criticize the performance of their director in external relations. It can be lonely out front.

What the director can use are outside allies. The trustees should stand with the head librarian, and they are shirking their trust if they do not. In the college and university library, the support or criticism of the faculty plays a role, as does that of teachers in the school. Even Friends groups and alumni and PTA groups can testify—or complain.

More than one library director has felt that he/she was standing alone in the budget fight. Staff is not sure how to help, and some members turn antagonistic as money becomes scarce. Users are not organized and can only stand idly by. When the pressure is on, library directors recognize the importance of outside relations, and may well wish that they had given more attention to them in the past.

It is interesting that the whole range of external relations applies as much to the small library as to the large. The organizational web may be simple within the very small agency, but not the outside connections. A small public library may have more board members than it has staff members. Even the one-person library—in a school or a small town—exists in a complex world beyond the library door.

The librarian cannot readily affect or change the external

organization. This contrasts with internal conditions, which can be altered if necessary. There is no choice except to live with the incumbent Mayor or the president of the institution or the principal in the school. The constituency chooses the librarian, not the other way around. The director's view might be solicited when a public-library board member is to be appointed, but even this is rare.

So library directors are confronted with an environment in which the library exists, and within which it thrives or languishes. Dealing with that larger world calls on their full capacity in diplomacy and public relations. Those who deal effectively with external organization have won half the battle. Indeed at a certain point the whole outside complex can be brought to work for the library, and library managers can turn their attention to the service which is their calling. As President Truman said: "A politician is a man who understands government." Or as a recent President of the American Library Association put it: "Libraries and the Political Process; an Opportunity for Developing Partnerships."[14]

References

1. Garceau, Oliver, *The Public Library in the Political Process.* New York, Columbia University Press, 1949, p. 239.

2. *New Jersey Statutes Annotated, 1967,* Section 40, 54–12.

3. *West's Annotated California Codes, Education Code, 1969,* Section 27351.

4. *Arizona Revised Statutes Annotated, 1956,* Section 9-416.

5. *Charter of the City and County of San Francisco.* San Francisco, John S. Dunnigan, Clerk, 1935, p. 24.

6. Joeckel, Carleton B. *Government of the American Public Library.* Chicago, University of Chicago Press, 1935.

7. Young, Virginia G. *The Library Trustee; a Practical Handbook*, New York, R. R. Bowker, 1978, p. 32.

8. Gertzog, Alice and Beckerman, Edwin. *Administration of the Public Library*. Metucken,, N.J., Scarecrow Press, 1994, p. 105.

9. Wheeler, Joseph L. and Goldhor, Herbert. *Practical Administration of Public Libraries*. Revised edition. New York, Harper and Row, 1981, pp. 278–279.

10. Wilson, Louis R. and Tauber, Maurice F. *The University Library; The Organization, Administration and Functions of Academic Libraries*. 2nd ed. New York, Columbia University Press, 1956, p. 38.

11. Hamlin, Arthur T. *The University Library in the United States; Its Origins and Development*. Philadelphia, University of Pennsylvania Press, 1981, pp. 45–59.

12. McAnally, Arthur M. and Downs, Robert B. "The Changing Role of Directors of University Libraries." *College and Research Libraries*, Vol. 34, No. 2 (March 1973), p. 110.

13. National Commission on Excellence. *A Nation at Risk; the Imperative for Educational Reform*. Washington, D.C., Congressional Record, May 5, 1983, pp. S6096–6208.

14. Sheldon, Brooke E. "Libraries and the Political Process: an Opportunity for Developing Partnerships," *Public Library Quarterly*, Vol. 4, No. 1, (Spring 1983), p. 29.

VII INTERNAL ORGANIZATION OF LIBRARIES

ORGANIZATION, as was stated at the outset, is the variety of relationships that hold an enterprise together and enable varied staff members to work in tandem for a common purpose. It is the structure and nerve system of administration. As such, it is an integral element of management, which, in Drucker's words, ". . . means, in the last analysis, the substitution of thought for brawn and muscle, of knowledge for folkways and superstition, and of cooperation for force."[1]

Take the elementary example of several men faced with the task of moving a very large rock. "Just where are we supposed to move it?" asks one of the men. Agreement is reached on where it is to go (the planning process is under way, with an objective set). They try to push the rock, but it is too large and heavy. One member says that they are not pushing at the same time, so the group agrees to have him signal just when to push (thus both coordination and chain of command emerge). But still they cannot move the rock. Worse yet, one of the men has strained his back in the second attempt, and must stand aside where he tries to offer helpful advice (a rudimentary staff officer). On his suggestion, the remaining men decide on a different approach, to have two of them make and activate a lever with a smaller rock and a wooden plank, while the others push in coordination (specialization of tasks appears). Sad to say, the rock still will not move. The staff officer (the man with the strained back) sees the futility of the effort (staff officers often have a perspective lacking to the worker on the line), and offers another suggestion: "Why don't

171

we get Joe's bulldozer and simply push it?" At which point the question of money must be considered, and the men constitute themselves a temporary task force on finance. Project the example many-fold and you have the organization that built the pyramids of Egypt—except that the bosses were pre-ordained and there were no bulldozers to provide an easy solution.

The example of rock-moving may be over-simple, but it illustrates several organizational relationships: planning, directing, specialization, coordination, line and staff functions. The catch is that in more complex tasks—running a library as a case in point—these elements become blurred and confused. Just where the rock is to go is not decided, the pushers do not have full confidence in the individual calling the signals, the staff officer has ambitions to be the boss, the specialized tasks used are those that worked in a different library, communication becomes disrupted, staff efforts go in different directions. The rock stays where it was.

Or take another elementary example. Assume a one-person school library in which the load has increased and a second position has been authorized. What kind of worker should be added? There are several possibilities. One is to add a second professional librarian who would share the various duties side-by-side with the chief. Another is to define the second professional position as specialized in nature, say as cataloger (not likely in a very small library) or as reference librarian. Or what about a person to handle the visual and oral material which a modern school media center possesses? Still another possibility is to add a clerical or paraprofessional worker, parallel to assigning a teacher's aide to the overloaded classroom teacher. This last alternative is a form of specialization, by level of duties and responsibility, although we usually do not think of an "aide" as a specialist. Thus there are possibilities even in the smallest library to organize by function, by level, or by form of resources. In any of these alternatives, the chief librarian would face a new responsibility, that of supervising the work of the second staff member, and of coordinating this work into the total service of the library.

The examples point up the two main components of organization: 1/dividing up a task into the separate pieces of work that need to be done, and then 2/putting the pieces together so that they jointly achieve the agreed purposes. Specialization and coordination—division of labor and combining of effort. The presentation here will be divided under these two broad headings.

Organization will be dissected in this and the next two chapters. The present chapter deals with functional and other bases for dividing work in libraries. The following sections go on to specialization by levels and to structures for direction and decision-making.

Building Blocks of Organization

The starting point is not at the top, with the director's office, but at the bottom, with individual tasks and jobs. The central question is what work is to be done. Supervisors, middle managers, directors come later to keep the enterprise going. It is conceivable that a project could do without administrators, but it could not do without workers.

Why divide the work into different jobs and specialties? Why not simply gather staff members with common interests and common sense and have them all pitch in to achieve whatever purpose is agreed upon? Because, for all the possible good will of staff, one would not come out with a finished automobile in the factory or a cured patient in the hospital or effective contact with recorded knowledge in the library.

Defining jobs permits a division of labor. One person designs the car while another person (or robot) attaches the fender; one person makes the hospital bed while another repairs the ruptured disc in the patient's back.

What kinds of jobs need to be done in the library? The A.L.A. Descriptive List includes no less than one hundred tasks, from putting books on shelves to evaluating the literature of a subject field, from stamping a book for circulation to analyzing the reading level of a user seeking guidance on resources to use. Libraries are by no means the most complex of organizations, but they have quite a wide variety of tasks to be performed and a wide range of skills is required for their provision.

That is where defining of jobs comes into the picture. With the establishment of positions with different responsibilities and capacities, the complex task of rendering library service is broken down into manageable pieces. By noting the distinctions among jobs, personnel with varying and constrasting capacities are hired, whether third baseman or catcher or fielder, whether cataloger or reference librarian or children's specialist. Having defined the positions and specified their requirements, staff members with the particular qualifications required can be selected. The pitcher needs control and cunning, the shortstop speed and flexibility, the fielder a sharp eye and a good throwing arm. Are we clear on just what special traits should be possessed by librarians in different positions?

Step by step the places on the team are being defined, and suitable team members can be recruited. We often speak of a team and of teamplay, but this does not only mean that the staff is made up of people who are compatible and prepared to work together; it also means that the staff is composed of people whose abilities fit together, employees who complement each other. Without this "fit," exhortations to be a "team" or a "family" can warm the hearts of those involved but will not necessarily result in better service.

Specialization of positions also permits the play of personal preference as well as of formal qualifications. Some individuals like to hold down the hot corner in baseball, and others not; some librarians prefer to work with children or with computers, and others not. There are individuals who aspire to command and others who are indifferent to power, and this is not necessarily correlated with either commitment or ability—witness the skepticism with which many university faculty members view department heads and deans.

Working with the building blocks of organization has other advantages. Each staff member has a part, an assignment, and knows what it is. He or she can concentrate on the assignment, not having to worry about tasks that are assigned to others. Further, skill increases with experience and repetition within the particular duties performed. Extra training or extra study can be pursued with a clear-cut goal in mind.

Specialization of tasks at certain points permits the introduction of labor-saving devices. If the task at a given desk is recording of circulation of books, the record-keeping can be mechanized; if extensive filing is involved, this can be done by machine. In manufacture we see the progression from craft skills in the pre-industrial period, to the assembly line in the 20th century, and now to robots. We all recall the dramatic example used by Adam Smith in *The Wealth of Nations* on the number of pins that a given number of workers could produce in a day when parts of the task were broken down and simple machines introduced, as compared with the number produced when each worker handled the whole process alone and without labor-saving devices.

Will robots have a place in libraries? Conceivably at the circulation desk, conceivably at the reserve-books station in the academic library. But specialization should not be viewed as a step toward mechanization of the librarian's job. On the contrary, the very process of specialization separates out the positions in which judgment rather than repetition is the controlling factor. The more judgment and the less repetition required in the librarian's job assignment, the less the likelihood that the librarian will be replaced by R2D2.

Robots aside, the process of job specialization results in a steady breaking down of work into limited, finite tasks. When carried to its logical conclusion, the incentive for performance may be lost; work becomes mechanical, the end product is not seen, and the employee lacks commitment. This is a deep-rooted problem in American industry today. We must shortly examine what job specialization has done to the morale and performance of library workers, but first the nature of job specialization in libraries must be analyzed in greater detail.

Predominant Functional Organization of Libraries

As noted in an earlier part of this presentation, organizational theorists have spelled out the different bases on which large-scale enterprise has been organized. Prominent among these have been organization by purpose, by function, by nature of material handled, by clientele, and by geographic location. No one was found to be superior or best, and most enterprises are organized on several of these bases rather than on any one.

But this does not mean that it makes no difference which is used. Each has some advantages and some disadvantages. It is worth knowing these in order to get full benefit from the particular kinds of building blocks used, and to watch out for and if possible prevent their detrimental effects. Further, the bases of specialization which predominate determine to a degree the nature of an enterprise and indicate what is considered most important by that institution.

What basis of organization predominates in libraries? The answer is function, although other kinds of specialization are of course used, as we will note shortly. By "function" is meant the breaking down of work assignments into the logical activities or services which enable the enterprise to achieve its goals. Usually this is a sequence; where all the functions are done in order, presumably the purposes of the enterprise are achieved.

Think of what goes on in a library as on a continuum. Materials have to be obtained to build the collections, so there is an *acquisition librarian*. The acquired material has to be organized for use, so there is a *cataloger*. When the collection is in place, users need assistance, so there is a *reference librarian*. If users elect to borrow material, they go to a *circulation assistant*.

These are the most frequent positions: acquisition librarian, cataloger, reference librarian, circulation assistant. And in a library of any size, these same functional specialties are built into departments.

It is interesting to note that these four functions were differentiated very early in the development of American libraries, and have persisted over a long period of time. Moreover, they appear in the several different types of libraries, even though the social purpose of, say, the academic library is different from that of the public library. The standard library functions have proven themselves over time and in a variety of establishments, and librarians rest easy with them.

But this alone does not prove that they are necessarily best. It is worth standing back and seeking perspective on the predominant functional basis of library organization. Some years ago two perceptive critics of library organization ran against the grain with their assertion that "The division between circulation on the one hand and reference on the other is not the most fruitful basis for organizing service to adults."[2] Our task is to see why the functional structure predominates, and what effect it has on library performance.

One thought that strikes the reflective observer is that the terms themselves are not very self-explanatory, but constitute more a jargon with which librarians are entirely familiar but which may be ambiguous or even confusing to users. "Acquisition" probably explains itself to the outsider. But to say that one is a "cataloger" often leads to the observation on the part of the uninitiated that the individual must file entries into the card catalog. The term does not clearly convey the task of analyzing the content and purpose of a publication and of assigning it a place in a body of organized knowledge. "Reference" librarian is equally ambiguous as a descriptive title. "Refer" to what? Or is the reference librarian someone to whom users should present their references, as in applying for club membership or a credit card? Some librarians have looked at this designation from the standpoint of users and have adopted the more descriptive label of "information librarian" and "information desk." "Circulation" also is an insider's term, which in the dictionary definition refers to some kind of passage or transmission, as of blood.

The fact that the labels used do not readily identify the functions performed does not invalidate the functions themselves. But users do puzzle over them. Their common usage within the profession suggests an inside-out rather than an outside-in orientation, emphasizing what librarians do as technicians rather than what they do for their clientele.

More important is to understand that functional organization breaks what started out as a unified mission into separate pieces. Perhaps the point can best be made by comparing the organization of teaching with that of library service. There are various functions connected with teaching: lesson preparation, assembling of teaching materials, lecturing, discussion leadership, testing, etc. If the classroom were organized like the library, each of these would be handled by a specialist, and the child would be handed on from one to another even as a book is handed on from one functional worker to another in the library. This of course would be nonsensical.

The school is organized by purpose—we say its mission is to teach, so we have a "teacher" who handles and integrates the several functions—while the library is primarily organized by function. This is a structure that is found more frequently in present-day fabricating activities, where the making of a product is broken down into the several functions involved.

In libraries the continuum is similarly broken down into pieces. What are the advantages and disadvantages?

The benefits apply that have been noted for job specialization. Tasks are clearly defined, persons with requisite abilities can be recruited, personal preference can be honored. The worker learns by experience within circumscribed duties (at least for a period, until few new challenges arise). One can only admire the skilled cataloger and skilled reference librarian plying their specialties, drawing on a depth of experience. Not only skill but also productivity should increase in function-based positions, as the worker at whatever level learns by trial and error what works more rapidly and efficiently. Still another benefit is that specialization by function permits employment of a larger contingent of clerical workers, who are paid less than highly-trained individuals; witness the greater proportion of non-professionals in acquisition and cataloging and circulation departments than in subject divisions and in user specialties such as children's and young-adult service.

However, in functional organization it is possible to lose sight of the end product, and the danger is larger the greater the distance of the worker from that product, whether a reliable automobile or a satisfied reader. Library workers in direct contact with the public often complain about the performance of those behind the scenes and removed from the inquiring seeker. Thus there arises the not infrequent friction between the reference librarian and the cataloger as to the classification and subject headings for particular books. One has the inquiring user in mind, the other the integrity of the organization of the collection. And even behind the scenes there may be friction between the acquisition staff and the catalogers, the first seeking to process materials on the basis of the chronology of arrival or on the basis of similarity of materials, whereas the latter want to respond to pressure for items particularly in demand. User needs may penetrate back as far as the cataloging department but not to acquisition. A considerable number of library workers never have direct contact with a user in the course of their duties.

When function determines structure, workers tend to become attached to the particular activity in which they engage and to think less of the eventual result of their work. The circulation assistant adopts the standards of performance of the circulation staff, which could be efficiency or indifference or even hostility. Further, functional specialists often are not sure whether their efforts result in service, even though this may be the goal to which they are truly dedicated. For example, catalogers do their best to make publications and their contents accessible to potential readers, but seldom know whether they hit or miss; they have little choice except to follow the rules and hope that these are in accord with use.

An additional problem of functional organization is that it requires an extra measure of coordination to keep the several steps synchronized. This adds to the hierarchy of administrators, and to management costs. We will shortly note the variety of coordinating officers in libraries.

All this does not mean that libraries are poorly organized because they stress function, or that basic reorganization should necessarily take place. Defenders of the prevailing structure can point out that it has stood the test of time. But it is worth remembering that functional divisions can become fiefdoms, cut off both from other divisions and from the people the library is designed to serve.

What are the alternatives? Libraries themselves use bases of organization other than function: subject specialization, form of material, clientele group, and geographic distance. Each cuts the pie in a different way and each has certain advantages and problems.

Organization by Subject

In larger libraries, both academic and public, subject specialization is likely to occur in some form, whether in separate
departments or at least in separate positions that are thought
of as devoted to one or another field of knowledge. Subject
librarians and subject departments more frequently exist in
addition to the traditional functional divisions—that is, there
are both functional positions and subject positions—but in
some cases they absorb all or part of the selection-acquisition-
cataloging-reference sequence.

It is interesting to note that subject divisions evolved differently in public as compared with academic libraries. In the
former these specialties were added to the functional base, at
first one by one and in time, in buildings constructed in the
last half-century, as a complete circle of subject departments.
The units added first were likely to be art-music, local history,
and business, one or more of these in response to predominant
interests of the locality served. The result is positions or departments devoted to some topics but not to others. The organization can be diagrammed as in Figure 5.

Later development, in larger central buildings, sought to
complete the spectrum or circle of subjects, so that all topics
were covered in the subject structure. This can be diagrammed
as in Figure 6. The earliest examples were the Cleveland
Public Library (1913) and the Los Angeles Public Library
(1914). The number of subject departments in the full development is usually six to eight, those shown in the diagram being
the original divisions in the trend-setting Enoch Pratt Library
in Baltimore.

Thus in public libraries the historical base was a central
functional organization to which subject units and branches
were added. By contrast, many university library systems began
as separate subject units, serving parts of the institution, and
then over the years a functional and coordinating center was
added. The center—that is, the university library—has gained
increasing control, in part because of the essential interrelation
of both resources and use, and also because of "tighter" admin-

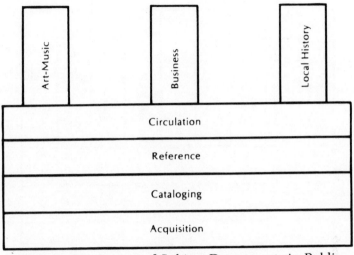

Figure 5 Emergence of Subject Departments in Public
Libraries

istrative control in the institution as a whole, which favored
one unified system rather than various autonomous libraries.
If this transmutation were diagrammed, it would show first a
series of separate subject collections, then these units supplemented by a central acquisition-cataloging-circulation agency,
and in time the joining of the two with unified administration
under the functional center.

For both types of libraries, the advantages of subject organization are apparent. All materials dealing with a topical area—
books, journals, reports, audio and visual materials,
microforms—are gathered together physically. Librarians are
assigned who have special background in the same topical
area. Users find conveniently assembled all the materials they
need. Building up these collections, and ministering to the
needs of readers, are specialized staff members who know the
content of their resources. Librarian and user are on an equal
footing, both across the service desk within the library and in
meetings outside with faculty and community groups, where
the librarian is recognized as possessing a background shared
by members of the group.

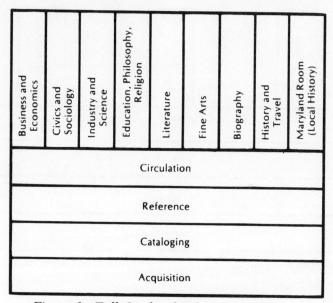

Figure 6 Full Circle of Subject Departments
(Original Plan for Enoch Pratt Free Library)

This is the theory. In practice subject specialization and subject departments have encountered difficulties. To begin with, this is an expensive type of organization. Some resources must be duplicated, because there are general materials that must be used with all groups of subject publications. Subject librarians cost more than general librarians. Separate rooms or divisions must be staffed even if the overall volume of use does not so require. For example, a public library with six or eight subject departments must have personnel available in all of them, even in slower hours in the morning or the late evening. On a slow night, with limited public inquiry, there may be a half-dozen specialized professionals waiting at service desks in the several rooms.

The cost of branch subject libraries is no less on the minds of university library administrations. Rogers and Weber express the prevailing view: "Perhaps the most persistent and difficult organizational problem ... is the degree to which branch libraries will be allowed to proliferate."[3] Considerably earlier,

Wilson and Tauber had this comment on the same issue: "Few questions concerning university libraries have been more extensively debated and less carefully studied."[4]

From the users' standpoint it turns out that subject departmentation is a convenience for some but an inconvenience for others. Readers working within a subject field as defined by the library have in substance a special collection and staff at their command. But the interests of many people—say in such areas as war and peace, environment, social trends, education, family affairs—spread across neat subject lines. A study in the Enoch Pratt Free Library showed 51 per cent of patrons had to use two or more departments in the central building.[5] In academic libraries shifting subject lines, new disciplines, and combinations of fields—biochemistry and computer science and space science and the interrelations of mathematics with physics and of psychology with education are only a few examples—render any traditional divisions invalid for some faculty and students. Rather than being helped, users may be confused and find themselves being shunted from department to department.

Even the shelf classification of materials poses a problem. A book ordered by one department comes through classified in another division, and this occurs more often as dependence grows on cataloging entries from central utilities (OCLC, for example). Of course any library can proceed to change the classification to accord with its service department structure, but this involves an expensive process of review and adjustment that negates the cost advantages of turning to the outside service in the first place.

Given the concern about the proliferation of departmental and subject libraries, it is not surprising that larger academic libraries have sought means to limit and pull back on separate, decentralized units. As new and cross-disciplines emerge, resources for them are typically added onto existing branches rather than creating additional departmental libraries—not without protest from the faculties affected. Recently there has been a trend toward inclusive science libraries on campus, sometimes involving new buildings that pull in and incorporate several different departmental collections. Rather broad subject divisional units, combining related fields such as the natural sciences, the social sciences, and the humanities, are now favored.

A few of the largest universities—Harvard is an example—have applied a different concept. Rather than trying to consolidate as much as possible, they have recognized the stronger of the departmental libraries and nurtured them as separate but federated units. This comes close to the "federal decentralization" pattern favored by Peter Drucker, in which he saw greater clarity of mission in each of the affiliated agencies, greater adaptability to varying circumstances and challenges, and a placement of decision-making closer to the end product of the enterprise. In this structure those service factors that first brought the separate collections into existence are preserved, and at the same time these collections are loosely coordinated in a single library system. Where this structure can be afforded, there is much to say for it as against a large monolithic center that has certain managerial conveniences and economies but which may not deliver as well at the point of faculty and student demand. Federal decentralization rather than consolidation is worth consideration in larger university libraries.

Even where considerable centralization and consolidation have occurred, separate autonomous or semi-autonomous collections often exist for law and medicine. Some university library directors look askance at such wayward units not in the fold, but they might better look upon them as an opportunity to practice federal decentralization, which has gained considerable favor in business and industrial circles. On some campuses a sort of *de facto* federal decentralization exists, with a few strong departmental libraries standing separate to a greater or lesser degree from the central coordinating unit.

Public libraries also have to a limited extent sought to reduce the number of subject departments. The Enoch Pratt Free Library did so after the study cited earlier. One of the most recently constructed of central-city public-library buildings, that in Atlanta, is down to four departments: a combined social science and science-industry unit, a humanities unit, an art-music unit, and a small local-history department.

Besides the inter-subject interests of many users, an added problem has been the recruiting and holding of subject librarians. Many a public library has subject-specialized departments but does not have subject-specialized staff members. In some fields (economics and the sciences, for example) it is difficult to obtain staff members possessing advanced subject training, transfers occur among the fields without regard to subject background, management career opportunities open up and prompt subject librarians to shift their goals, and the salary ceiling is soon reached in subject assignments—all these conspire against building and retaining strong subject staff groups. Also, several larger public libraries that placed periodicals with books in subject rooms have gone back to a separate magazine unit, reversing the earlier decision because subject staffs find it a burden to handle the subscription material. Thus, the positive factors that brought subject departmentation into the public library—convenient assembling of resources regardless of form, and staff with special book knowledge—are in process of being lost. This is unfortunate, for specialized subject service has been a distinctive feature in some larger public libraries, and the step backward comes at a time when the agency is uncertain about its mission and searching for focal points in its fragmented service program.

Early in the trend toward subject specialization, a few voices were raised advocating staff subject specialization without separate subject departments.[6] This idea is intended to preserve the unity of the collection and still provide personnel who are on an equal footing with more advanced users. To a degree many libraries follow this practice in that staff members with particular interests concentrate somewhat, being responsible for selection of acquisitions and for difficult reference questions in designated fields, but this coverage is likely to be sporadic and is not very evident to users as a resource that they can call upon; they do not know who the informal subject specialists are. The concept is not widely applied on a systematic basis.

In a few cases, subject specialists, rather than supplementing functional departments, have taken over at least part of the functional base, conducting all or some of the functional operations. An example is the Los Angeles Public Library, which has no reference department as such, which depends on subject librarians for most materials selection, and which refers difficult classification questions to these same individuals. In most systems with subject departmentation, a push and pull exists between the two forms of organization, with one type dominant in some and the other type dominant in other libraries. The general reference room is often caught between, with its scope and duties uncertain vis-à-vis the subject service rooms. This unit may experience a revival as computerized data sources come into greater play and are placed in general reference rather than dispersed in subject rooms; the pendulum may swing back.

The factors which originally prompted subject specialization remain relevant today, in a time of publication overload. Advanced and professional students and faculty in universities welcome access to working collections in their fields. General readers with developed interests welcome subject rooms in city libraries that cater to these interests. In a sense these are "special" libraries for the unaffiliated specialist. This is one role that central public libraries could serve, that of a congeries of special collections for advanced readers in the general society.

But over the years the concept has lost some of the force claimed for it by early advocates.[7] Decisions forced by the dollar sign have taken their toll. Uncertainty as to purpose or mission has dulled the earlier dedication. Subject librarians have seldom gone out of their way to associate with their counterparts either on the faculty or in the community at large. Subject departments have often been content-oriented rather than focused on user groups; subject librarians know more about the insides of books than they do about how they are used. In the push and pull with traditional functional departments, the latter have usually prevailed. It would be premature to say that a promising idea has run its course, but like other parts of the library service organization it seems to be rocking along without the vitality that marked its earlier years.

One short-lived variation on subject specialization is worth noting. In the 1940s and 1950s the idea of "interest groupings" was advanced and tried in some locations (Detroit and Chicago, among larger cities). The concept was to group materials not by standard subject categories (a content-oriented approach) but by predominant public interests (a user-oriented approach). Examples were current social problems, personal relations, community affairs, family concerns, leisure-time activities, career development, the arts, etc. Materials from various parts of the standard classification, from fiction as well as non-fiction, and in whatever form, were brought together, and library "specialists" assigned to each interest. There was some evidence that this organization stimulated use, but the concept fell into disuse as interests changed and this unorthodox plan impeded students following accepted subject categories.

The reader-interest experiment in particular, and the whole trend to subject specialization, were efforts to organize libraries for use, to facilitate the joining of searcher and resources. It is an effort not yet successfully concluded, for all forms of service organization prove in practice to have problems and shortcomings. Where is the library that is really easy to use?

Organization by User Group

If difficulties arise in organizing service by the content of publications, why not approach this from the standpoint of the clientele served? After all, service to users is the goal of libraries. If positions and departments could be organized around distinct groups, it should be possible to fit resources and activities to their needs. Libraries have tried this to a limited extent, and with some degree of success when it does apply. The more common examples are children's librarians and young adult librarians in public libraries, and undergraduate-oriented personnel who emerge in college libraries and in some university libraries. The concept could be extended to other identifiable groups, such as preschool youngsters, parents, senior citizens, the "disadvantaged" with limited education, vocational as distinct from academic majors in secondary schools, professional students in universities. The requirements are only that the group be distinct, have sufficient numbers to justify special attention, and have interests to some degree different from the bulk of users.

The most established of the clientele-based positions is that of children's librarian. Large public libraries have substantial divisions devoted to this age group, and even small libraries have a children's position, often before they have a separate reference post. What have been the results?

The Public Library Inquiry many years ago singled out children's service for commendation. "Altogether, public library service to children and young people is an impressive achievement."[8] This aspect of service has held its place over the years, right through the recent period of austerity. A recent treatment, after noting a period of decline in children's service, concludes that ". . . new exigencies have once again catapulted children's librarianship to the forefront of public library attention"[9] Some people even think of the community library as primarily an agency for children.

It is worth noting the characteristics of organizing service by the young age group. To begin with, a clear-cut purpose animates children's service, a definite goal that children's librarians seek to achieve, as distinct from the "give them what they want" philosophy that controls the rest of public-library ministrations. This purpose is to introduce children to the best of juvenile literature, a simple yet compelling objective.

Children's librarians have developed techniques for this purpose: story hours, plays, films, reading games. Because they are dealing with a distinct group, they come to understand its psychology. Because they are dealing with a finite group, they come to know many of its members individually. This contrasts with adult service, where it is unusual for the librarian to be versed in adult psychology, and equally unusual for him/her to be acquainted with more than a handful of users. Children's librarians have what can be called a genuine professional relationship with their clientele, in the sense that a continuing rather than a one-shot connection is established, and in the sense that professional judgment is applied to youngsters as known individuals.

A parallel depth applies to children's librarians' knowledge of their collection. It is indicative to observe juvenile librarians go directly to the shelves in response to inquiries, knowing what is there, whereas the adult librarian more typically has recourse to the catalog. Further, professionals serving youngsters have a considerable understanding of the insides of their books, as to reading level, reader appeal, and values promoted.

All this is not lost on the general public. In the public mind children's service is one of the notable achievements of the public library; if one doubts this, try to cut back on service to youngsters and note the reaction. A definite part of the esteem accorded the agency derives from this source.

Yet there is another side to the picture. Juvenile circulation has been decreasing in public libraries. Various factors account for the decline: a smaller number of children in the population, more adequate school libraries able to supply free reading as well as curricular resources, purchase by families of books for their youngsters, perhaps the lure of television, videos, and computers. Moreover, children's librarians, while nourishing enthusiastic young readers, have not been able to reach the large group of reluctant readers.

From the librarian's standpoint, a problem arises that is found in many kinds of specialization. Children's professionals often find themselves in a dead end in terms of careers. Their very dedication and devotion set them apart, a little out of the career mainstream. Many have difficulty in shifting over to the general administrative ladder. To some extent the bottleneck has been broken with children's librarians being appointed to head branch libraries in cities, but it is exceptional to find them in the front office of a large system.

Children's service, like other forms of specialization, is expensive. It would be cheaper not to have a juvenile department. But the money is found, even in hard times. This can be attributed to the appeal of a goal-oriented form of organization that focuses on a distinct clientele.

A similar effort was made over the years to serve teenagers, under the rubric of young-adult or young-people's service. At one time many public libraries had young-adult professionals and separate collections and activities for the group. In the last dozen years this service has faded, and in some places now amounts to no more than a few cases of books which are little used.

Part of the problem was to define purpose. The teen years are a restless period, a searching period, for some young people a period of rebellion. With relaxed standards in the society as a whole, and with more tolerant family discipline, teenagers try to find their way in an exciting, complex world. Some young-adult librarians sought to protect them from the great unknown by stressing reading without too much conflict or sex or unorthodox values. The effort was doomed to failure with all except the most compliant of young people. Young-adult librarians with greater insight sought not to protect but to lead teenagers into the adult world, helping them to mature, providing resources dealing forthrightly with the questions young adults face. This was not much more successful. Young people by the late teens are becoming individuals, going their many separate ways, so that there are few well-marked roads of development, and the restless spirit just will not be contained.

Another negative factor was primary dependence on the medium of print. These last years have seen the first fully multimedia generation, fostered on visual images on television and on the aural excitement of rock-and-roll music. Librarians, and particularly public librarians, did not learn how to use these newer forms—in fact some saw themselves as standing in the path of trends which they considered undesirable or offensive. The bulk of young people found their offering to be plain dull.

Other librarians serve both children and teenagers in schools; the school library is a unit organized by user group. Ideally the client-staff relationship is regular and close, starting in the early grades with introduction of the magic of reading, going through the years when resources can match any interest which the growing child develops, and continuing through high school with the library furnishing materials for academic achievement. Some school libraries have become media centers, calling on the full range of printed, visual, and aural resources; or, in the newest terminology, are called resource centers.

Yet in practice not many school libraries have become central either in the work of the classroom or in the life of the growing person. Too many function as supply rooms rather than educational forces. Neither administration nor teaching staff draws the library into planning and teaching projects. The student associates the library with an imposed learning experience, so that few develop a lifelong library habit; one of the smallest user groups of public libraries is the post-high-school contingent in the population.

It is heresy even to bring up the question, but one wonders whether the organizational concept of the centralized library in the school has in the long run been the wisest course of development. Classroom collections are considered passé and old-fashioned. But, as noted earlier, schools are basically organized by purpose; the teacher combines the various functions from lesson preparation to testing. Provision of curricular materials is one of the few functions that has been pulled out and placed in a separate unit called the library. This organizational decision affects the role of the librarian, the place of resources in the teaching process, and the impact on growing young people. Heresy or not, it is worth remembering that the school has been found wanting—witness the recent critical reports— and therefore worth considering whether some other structure for resource provision would be more effective. What of an experiment in which materials are placed primarily in the classroom, to be used as an integral part of the teaching and learning process, with the "librarian" functioning not as the custodian of a collection but as resource specialist, selecting materials, planning with teachers for their use, participating in classroom instruction when the materials are involved, and working individually with students starting term papers and senior reports?

Not playing an essential role, school librarians are ready targets when the educational budget gets tight. Secondary-school libraries have difficulty getting adequate clerical help. Elementary schools are losing librarians, with one professional handling several schools, functioning more as overseer than as practicing librarian.

Going back to public libraries, a promising kind of user specialist appeared in the 1920s in the form of the reader's adviser. This was a librarian for adults systematically following their individual interests, informal students in a sense. The individual came to the librarian with personal concerns or curiosities. One wanted to understand modern art, another to explore expanding career areas, another to grasp Eastern philosophy and religion after a visit to India and China, still another to prepare for the development stages of a forthcoming child, while another wanted to prepare for a house he planned to build—and on through the spectrum of interests of the inquiring mind. They were prepared to devote a reasonable amount of time to the pursuit, not in one quick fix but in a sequence of reading. The librarian sat down with the patron, helped clarify objectives, ascertained reading ability. Psychological insight was called into play. An individual course of study was outlined, with the student going through a half-dozen or a dozen books over a few months. Each successive volume was waiting at the reader's adviser's desk according to schedule, and the visits to get them afforded opportunity for informal follow-up interviews on progress and problems along the way.

This was adult education in more clear-cut form than libraries have usually achieved. It also was professional service closer to the model that prevails in other professions: ministration to individuals, diagnosis of each person's needs, prescription of a course of action, continuous contact to monitor progress. Relation of librarian to client was similar to that of doctors, dentists, lawyers, accountants, psychologists, etc.

But in time the basic functional organization prevailed. By the 1960s the work of the reader's adviser was absorbed into the reference desk. In time it disappeared except in the most rudimentary form. The library fell back into its traditional service organization.

A few libraries have tried a device that is definitely second best for reader guidance. They select a few topics of particular interest to their constituencies—consumer materials, for example, or environment or community development or family problems—and mark volumes on these topics with a color code. The volumes stand in their regular classified order on the shelves. Users going through can watch for colors corresponding to their interest—say, for consumers, under food and clothing and housing and automobiles and vacations and other products which people consume. This device adds a rainbow hue to the shelves but it is no substitute for a librarian on one end of the log and a reader on the other.

Business departments or branches within larger public libraries represent an interesting combination of user-group and subject organization. Their orientation is more toward business people than towards economics as such. They stock those materials in which the local business community has a particular interest, even though this may extend to some technological sources, to legal problems, to parts of the world that are markets for local products. A few have even included "fiction for business persons"—whatever that may be. As larger corporations have built up their own special libraries, the units in public libraries have become somewhat more agencies for smaller-scale business. Whatever their scope or level, as user-based special units they have, like children's service, been one of the distinctive features of public libraries, and have built a measure of esteem for the institution.

In academic libraries subject departments are also in some cases units specialized by user groups. Separate collections for law and medicine serve circumscribed clienteles with particular needs and use habits. The library can become attuned to these clientele needs. It is not unusual, for example, to have individuals with legal training in charge of law libraries. In a few very large universities, undergraduate units have been established for students who are not deep into research. Yet organization by user group is not prevalent in academic libraries; the emphasis is either on centralized function or on subject content of resources.

Overall organization by sub-groups of clientele is exceptional in libraries. Like other forms of specialization, it is expensive. It works against the economy of a centralized functional structure. Most users of libraries share one organization with readers very different from themselves, the professional with the high-school drop-out in the public library, the Ph.D. candidate with the freshman in the university, the serious student with the casual browser. One function-based service plan is supposed to work for all. Whether this contributes to the frustrations which many people experience with libraries is difficult to say. What can be reported is that lack of organization by user group results in the impersonal and discontinuous nature of most library service.

Organization by Form of Materials

As the quantity of non-book and non-print publication mounted over the years, libraries established positions and departments devoted to these newer formats. First came magazines and journals, then government documents, a little later slides and films, followed by microfilm and other microforms, and most recently data-based resources. A small number of libraries set up photograph and print units. Sound recordings also entered collections but usually did not bulk large enough to result in specialized positions.

It was natural to utilize form of material as one basis of organization. Libraries are collections of resource materials for which they carry responsibility for accessible arrangement and for proper protection and preservation. These objectives could more readily be achieved in separate units staffed by experts, with suitable equipment and special classifications of resources. Documents, for example, require shelf arrangement different from that for the book collection, prints call on an expertise not possessed by most librarians, films posed a particular problem in handling and storing, but today's libraries now provide videos which are handled more easily.

Where libraries are large enough to have not just single positions but whole departments devoted to forms of material, the departments tend to take over the basic functions rather than just operating as supplements to the rest of the library. Document and film and print divisions often handle selection and acquisition, cataloging, reference service, and even circulation for their particular resources. When users inquire of reference staff about the non-book and non-print forms, they are typically referred to the separate department for each. Thus, the form divisions often operate as complete, self-contained libraries within the larger system. This is one application of the principle of federal decentralization.

As form departments increased in number, they complicated the task of many users in locating what they seek. If one believes that libraries exist to bring materials conveniently together by subject content, then specialization by format violates this principle. One can hardly think of a topic—whether in geography or history or science or whatever—where relevant publications would not be found in all or most of the non-book sections. Specialization by format spreads related resources all over the building.

This criticism would be challenged by the minority of users who seek resources by format. Those who come into the library seeking videos—say for a class session or a community meeting—find it convenient to go to one location; or a journalist seeking an illustration for an article will know to go directly to the print division. And there are those who drop by to browse through current magazines and appreciate having them all together.

But these are exceptions. Many readers come in looking for information or background on a topic. They either go to the section of the book shelves with which they are familiar or they consult the catalog. In each case they will locate books but not the several other forms. Or they may ask the librarian where material on the topic is located, and be directed usually to the shelves or the catalog. Yet the inquirer might welcome a video or a government document or information from a computer data base; in fact, the non-book material might have exactly what is sought. Readers are expected somehow to find their way through the labyrinth of formats.

Some libraries have made efforts to help. Pamphlets have been shelved with books. In some cases dummies on the shelves have reminded searchers that there are compact disks or videos available on the same topic. Posters may direct visitors to the database terminal. After an initial period most of these efforts fall by the wayside, for they are an inadequate cure for a complex organizational problem. The format divisions endure, but not the guideposts to them.

So most libraries depend on the catalog to direct both user

and staff to non-book sources. This is a less than perfect instrument for the purpose. Usually only one generalized class entry is used ("see also Pamphlet File"), which some searchers do not see and which those who do may disregard. The various non-book media get less than thorough cataloging and subject headings, and this is more constricted the greater the emphasis on cutting cataloging costs and the greater the dependence on outside purveyors for catalog entries. In terms of bibliographic organization, non-book materials tend to be step-children in the collection.

The exception is periodicals, for which an elaborate index structure exists. But in libraries of substantial size, periodicals are likely to stand separate from books on the same subject. Some libraries have sought to bring this material back into subject rooms, so that content in a book binding and content on the same topic in a magazine binding stand near each other. However, more than one library that has tried this goes back after a period to a separate periodical section. The tasks of checking-in issues, keeping journals in order, noting and locating missing issues for binding prove onerous, and are pushed back to a staff devoted exclusively to these headaches. This is convenient for librarians in the subject rooms, but it is not convenient for users.

The newcomer is machine-readable information in data bases and accessible through terminals. Originally the information stored was mostly bibliographical (that is, it tells where to find the information sought, but does not usually give the information itself), but this has changed. Telephone directories, encyclopedias, financial services, scientific data and much else are now in this form. Rather than supplementing the print collection, such computerized information is replacing some parts of present resources.

How libraries organize this newcomer will go a long way toward determining the role that they will play in automated information. Thus far the tendency has been to establish a separate unit for computerized data. This is the road followed when other forms appeared earlier. The format is new, its use requires some skill, special equipment is involved—so specialization by form prevails. The user has one more part of the library to consult, another service source that he may overlook.

But data-based information has a unique quality. Both the bases and the computer can in a sense be placed anywhere. Multiple access can be gained simply by installing terminals. Will the pattern of the future be the prevailing one of a separate and single computerized information station, or will there be a terminal at every service librarian's desk? Only when the latter is achieved will libraries move confidently into the computerized information age.

For all the proliferation of non-book formats, few libraries have become genuinely multi-media. Their primary effort is focused on print material. The basis and core is books, closely supplemented by journals; non-print materials stand on the fringe. Money goes first to print, as does space allocation in the building. As a result the public thinks of libraries as places of books, with some special material off in a corner or on the second floor or down in the basement. Some school libraries come closest to being multi-media, where material most useful on a subject is purchased without regard to format, and where the several forms stand together and are used together in the school media center.

The rare book room is a special case. Actually, in most instances it is another book unit rather than a unit organized by format, for resources are likely to be in print form. Here protection and preservation take priority because of the unique character and high value of holdings. A small but regular group of users seeks them out, and they sometimes attract private money both for acquisitions and for distinctive furnishings. Here again the advantage of specialization of personnel is evident, for special collections call for special talents on the part of staff. Even more than format rooms, these divisions stand separate in the library organization, sometimes with different conditions of use and different hours of service. Despite the fact that rare book rooms are used only by a small and select group, both public and academic libraries like to call attention to them, featuring them in descriptive folders and annual reports, much as some families like to mention their special jewelry even though it may not be very evident.

Organization by format cuts the collection in a way distinctly different from the basic arrangement represented by subject classification of holdings. This is an effort to respond to a multimedia age. At the same time it complicates organization, adding to the number of departments that must be maintained and the number of specialized positions that must be filled. For some staff members it is a convenience, and for many users it is an inconvenience. This is not to condemn organization by format; there are no final and best answers for the structure of complex enterprises, but where a design is as pervasive as this, both administrator and staff should be acutely aware of the problems posed and be ever alert to mitigate shortcomings. Failure to do so results in a library-oriented structure that lets users flounder as best they can.

Organization by Geography

Distance from the center prompts some specialized positions and departments in libraries. Examples are branch public libraries and departmental academic libraries. There are city libraries with fifty or more branches and university libraries with an equal number of departmental units.

The organizational questions that arise are how many detached units to have, and how closely to tie the outposts to headquarters. Supervision and coordination of branches is a related question that will be considered in the next chapter.

One school of thought stresses uniformity, both among the detached outlets and with the central unit. Policies adopted are made to apply to the distant agencies as well as to the central unit, regulations are passed to keep them in line, intermediate supervisory positions are maintained. Larger public libraries, for example, may have not just one supervisory-coordinating officer (Head of Branches) but also subordinate officers under the Head who are responsible for the outlets in one section or region of the city. Some academic libraries group departmental libraries in a broad subject area (science, social studies, etc.) and assign a middle manager to oversee and keep them in line. Such libraries would no doubt protest that the intermediate officers are there to guide and stimulate and coordinate the territorial units as much as to regulate them, but control is basically the purpose in this concept.

A contrasting school of thought sees an opportunity for variation and innovation in units that are detached from the central structure. Collections could be particularly tailored to the group served, classification schemes could be adjusted if desirable, experiments could be tried, staff with unusual talents could be assigned. However, not much of this occurs. Emphasis is usually on conformity, keeping the remote units in step, avoiding the complexity and confusion that could result from too much individualism in members of the family who are not living at home.

The result can be seen in the branch systems of most city libraries. Neighborhoods may differ sharply, from affluent to poor, from highly organized to deteriorating, from an excess of old people to an excess of children. Yet the branches are remarkably similar. Come in through the door and there will be a few cases of current best sellers in hardback and paper bindings. To one side is a children's room, crowded with youngsters or bereft of youngsters, depending on the neighborhood. To the other side is an adult fiction collection with a selection of classical authors, some titles of established 20th-century novelists, titles in demand for school book reports, and copies of yesterday's best sellers. A parallel non-fiction section holds a more or less balanced subject collection, with a few titles on topics from philosophy to government to science to the arts and on to history. Tucked in at a prominent point are a few cases of mystery stories, science fiction, and romances. The visitor would get very little idea of the neighborhood served, either from the collection that stands on the shelves or from the service program and kind of staff provided. Similarly, the same policies and regulations apply to all: there will or will not be films or recordings in branches, each will have a children's librarian whether or not a neighborhood of families is served, loan periods will be the same in high-education as in low-education communities. The units serving very different clienteles have been struck from a single mold.

Branch librarians would protest this picture and point to

more how-to titles in one collection and more arts and travel material in another, a case or two of publications in Spanish or on black culture in some units but not in others. In most cases these are fringe additions to the standard balanced collection. One searches long and hard for community branches that start from the community, following its interests, resisting expenditure for titles that fill a "gap" in resources but that when purchased will stand unused on the shelves.

The result of conformity in branches is markedly different amounts of use in different sections of the city. The standard unit fits some neighborhoods and they respond, but it does not fit others and use is low. Then as circulation declines, less book money and fewer staff members are assigned to the branch, and use goes down further; such agencies are caught in a downward spiral.

There is a further result. As use goes down, the cost for each patron served and each item circulated goes up. Unit costs in heavily-used and little-used outlets in the same city can vary in a ratio of one to ten. In a study in Atlanta the figure per item circulated varied from $1.32 to $13.52 in different branches.[10] A report on the San Francisco Public Library, finding costs per use (not per user, but per visit by each user) to be $10.28 in one instance and $10.95 in another, could not resist a snide comment: "Without being cynical, one is tempted to suggest that each local user be provided with a taxicab ride back and forth to the nearest larger branch, where the individual would get better service and the dollar outlay even with the taxi fare for that service would be less than at present."[11]

It would be unrealistic to claim that an organizational policy that permitted and encouraged branches to pursue individual service programs would automatically generate equal use in all neighborhoods. Studies show that persons with greater education engage in more reading, and that different groups attach varying amounts of prestige to books. But certainly the publications in a neighborhood outlet should reflect the level and concerns of the people served; every librarian would subscribe to this principle, but in practice it is often forgotten. It may even be that books should play a less central role in collections for some communities, and be replaced by a foundation of visual and aural materials and, in the future, by computerized resources.

In the last decade or more, the inherent competition for money between the central unit on the one side and branches on the other has become more apparent in public libraries. When funds were growing ten percent or more a year, and inflation was low, the pinch did not particularly hurt. With smaller increases and mounting inflation in the 1970s, cries of pain were heard. Should central be favored so that the basic collection is maintained, or should neighborhood outlets be favored so that community service is sustained—or should both be treated equitably while quality of service declines across the board? Public library directors have divided on this issue. Where a middle road was sought, with the closing of lesser-used branches while maintaining the strength of larger outlets, neighborhoods have protested and very few closings have occurred. For library distribution, local grocery stores rather than supermarkets have been favored by the populace, even though stock is limited and hours are curtailed. Branch libraries have shifted in the public eye from being outlets for books and education to being symbols of neighborhood service, and any word of closing rallies those who never use the local agency as well as regular users. Most existing city branch systems were developed before the present-day prevalence of the automobile, and before the recent dramatic upturn of public transportation in some cities, and the earlier configuration remains firmly in place. Thus the competition continues between functional centralization and geographic decentralization, with officials seeking to do a balancing act that somehow is expected to get more for less.

Geography also prompts maintenance of departmental library units on college and university campuses. The territory covered by academic institutions expanded with increased enrollments and accelerated building programs of recent decades. Moreover, extension units at a distance have been established in many states, seeking to bring opportunities for higher education within commuting distance of most students. Medical, dental, pharmacy and other colleges have been located off the central campus, occasionally as far away as another city.

Academic library directors have sought to restrain the development of too many distant agencies. Considerations of both cost and control were in their minds. Where an instructional site grows up at a distance, the directors try to prevent undue proliferation by setting up one larger collection rather than several smaller ones. Further, they seek to hold down the remote unit to direct curricular support and to encourage dependence on one comprehensive and research collection for the whole system.

This does not always go down well with officers and faculty in the decentralized locations. They naturally want as much service as possible to carry their course instruction and also their own research. No doubt an element of pride and rivalry enters the picture. The additional campuses may gain considerable strength and leverage, so that the central-branch competition for funds is played out in the academic as well as the civic world.

In the most populous states, public university systems develop a nexus of semi-autonomous institutions. The University of California has nine campuses, each with a library of some stature, and indeed with decentralized departmental branches of their own. In New York State the SUNY system has no less than 64 units (including the public colleges and universities in New York City which were incorporated into the statewide institution). Whether such development represents over-expansion is an educational consideration outside the scope of the present discussion, but it clearly has resulted in proliferation of academic libraries. The divisions and branches grew up to provide access to resources. It is interesting to speculate, if the statewide systems were being developed today, whether there would be fewer and smaller "complete" libraries, and greater dependence on specialized resources made available through networks already in existence and through communication-transmission technology coming into place.

Decentralized organization by geography or territory was inevitable. Once established, detached outlets prove most difficult to close or modify. Library directors carry a burden they did not make, but which strains their budgets as well as their backs.

Conclusion

There are other bases for specialization and departmentation in libraries. A few units are organized by language, or more properly by special alphabets, such as the Jewish and Slavonic divisions of the New York Public Library and the Oriental divisions in some universities. Idiosyncrasies of buildings can prompt and perpetuate unusual departments. Even the enthusiasms and peculiarities of individual staff members and department heads can affect structure.

But the functional foundation usually prevails. Other forms of specialization play more a supplementary and supporting role. Services started with the aim of breaking away from limitations in the traditional structure often come back in time to the base in function. An example is service to the "disadvantaged," launched with such hope by various public libraries in the 1960s. This specialty involved selection of materials unlike those in the regular collection, their arrangement in unorthodox fashion, new "outreach" methods, personnel with evangelistic motivation. The traditional separation by function was to be breached by concentrating one arm of service on a portion of the population. Come back a decade later and in most cases the special service is hardly visible; what little remains has been re-absorbed into the long-standing cataloging, reference and circulation departments. Business as usual prevails.

Libraries have made limited use of the basis of organization favored by such present-day theorists as Peter Drucker. He stresses a goal-related structure and result-producing divisions. Ask what the agency is for, why it exists, and build on that basis.

Applied to the public library, for example, this would result in one division for education, another for information, and still another for recreation: that is, positions and divisions focused on the purpose for which the institution exists. In the university library the categories would be the instructional division and the graduate or research division. The result would not only be emphasis on objectives but also specialization of staff, in education or information or recreation in the one instance, and in instruction or research in the other, and emphasis also on how and why people pursue these aims. There would thus be a shift from function and from collection to purposes and to users.

Objections to such structures can be readily advanced: the overlap in the goals themselves, the relevance of the same materials to two or more of the purposes, and the orientation of librarians more toward books and their contents and less toward people and their motives. While a result-producing structure is unlikely to be developed in libraries, it is worth reflecting on its possible advantages to see how they might be achieved, at least in part, within the more familiar organization.

Whatever the basis of internal organization, a few elementary principles should be kept in mind. Keep organization as simple as possible; question every proposed new specialty, department, or branch. Consider how much coordination each unit requires; don't be tempted by intriguing divisions that need constant oversight. Once a position or department is established, define jobs and responsibilities clearly; beware the ambiguous position or unit. Cherish flexibility and responsiveness; don't let organization become a strait jacket. And avoid evaluation based on orderly structure; the ultimate measure is performance at the library-user interface.

References

1. Drucker, Peter F. *Management: Tasks, Responsibilities, Practices.* New York, Harper and Row, 1974, p. 454.

2. McDiarmid, Erret M. and McDiarmid, John. *The Administration of American Public Libraries.* Chicago, American Library Association and the University of Illinois, 1943, p. 74.

3. Rogers, Rutherford D. and Weber, David C. *University Library Administration.* New York, H. W. Wilson, 1971, p. 73.

4. Wilson, Louis R. and Tauber, Maurice F. *The University Library; the Organization, Administration and Functions of Academic Libraries.* New York, Columbia University Press, 1956, p. 47.

5. Martin, Lowell A. *Space in the Pratt Central Building.* Number 2 in the Deiches Fund Studies of Library Service. Baltimore, Enoch Pratt Free Library, 1964, p. 3.

6. Hurt, Peyton. "Staff Specialization; a Possible Substitute for Subject Departmentalization," *Bulletin of the American Library Association,* Vol. 29, No. 7 (July 1935), pp. 417–421.

7. See, for example:
   Warren, Althea. "Departmental Organization of a Public Library by Subject," in Joeckel, Carleton, B., *Current Issues in Library Administration.* Chicago, University of Chicago Press, 1939, pp. 110–134.
   Phelps, Rose B. "The Effect of Organizational Patterns on the Adequacy and Efficiency of Reference Service in the Large American Public Library," *Library Quarterly,* Vol. 17, No. 4. (October 1947), pp. 281–295.
   Maizell, Robert E. "The Subject-Departmentalized Public Library," College and Research Libraries, Vol. 12, No. 3 (July 1951), pp. 255–260.

8. Leigh, Robert D. *The Public Library in the United States; the General Report of the Public Library Inquiry.* New York, Columbia University Press, 1950, p. 99.

9. Gertzog, Alice and Beckerman, Edwin. *Administration of the Public Library.* Metuchen, N.J., Scarecrow Press, 1994.

10. Martin, Lowell A. *A Public Library Equal to the Potential of Atlanta and Fulton County.* Atlanta, Atlanta Public Library, 1985, p. 86.

11. Martin, Lowell A. *A Plan of Development for the San Francisco Public Library.* San Francisco, San Francisco Public Library, 1982, p. 40.

VIII SPECIALIZATION BY LEVEL

THE PREVIOUS CHAPTER dealt with the logical first step in organizing a library: determination of tasks to be performed and of the positions and departments needed to carry them out. Thus the cataloger appears on the roster, and the circulation assistant, and the subject librarian and the map specialist and all the others. The various tasks and positions and departments are laid out.

Are all these positions at an equal level in skill, calling for the same amount and kind of training? The answer of course is negative. The bookshelver and the science bibliographer differ in level, as do the circulation clerk and the children's librarian. Grouping positions by level is a part of organization, leading to a hierarchy of expertise.

This chapter will deal with the several distinct levels of positions that have arisen in libraries: i.e., professionals, paraprofessionals, and clerks. The following chapter will go on to another type of specialization, for supervision and management, and on that basis will examine the administrative functions of direction and coordination.

In libraries distinct clerical and professional levels gradually emerged over the years, and in time became solidified in the position classification structure. Graduate schools grew up to prepare personnel for the more advanced posts. More recently an intermediate level has appeared in the roster, that of paraprofessionals of different types. Each of these will be examined, along with their interrelations.

First, it is worth noting that libraries have an uncommon

distribution of advanced and highly-trained personnel on the one side, and semi-skilled support staff on the other. Typically a manufacturing plant has a very large proportion of workers with limited skill and a very small proportion of engineers and designers. Some workers on the line may develop a specialized skill on the job—finish painting of the automobile, for example, or the mixing of specialized steel in the mill—but we do not think of them as "professionals." A parallel description could be given of the staffs in record-keeping enterprises such as banks and insurance companies: a large number of clerks and a small number of financial experts. In contrast with fabricating and record-keeping enterprises, educational institutions typically have a high proportion of professionals and a small proportion of support staff. This is true from the elementary school through the university; the mission being education, the bulk of staff members are educational specialists.

Libraries fall somewhere between. They have a larger proportion of professionals than the factory or the bank, but a smaller proportion than the school. This follows from the dual nature of the library. It is in part an educational agency, requiring experts, and in part a repository of materials, requiring routine handling and a considerable volume of record-keeping. It is not easy to think of an organization with a similar mix. Perhaps the hospital comes closest, with its medical staff, its variety of paraprofessionals, and its considerable number of attendants and other semi-skilled workers. Because of the unique mixture in libraries, attention to each of the three levels, and to their interrelations, takes on greater importance.

The Professional Level

What is a library professional, how can you identify one? What work do they do? How many does a library need?

Applying management principles, the answers to such questions would be determined by the tasks actually performed. The number of positions and training required for them would follow from this base. However, librarians typically answer the question of who is professional the other way around, by pointing to those who have completed library school. Professional work in this view is what these individuals do. And the number needed is determined by how many positions are occupied by staff members with this qualification.

Using library-school graduation as the criterion leads to questionable conclusions, both in logic and in actual staffing. Were there no professionals in libraries before there were library schools? Does any position become professional if a library-school graduate is hired to fill it? And is the work that person does by definition professional? Affirmative answers to these questions leave one uneasy, and prompt a search for other factors that distinguish professionals and professional work.

One consideration that must be recalled for a moment is the natural tendency for workers to exalt the nature of what they do. One way is to claim that it is professional. We know of sanitation "engineers" (garbage collectors) and lawn "doctors" (gardeners) and stationary "engineers" (janitors). Prestige attaches to the professional-sounding label, so it is used to inflate the nature of the job.

It would be unjustified to charge that librarians seek to exalt their positions by means of a label. They are in posts formally classified as professional, so they already have the desired designation. Unfortunately the label they use — that of "librarian" — does not carry any great measure of prestige. In the public mind, this profession falls somewhere below the distinction accorded physicians, lawyers, and engineers. Most library practitioners have at some time been questioned by friends and acquaintances on just what they do and why that requires graduate education — and have not always given convincing answers.

Another extraneous factor that must be considered is the element of service that animates much library work. This motivates many a staff member in the professional ranks and some in non-professional categories, giving them a sense of dedication. And why not? Where else can the citizen and the student turn in the community or in the academic institution with assurance that they will usually get a considered and informed response to an inquiry? The service orientation of libraries accounts for much of the esteem in which the institution is held, even by

those who would think twice about applying the term professional to that service.

But service alone does not make a job professional. Toilers
in many walks of life satisfy the customer. There are polite
bus drivers who perform with skill, and telephone operators,
and carpenters, and bank clerks. We return to merchants who
give what we call service. But we do not describe them as
professionals.

Analysis of other attributes, such as intelligence on the job
and adherence to ethical standards, leads to similar conclusions. These are involved in professional performance—and
also in non-professional performance. They are not what sets
the highly-trained expert apart.

What then are the distinguishing marks? Brought down to
the core, professional work is judgment based on an extended
intellectual discipline. The phrase "and applied to the well-
being of human beings," could be added but various jobs
improve the human lot without being professions. The essence
is judgment based on a discipline. The two go together: not
judgment alone, for this comes down to common sense, which
is a quality possessed by people whether in or out of the
professions; not discipline alone, for this is a quality possessed
by the scholar who may never stir out of his study. And the
discipline must be intellectual, not manual, as in the case of
the extended training that goes into the preparation, say, of a
cabinet-maker or a topflight tennis player.

Does library service involve judgment based on an extended
intellectual discipline? The answer is affirmative, even though
some nonlibrarians would have to be convinced. Judging publications for accuracy, balance, effectiveness of expression and
suitability for the clientele served certainly qualifies, as does
building a collection attuned to this same clientele. Similarly,
the organization of resources, constructing a logical and usable
structure, and fitting individual titles into this scheme, call for
decisions based on considerable training. The same applies to
identification by the reference librarian of the particular items
in a collection needed to meet the individual user's needs, and
here an extra measure of understanding of human psychology
comes into play. The children's librarian and the school librar-

ian, guiding the reading of youngsters, combine knowledge of resources on the one side with understanding of the learning process and child development on the other. Examples could be extended to the scholarly library and to the business information center.

Gain the discipline, exercise judgment based on that discipline, and inquiring minds and the record of knowledge are joined. Unless one deprecates learning, a professional service has been performed.

The next question is whether library *positions*—those labeled professional—call for judgment based on an intellectual discipline. Here the answer is yes and no, at some times but not at others. Practicing librarians are the first to point out that a considerable portion of what they do is not professional. The cataloger is caught up with records and filing, the reference librarian with directional questions requiring little of the discipline, the school librarian with the housekeeping activities needed to keep a materials supply room in order. Users observe the situation, and thus their uncertainty as to what level to ascribe to the staff member.

This equivocal public perception reflects back on the librarian's self-image. The 1983–84 President of the American Library Association, in her inaugural address, referred to ". . . a pervasive and growing uneasiness about who we are and what we as a profession are all about."[1] If librarians doubt themselves, no wonder that others share that view. It would be a mistake to ascribe all of this to organization within libraries, but how librarians conceptualize their functions and how they group these into jobs are a contributing factor.

Positions that combine a range of levels, from simple to complex, from routine to extraordinary, violate one of the principles of specialized organization in enterprises, that of putting like work together in designating positions. One does not combine filing and typing with corporate decisions in the executive suite, nor record-keeping in the physician's position, nor housekeeping for the aeroplane in the pilot's duties. The reasons for division of labor are efficiency, economy, skill, and morale. All are diluted if contrasting levels are combined in one job.

The question is how the range of duties in professional positions in libraries came about, why the inclusion so often of clerical duties. Part of the answer is the nature of library work. It entails handling of materials and keeping of records; sometimes it is quicker to have the reference librarian who selected the book from the shelves also put it back, and for the cataloger who decides on a subject heading to type it on the catalog card. But more of the reason is a combination of the tradition of service in libraries and the tendency to maintain as many professional positions as possible. Various earlier organizers of libraries wanted users to be fully served at whatever point they made their first contact, whether at the door or the circulation desk or wherever. In this view all staff members should be able to respond and to respond fully. The user was not to be referred or shunted about.

This was a little like saying that patients are to be treated at their first contact in the doctor's office or the hospital. Patients would be astonished to have the admission clerk in the hospital or the nurse in the doctor's office identify their illness and prescribe what should be done about it. Where clients conceive a service to be specialized, they want to see the specialist, no matter how many referrals this may involve. Where they do not conceive of a service as being very specialized, say when they enter a department store, they are satisfied with a polite and reasonably-informed salesclerk. The tendency has been to organize libraries like department stores, not like specialized service agencies.

That earlier tradition carries over into present-day organization for guiding use of facilities. Libraries are not strong on directions and folders for guidance when one enters the door; this is considered impersonal and not in accord with the personal service aim. For some reason signage is limited or nonexistent in library after library. Seldom is there a non-professional information assistant near the entrance; questions might arise which this staff member could not handle. As a result quite routine questions are asked at the circulation desk, interrupting the flow of work there, or at the reference desk where they are sandwiched between complex bibliographical inquiries, or of any staff member working near the catalog.

Besides confusing the duties at service stations, this arrangement is labor-intensive and costly. Where professional work predominates—say in the reference room or the subject department—little provision is made for the clerical work also involved. One comes on sizable libraries where the whole range of public service units (other than the circulation desk) have very few clerical support positions. Someone has to type reports, label shelves, keep materials in order, and tell patrons where the washrooms are located, and for lack of support staff this falls to professionals.

Alternative arrangements are conceivable. Take a subject-organized public library as an example. There could be a central informational and directional station staffed by paraprofessionals and with a core collection of reference sources. This desk would handle the entering flow of traffic and answer routine information inquiries. Subject librarians at decentralized stations would deal with complex searches, those requiring judgment based on intellectual discipline. Within the subject areas or rooms, the non-professional tasks of maintaining the areas and the professional tasks of consultation with users could be separated, the first to be handled by non-professionals at the entrance, the second by specialists in offices (which is where professional consultation in other fields occurs). There is even an element of economy in this plan. In periods of limited user traffic (morning and evening hours), rather than having staff stationed in each of the subject areas or rooms, the central directional desk could handle much of the demand, with subject librarians engaged in other activities (such as building the collection) and on call when needed.

Librarians themselves are of two minds about the confusion of levels of work in their job assignments. They complain of the clerical tasks imposed on them. But they resist any recommendation that the number of professional positions be decreased and the number of clerical and paraprofessional positions increased. A sense of security comes into conflict with a sense of professionalism.

Another effect of the jumble of levels in professional positions is the public's ambiguous conception of the librarian. The user is helped to find obscure information and admires the skill and knowledge of the staff member. Then the user sees the same person putting the magazines in order or typing up reserve requests. To many people librarians are pleasant individuals, inclined to help, probably familiar with the books and other sources around them, usually spending considerable time at what appear to be housekeeping activities. Their visual image is of a neatly-dressed woman of settled years, and they are vaguely surprised when the librarian is an aggressive young man or young woman. The public view is equivocal: are they dealing with a friendly attendant or a trained specialist?

Still another question that can be raised is the nature of the discipline provided by library schools. This is not the place to offer a critique of education for professional library service. Suffice it to observe that this too is a considerable mixture. Four years of college are required, but with undergraduate content so varied that little conception exists of definite "pre-professional" preparation. Within the fifth year of study, attention is given to history, to practice, to techniques, to analysis of resources, to what libraries do, and to what libraries might do. Whether this amounts to an intellectual discipline based on a body of verified principles is a moot point.

In the 19th and early 20th centuries, the number of clearly designated professional positions was quite small. The bulk of work was done by workers who might or might not be designated as "librarians." Around the turn of the century, the range and volume of publication increased, and the objective of aiding and guiding readers came to the fore. Trained librarians were needed. They received formal instruction either in training classes within libraries or in divisions established in technical institutes and universities. Separate identification and designation of professional positions increased. Some larger libraries held out into the 1920s and 1930s before distinct jobs requiring advanced training were established.

Once the wave spread, it took in many positions in libraries. After all, it was not very expensive at that time to convert a job to the professional level. More women were going to college and coming out with relatively few opportunities for careers. They could be attracted to genteel library positions with very modest salaries. In time many libraries had half or more of their jobs in the advanced classification, and this whether the tasks performed required college and graduate study or not.

The challenge to this large proportion of professionals came first in reviews of cataloging departments. Many had a marked majority of professional positions, with limited support staff. In surveys of academic libraries, Maurice F. Tauber and others pointed out that the proportions should be reversed.[2] Rather than the professional making a decision on classification or subject headings, and then carrying through to get the designations on cards and into the catalog, such specialists should concentrate on the decisions and have adequate clerical help to complete the process. To a degree this change has occurred in both public and academic libraries, and has been abetted by the increase in centralized cataloging services (OCLC, for example). Application of the same principle has been slower in reference departments, even though most analysts agree that a majority of inquiries could be handled by personnel without graduate professional education.

Typically, the proportion of professional positions in libraries is now down to about one-third, the proportion recommended by standards of the American Library Association.[3] The percentage of clerks, rather than increasing, has actually decreased to some extent, as an intermediate class of paraprofessionals has come into the picture. There is a tendency in libraries to push duties as high as possible among the levels of workers, whereas management principles—and the interests of economy—point in precisely the opposite direction.

No neat formula can be laid down for the proper proportion of professional positions in the staff. Larger libraries with research capacity may well need more than the average; at the other end of the scale, libraries of moderate size and a good level of income may also need more to fill the specialized service positions they can afford to maintain. But it follows from the continued element of clerical duties mixed into professional positions that the percentage is high and could be reduced with re-thinking of service structure and re-allocation of tasks.

While no exact formula can be prescribed, a model worth bearing in mind is a staff made up one-quarter of professionals, one-quarter of paraprofessionals and one-half of clerks. Present professional staff members are made uneasy by any suggestion that the number in their ranks be reduced. This is viewed as a threat: who would be fired? Actually the adjustment could be made without any dismissals, by attrition over a period of time. The positions remaining would be genuinely professional, with the bulk of routine tasks at this level and the work not requiring the intellectual discipline transferred to others. Internally, librarians would feel that their full capacities are used. Externally, the public would perceive the librarian as an expert in learning and resources and not as a record-keeper and housekeeper.

The Paraprofessional Level

Librarians have long had an intermediate level of staff, not professionals in any formal sense nor clerks in the usual meaning of the term. They have been able to hire intelligent individuals, usually women, who are high-school graduates and may even have some college. In academic libraries, faculty wives filled this role, and might well be college graduates. Like other institutions, libraries would be the poorer if they had not had the services of married women.

Once on the staff, such individuals were often given additional responsibilities as needs and vacancies occurred. They assisted in the cataloging department, filled in at the reference desk, in time became head of circulation or serial or other units. A number have cut out both a place on the staff and a career for themselves.

Some library administrators realized that this intermediate group constituted an asset and at the same time afforded an opportunity to stretch the personnel budget. Also, for a period, graduate librarians were not easy to find. Formal recognition was given to the group with a separate class of positions in the personnel plan, under such titles as Library Assistant and Library Associate.

At first the emphasis was more on graduates with two years of college. Junior colleges and community colleges established curricula in library techniques, which flourished for a period and then declined. Assistant positions at this level were squeezed between clerical workers on the one side, who could be taught techniques on the job, and more advanced work on the other, that as a minimum required further subject education and a college major.

More recently an Assistant or Associate is typically a four-year degree holder. This has several advantages for the library. Persons with wider background can be recruited. There is opportunity to be selective as to college majors of the graduates chosen, depending on service needs, although science and business majors can seldom be attracted. To provide further prospects, some libraries encourage paraprofessionals to go on to library school, providing flexibility in schedules and financial assistance to smooth the path. If the agency has professional vacancies, this is a choice source of recruits, for their performance on the job has already been tested and proven.

By 1970 the intermediate class was recognized in the Education and Manpower statement of the American Library Association. A study published in 1980 reported that 88 percent of 136 larger public libraries had a paraprofessional group with college graduation as the educational prerequisite.[4] Typical duties of associates included assisting children's librarians, processing cataloging records, and revising filing in the catalog. A provocative finding was that 75 percent or more of libraries had the paraprofessionals discharge such duties as "assists readers in locating specific information," "assists readers to use the catalog," "teaches readers to use reference materials," and "suggests titles for purchase"—all tasks that appear in the A.L.A. list of professional responsibilities for librarians. Further, supervisors consistently gave high ratings to the performance of library assistants in these and similar duties.

Another example of reorganization of positions occurs when public libraries set up a separate telephone reference unit. Calls come directly to a staff assembled specifically for the purpose rather than going to the librarian at the public desk, where they interfere with service in person. The instructive point is that many libraries moving in this direction find that the telephone inquiries can be handled, and handled adequately, by assistants without library-school training. Applying the principle of uniformity rather than diversity of levels in positions, a service can be given effectively at less cost. The per-question cost in such telephone units turns out to be less than at regular reference desks, because less-expensive staff is used, because resources can be arranged for rapid response, and because demand is steady rather than being intermittent, with periods when the professional at the public desk has no clients and fills in with other work.

The satisfactory record of library assistants in handling duties usually assigned to library-school graduates raises the question of what distinction, if any, exists between this level and the lower professional grades. Presumably the distinction is in the potential of the junior professional for growth, but no one is sure whether or how the graduate library school imparts this. And unfortunately, potential for professional growth is not really tested in most libraries because they have few genuinely advanced professional positions; the only opportunities for growth are over in the administrative sequence.

The paraprofessional level has cut out a place in library staffing patterns. What started as an expedient response to a shortage of professional recruits has become a formal part of position plans. In larger libraries, assistants and associates form a cohesive group within the roster, and some have organized into associations or affiliated with labor unions. They request salary increases and present grievances. The recurring source of concern is the dead-end nature of the intermediate level. The option of going on to library school may not be practical for some, the library is often unable to guarantee a position on completion of professional education, and the general job market for librarians is not favorable. Another concern is that assistants and associates feel that they do work equivalent to that of the professional, but without recognition or salary; interviews with members of this group often reveal a considerable amount of resentment on this score. The study cited earlier, showing that paraprofessionals perform reference and guidance functions, lends credence to this complaint. In time there may well be legal action on this score, with paraprofessionals charging discrimination in that they do not receive equal pay for equal work.

Paraprofessionals have been brought into the ranks not so much as a source of workers for advanced clerical duties but more as a source of personnel to handle services that in the past were assigned to professionals. Where they have been adequately trained on the job, they have proven that they can handle tasks that were thought to require graduate education. This has not gone unnoticed by larger government employers. The Office of Personnel Management has challenged the need for Master's degrees in some federal positions for librarians. From the long-range standpoint, the sounder response is to organize tasks within libraries so that some positions clearly call for the discipline represented by graduate study, thus meeting the challenge, rather than defending the existing mixture of duties in professional assignments. Then paraprofessionals can properly be used for the work they are capable of handling.

Libraries have gained a source of qualified personnel for which they do not have to pay professional salaries, but at a hidden price. Here is another level of personnel — in addition to professionals and clericals — that has special needs, aspirations, and complaints. And this level of positions has raised questions about requiring the professional degree for a wide range of tasks that must be done. The cup of the administrator runneth over.

Clerical Staff

Finding suitable clerical staff is a growing problem for both business and government. A service economy requires armies of workers to handle the paper generated and to deal with users of the services. It is a mistake to assume that such jobs can be filled by employees with few if any qualifications. Word and number ability are often necessary, as is competence in personal relations. Yet the worker supply divides more and more into two extremes: those with specialties acquired through additional education or apprenticeship, and at the other extreme those who have verbal and/or personality deficiencies and do not fit into any part of the economy. Hence the substantial measure of unemployment even in localities where the newspapers carry long lists of job vacancies. Even those with no deficiencies think twice before entering clerical service because this is the level of work that has been hit hardest by automation; the new clerical recruit looking ahead is unsure about job security.

Libraries compete in this market. There is some attraction to working in a library: the environment is pleasant, the pressure of work is not great, and recruits may look forward to associating with people at their best as they seek out knowledge. Reality brings disillusion, as clerks unpack boxes and boxes of materials, type reams of cards, shelve thousands of books, and endlessly stamp out books for circulation. The development of the paraprofessional level further hems them in, for the latter are available to handle tasks requiring a little more initiative and judgment. City libraries must usually take clerks from general rosters prepared by the civil-service authority, and thus are restricted in searching out and selecting individuals best suited for their particular jobs. A common report from library administrators is of unrest in the clerical ranks, and—even more serious—of discourtesy at the circulation desk.

Schools and colleges have a built-in source of clerical help in the form of students. Use of this source serves several purposes. Not only does work get done, but at the college level it provides financial assistance, and some students may develop an interest in library careers. Libraries that devote reasonable time to motivating and training student help often get substantial return for the effort, and may even bring out some exceptional performers who can be given more advanced duties before they graduate.

But it is difficult to hold clerical staff. Turnover is heavy, as some of the best recruits move on to more promising opportunities and some of the worst drift from job to job. The particular techniques in libraries require time and effort in training on the job, which is lost when some clericals shortly move on or out. Discontent feeds on discontent within the ranks.

What to do? In recruiting, alternative sources might be explored, in the form of more part-time workers and of older citizens interested in earnings up to the limit allowed under Social Security. Library administrators are quick to question the dependability of part-time personnel, although they have limited experience with them, and do so just after complaining of the actual unreliability of full-time clerks. Academic librarians get many of their routine tasks done by student workers who are attending classes. Enterprises with peak-load periods, such as department stores, make extensive use of part-time clerks. There are competent and reliable people who wish to moonlight and others who for one reason or another can work only for brief periods. The number of part-time workers in America has been increasing in recent years.

Once hired, clericals should not be taken for granted nor treated as second-class citizens, but should be respected for the work they do and listened to when they have suggestions or grievances. Flexibility in schedules should be allowed for continuation of education. Like others, they need tangible rewards for service well done, in the form of a salary scale with reasonable increments, and they need the prospect for advancement, in the form of promotions to which they can aspire. These are platitudes in personnel management, but a careful look at libraries often shows formal violation of them by supervisors, and informal violation by fellow workers who like to put down anyone who is a rung or two below them.

Conclusion

To this point we have reviewed specialization by function and specialization by level of expertise in libraries. These can be thought of as horizontal and vertical job organization. It is where horizontal and vertical meet that administrative problems may arise.

We start with the functional base. Now add other specialties, say subject librarians and children's librarians. They may perform several of the functions, from selection to reader guidance. The intersections in the staffing matrix are increased, and with that comes an increase in the administrative coordination load. The subject librarian must be related to the cataloger, and the children's librarian to the circulation assistant. Interdependence increases at a geometric ratio, as do opportunities for conflict.

Next put specialization by level into the mix and the many interrelations are hard to follow. How does the clerk in acquisitions relate to the paraprofessional in cataloging, and this worker in turn to the professional in documents or films? Where do branches stand in the pecking order with the several specialties and levels at central? These are questions of coordination, to which attention must shortly be given.

Two principles that emerged in the preceding discussion bear repetition. So far as possible, don't mix unlike duties and unlike levels of work in the same position. For example, the reference position in a branch library that calls for circulation work and also for record-keeping and housekeeping (a not uncommon combination) is less than desirable both from the standpoint of the incumbent and from the standpoint of return from the personnel dollar spent. The related principle to stress is that duties should be placed as low in the personnel hierarchy as possible and the tendency to exalt and sublimate work should be resisted. If a task can be handled by a clerk, don't assign it to a paraprofessional, and if it can be handled by a paraprofessional don't assign it to a graduate librarian. In keeping duties at the lowest feasible level, it is a mistake to underestimate the capacity of the clerk or the assistant until this has been tested. Going the other way, assigning tasks to more advanced personnel on the grounds that this ensures performance really fools no one, neither the employee involved nor the patron who uses a service nor the taxpayer who foots the bill.

Organization of positions by levels of expertise is all to the good, as far as distinct levels can be identified. Orchestrating of levels is no small task for the administrator, and problems will inevitably arise. But that is why we have managers. The benefits are in service given and money prudently spent.

References

---

1. Sheldon, Brooke E. *American Libraries*, Vol. 14, No. 7 (July-August 1983), p. 483.

2. Tauber surveyed over 70 libraries in his active career. See Szigethy, Marion C. *Maurice Falcolm Tauber; a Bibliography.* Metuchen, N.J., Scarecrow Press, 1974, pp. 61–74.

3. *Public Library Service; a Guide to Evaluation, with Minimum Standards.* Chicago, American Library Association, 1956, p. 39.

4. Mugnier, Charlotte, *The Paraprofessional and the Professional Job Structure.* Chicago, American Library Association, 1980, p. 105.

IX DIRECTION AND DECISION-MAKING

THERE IS STILL another hierarchy of positions in libraries, and in fact it is the structure that first comes to mind when organization is mentioned. This is the managerial structure of supervisors, department heads, division chiefs, and directors or chief librarians. From this specialization of duties comes the familiar organization chart.

With this topic we return to the concept of organization stressed by the early theorists such as Max Weber. Here are decision-making and control and coordination. Here is "bureaucracy" as originally conceived, the structure that holds an enterprise together.

Here also the criticisms that have been leveled against that earlier theory come into play. It is worth recapitulating those criticisms. Organization was seen more as control than as stimulation and inspiration. Chain of command was emphasized and not a matrix of communication. The scalar principle prevailed, not the psychology of human relations. The view was from the top down and not from the bottom up. Decision-making was thought of as centralized and fairly precise, when in reality decisions are made at many levels, and unfortunately often without adequate information. The role of peer groups and peer pressures was not recognized.

Yet despite such criticisms, libraries, like other enterprises, still utilize bureaucratic structures. There are levels of command, decision-making is centralized, running a tight ship is often praised more than opening up a flow of communication, general regulations prevail over local options. Libraries are not

225

necessarily more control-oriented than most other agencies, but for the most part they have to be categorized as autocratic rather than democratic institutions.

This is reflected in the place of administrative positions in the career sequence of librarians. For many the taking on of managerial responsibilities is the only alternative if they seek more monetary reward and/or more prestige. Department heads and chief librarians are chosen from among professionals (service experts) and not from among experts in management, even though the work of the director is primarily or exclusively administrative. In larger libraries the director may earn three times as much as the established professionals, which indicates the importance that is attached to this responsibility.

Drawing of general administrators from among the ranks is uncommon in present-day enterprises. This seldom occurs in business or industry, where the president is more likely to come up through a management career in sales or finance than from a professional or specialized position as scientist or engineer or designer. Hospitals typically have separate career administrators rather than doctors in charge. In these and other cases management is viewed as a separate skill, for which education and experience in administration are the usual prerequisites. Socrates said it long ago, when he observed that management is a skill separate from technical knowledge and technical experience.

School administrators do come usually from the ranks of teachers. The same holds true for colleges and universities, but here professors do not typically aspire to head the institution—in fact they often have a certain disdain for administrators. I once had the title of Associate Dean, and faculty members would delight in repeating one of the expressions heard in the faculty club, that an Associate Dean is a mouse trying to become a rat. In some universities, there are professors with salaries higher than that of the president. This contrasts with library service, where the career ladder, the pecking order, and the more substantial monetary rewards are all in the managerial sequence.

Very occasionally the typical library pattern is broken and directors are brought in from other fields. Interestingly enough, this applies to some of the largest and strongest agencies, notably the Library of Congress, the New York Public Library, and the Harvard University Libraries. Appointees from the outside do not usually manage internal operations but concentrate more on external relations and fund-raising; they can be thought of as high-level public relations officers in the scholarly world. An advertisement for the directorship of a major public library (*New York Times*, October 2, 1983) straddled the issue with this sentence: "A graduate degree in Library Science is desirable but not required." Librarians look askance at such breaks in the prevailing practice of selecting directors from the professional ranks.

We must examine the rungs on this management career ladder in librarianship, then look at how decisions are reached in libraries, and finally at the complex problems of coordination needed to get the enterprise and its staff to work together for the common ends.

Department Heads and Branch Librarians

In larger libraries the first step for many potential managers comes when the professional is appointed to the position of assistant department head or assistant branch librarian. This may come fairly early in the period of service, for libraries have only a limited sequence that is purely professional and without some supervisory responsibilities.

Young librarians may hardly get seasoned at the service desk before shifting to a road that they will follow for the rest of their lives, perhaps looking back nostalgically at the book and user contacts that originally attracted them to the field. Or if such an opportunity does not open, because turnover in libraries has declined due to a surplus of librarians on the market, the left-back professional feels misused and unappreciated. It is a dilemma: stay in professional service that you want to do, but with limited salary and esteem; or shift over to administration, which may be what you do not want to do. This dilemma is the ground from which disgruntled and ineffective managers can grow.

The task of the assistant head of a unit is supervision, defined as the direct control of a group of workers assigned specific duties and responsibilities. Making of schedules, checking on work done and not done, training and re-training of personnel, handling changes in routines that have been decided on, counseling of staff—all these are typical activities. Assistant heads would probably add that another part of the franchise is the filling-in of whatever gaps appear, a kind of line-backer role, including filling-in for the department head when necessary. Except in departmental discussions or when specifically asked, assistant heads customarily do not have much input into policy review or budget requests. Their job is to keep the store open and the show going.

It is not an easy spot to handle. Assistant headships are likely to be the first management assignments for librarians. They are testing themselves and at the same time being tested by the library. They are expected to produce and control under circumstances they did not create. Normally they have little latitude for change; it is theirs to follow, not to lead. They seek to be recognized as "good managers" in the narrow sense, and if they make too many waves will not get this rating. At times they even have to compensate for department heads who are not equal to their task.

Libraries, like other agencies, give very little in-service training at this level. The assistant headship is the fateful fork in the road for young professionals, the choice that will affect the rest of their lives, but they are given little help on the new pathway; one learns to supervise simply by trying to do so. Where managerial instruction exists, in a city or in a university, it is likely to be for the higher echelons, and covers such topics as planning and budgeting. The library's own collection has shelves of books on supervision, each trying to express the platitudes of common-sense work planning and good human relations in a slightly different way. There is *The Effective Supervisor* and *The OK Boss* and most recently the popular *One-Minute Manager*. Some one should produce a volume entitled *How to Supervise and Still Be Loved*. In the voluminous literature on the subject, the work of Rensis Likert stands out as sensible yet inspiring.[1]

Libraries would do well to pay particular attention to assistant department heads and assistant branch librarians, the embryonic managers of the institution. They are out there alone, subject to the whims of their department heads on the one side and the tolerance of the staffs from which they have just been promoted on the other. While one hesitates to suggest any more staff meetings in libraries, this group might well be pulled together from time to time, if for no other reason than to give them identity outside their little enclaves. They should be prime candidates to attend conferences and training classes, for they have the most to learn and the longest time to give back benefits to the library. Cherish the assistant heads; they are the middle managers of tomorrow and they may be candidates for a vacancy in the director's office not too many years hence.

Moving up a step, department heads and branch librarians are critical cogs in the structure in both public and academic libraries. "Cogs" may be the right term, for they hold the agency together and keep it going. They are the junction points between general aims and policies and actual performance. All officers above department heads and branch librarians are removed from users; facetiously, one can say that they shuffle papers, hold meetings, and add up figures. All workers below this level follow the lead of middle managers, reflecting whatever standards and notions are held by the middle group.

The work of department heads can be thought of in three dimensions. They keep the agency on course, delivering service day-to-day. They cut out new paths and clear the underbrush, assuming the library is changing direction or adjusting to new circumstances. And they provide immediate leadership for staff, both professional and non-professional. "Cog" is not quite the word; maybe it should be "Kingpin."

Of the three responsibilities, the one most effectively discharged is likely to be the first, that of day-to-day performance. Department heads and branch librarians have in most cases proven themselves before appointment. They have done some supervising, whether formally as assistant heads or otherwise, and discharged these tasks effectively or they would not be considered for promotion. They have demonstrated that self-motivation and dedication that keep a person going without close direction. They are team players, subscribing to the aims and standards of the agency, or they are not likely to be entrusted with a middle-management assignment. Department heads and branch librarians are sergeants in the best sense, leading platoons, and usually doing so satisfactorily. Departments and branches in libraries differ in strength, but it is uncommon to come on a completely ineffective or sloppy unit, for there is pressure to produce both from management above and from staff below.

Not as positive a statement can be made about the flexibility and willingness to change of department heads. They have advanced in a sense by hewing to the line. After a period they have built "their" department, molded to their model. Many a forward-looking director has foundered on middle-management inflexibility and recalcitrance; seeking to turn the wheel, the head librarian finds that it is locked in position. Of course, this may also be a two-way street, because often department heads and branch librarians are given little freedom and little encouragement to show initiative. As Wilson and Tauber put it: "One of the glaring faults among university librarians has been their unwillingness to permit the department heads to experiment with new devices or introduce new practices."[2]

At this point we come again to the question of centralization versus decentralization in libraries, the degree to which staff at any level feel free to propose or criticize or experiment, a topic that must shortly be examined.

As to the critical third responsibility of department heads and branch librarians, that of leader and counselor of staff, both styles and achievement differ widely. There is no one pattern or set of principles. One comes on department heads who are martinets and others who are den mothers—and both of these may succeed. The two essential qualities are belief in the library and in the importance of the department, and empathy with individual staff members in all their variety.

Unlike chief librarians, able department heads and branch librarians can quickly infuse a staff with purpose and high standards. Contact is close enough that leadership can be felt directly. The unit chief is observed at work, sometimes alongside the staff member, so that dedication and thoroughness and sensitivity are conveyed by example. As problems arise they are shared by a close-knit departmental staff, rather than seen as some far-off issue that a remote administrator has failed to anticipate or handle. That is, all these benefits of a close working relationship accrue if the unit head is equal to the task; if not, the very closeness tends to exacerbate problems. Pray for a library with able department heads; directors can be replaced, but middle management cannot readily be re-made.

Division chiefs, as distinct from department heads, have responsibility for two or more departments, as in a technical processing or a public service unit, or the position of coordinator of branches. As such their responsibility takes on the aspect of a library headship. They still are fairly close to operations, but they seldom sit down to work at a service desk. They know staff by sight and name, but customarily leave direction and training and discipline to the department heads. The division chief is occupied more with coordination between units, with costs and budgets, and with evaluation of performance; that is, they are administrators in an office rather than supervisors on the floor. The division managers are likely to be members of the director's "cabinet," if such exists, but this is uncommon for department heads and branch librarians. The nature of their assignment is indicated in the title of assistant director or associate director which is sometimes attached to these positions.

Directors and Assistant Directors

The work of the chief officer should be focused on planning, on coordination, on evaluation, on costs, on inspiration — in short, on "leadership." Here in the end is where decisions occur, whether they grow naturally from within the organization or appear categorically from the director's office.

That is what the director should be doing: looking ahead, leading the way, fine-tuning a productive organization, stimulating the staff. Practicing chief librarians know differently. Arriving at the desk in the morning, they are informed of the newest crisis: a robbery in a branch unit, the serious illness of a department head, the failure of a heating boiler or large air-conditioning unit, a Letter to the Editor protesting certain titles in the library, breakdown of the computerized circulation system, a memorandum from the President's or the Mayor's office warning of an impending budget cut, a protest from a staff group on criteria for promotion. Once steps are taken to begin to deal with the immediate issue of the day, the appointment calendar is consulted. A board member who has been acting more and more irascibly at board meetings or a dean whose nose is out of joint will be arriving in mid-morning; there is a luncheon with a visiting fireman; the weekly "chiefs and coordinators" meeting occurs early in the afternoon; and a choice will have to be made between a late-afternoon reception for an incoming city or university official and one for an outgoing staff member. Underlined at the top of the sheet is *"Preliminary budget request due today."* The director takes a big breath and glances quickly through the mail. For a moment the chief wonders how dealing with all this will somehow inspire the staff and spur them to greater accomplishment, but then the thought is put out of mind. As one recent presentation put it: "Clarity of purpose — vision — is usually lost in the myriad daily preoccupations that confront library directors".[3]

Part of the problem is organization. Some of these matters should not come to the director's desk. Some problems could be handled where they occur, if proper authority has been delegated. Some should go to specialized officers, as for personnel, or finance, or buildings and grounds. A number of years ago Wheeler and Goldhor asserted that "In many libraries more than half the things a key executive does could be done by his assistants."[4] Recent research confirms that the problem remains today.[5]

The sensible director sits back once in a while and goes over the activities of the last few days. What was done that could have been done by others? What was done that need not be done at all? The first question is a matter of organization, the second a matter of objectives, and the two are related. After putting out fires, how much time was left for building houses?

Despite the title of director, the essence of the job is not direction. A wise university librarian put it this way: "Co-ordination rather than supervision and direct management is, in my opinion, the great task of the chief librarian, particularly if he has perfected a reasonably good organization and in all his work given sufficient attention to the selection of personnel."[6]

Coordination is a preeminent responsibility of the executive, and will be dealt with shortly. But decisions must be made. As a former U.S. President said, "The buck stops here"; and then he added something about the heat in the kitchen—evidently he didn't have a well-insulated oven in Independence, Missouri.

A key factor is the management structure just below the director. With up to 25 or 30 staff members, the chief can usually get along without an Assistant Librarian, although carrying out the many different management duties will be far from easy. A staff of this size can be organized into four or five departments, each with an equal number of employees, with span of control kept well within limits. The simple model is shown in Figure 7.

In staffs two or three times this size, an Assistant Director is desirable. A theoretical model is pictured in Figure 8. Note that to accommodate twice the size of staff, span of control had to be broadened, and the management levels in the structure had to be increased from two to four, substantially increasing the distance in the hierarchy from individual worker to director. This plan normally assigns internal management to the Assistant Director, with the chief officer carrying planning,

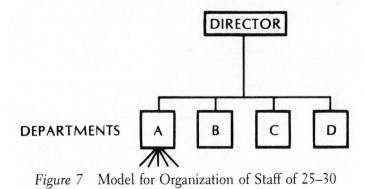

Figure 7   Model for Organization of Staff of 25–30

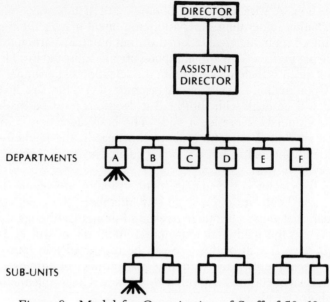

Figure 8 Model for Organization of Staff of 50–60

financial control, and exterior relations. If the two general executives nicely complement each other, this can be a smooth-running combination without too many complications. But there can be opposition of objectives or style, which both parties are disposed to keep hidden until there is some kind of explosion and an adjustment must be made.

Normally, the less-seasoned Assistant Head follows the lead of the front office, and receives guidance from that source, growing over a period of time in assurance and authority. Once settled in and in control, incumbents might better be called Deputy Directors, suggesting a role in their own right and not just as an auxiliary of the "big boss."

An alternative approach for staffs of 100 or so is shown in Figure 9. Instead of one Assistant Director there are three general officers below the chief, each responsible for part of the total enterprise. This complicates the task of the Director, who must coordinate the three divisions, but it controls prolifer-

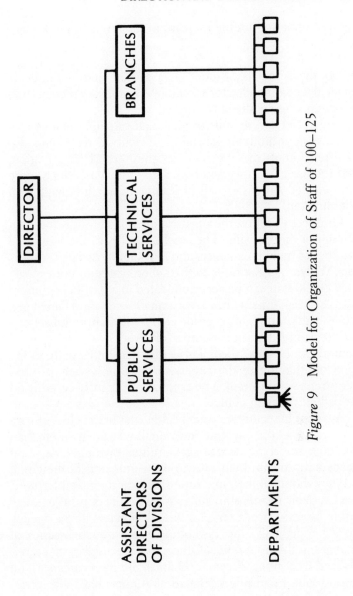

Figure 9 Model for Organization of Staff of 100–125

ation of units and undue increase in the levels from Director to individual workers.

Most libraries of small or medium size can be fitted into one of these models. "Model" as used here does not indicate an ideal recommended for adoption but rather a representation of patterns frequently encountered.

Above 100 staff members, additional variations and combinations occur. Both an Assistant or Deputy Director and also Division Chiefs may be used for purposes of coordination, and the levels of supervision are sure to increase. Such more complicated structures will be examined in the chapter on coordination.

Of direct effect on the organizational structure is the span of control that prevails. The smaller the span, the larger the number of middle managers and Assistant or Associate Directors. With a range of three to five subordinates on the average, only 80–90 staff can be accommodated in a four-tier structure (workers, department heads, Assistant Directors and Directors), while with a range of seven or eight, 400 staff members can be fitted into the same number of levels. No exact span of control can be prescribed. This varies depending both on the span of attention of the supervisor and the variety of tasks performed within a unit. The criteria are adequate control and empathetic human contact.

Assistant Directors are usually alter egos of the chief officer. They range all the way from individuals who are no more than executive secretaries to managers in their own right. Assistant heads have to trim their sails to the commands of the chief, yet they should at the same time stake out their own territory. It is a suitable relationship that may take some time to coalesce. Some assistant heads serve as virtual directors of the agency for a period while the institution goes through a series of changes in the front office. Others find themselves in a sense blocked by a strong director and finish out their careers in the second spot. Promising young administrators have sometimes been advised to seek appointment as head of a smaller agency rather than as assistant head in a larger one, in order to avoid a possible dead-end. In the past a common combination was a male Director and a female Assistant Director, but this sexist pattern may be changing.

Division chiefs fall somewhere between, with primarily supervisory staff below them and coordinators above. Their work tends toward the latter, for these positions are usually created to get two or more departments to work together. As coordinators, division chiefs move from the direct flow of service and production, and like other administrators who move up the ladder, seek to get work done through others. They are subject to pressures similar to those on Assistant Directors.

Decision-Making and Centralization of Authority

To a degree the sound organization staffed with well-trained personnel runs itself. Workers discharge their duties, they fit their efforts into those of others, production occurs, and supervisors are around to step in when the unexpected happens, putting matters back into the established order.

But only to a degree. Sole dependence on the established order results in resistance to change. Institutions, like physical bodies, have a tendency to continue in a straight line; without a sense of direction they can march straight to oblivion.

Decisions must be made, planning must occur, budgets must be finished. Problems that arise may be beyond the experience or authority of the supervisor down the line. Coordination may occur naturally between adjacent workers but not between adjacent departments. Money may be available to expand, or may be cut and force contraction; both require central review. Changed circumstances and new opportunities may prompt a change in emphasis or in objectives. Upper management necessarily comes into play.

Good administrators know the formula for decision-making. Clarify your problem or goal, hypothesize alternative solutions, gather relevant information, involve the interested parties, and on this basis reach a conclusion in conformance with the logic of the situation. But real life does not follow formula. Under the pressure of time, in libraries as elsewhere, breakdowns and deficiencies occur at each step in the process. Goals are left hazy, information is incomplete and biased, a hunch is favored. Only some, or perhaps none, of the informed and affected parties are consulted. Research in recent years has underscored the vagaries of decision-making in group endeavors.[7]

Consider the individual decision-maker in the library. The matter under consideration may be as specific as revising a classification number on a single publication or as broad as adopting a different classification scheme for the whole collection, as specific as selecting an individual title or as broad as adopting a book-selection policy. What factors bear?

- The goals and purposes of the library, whether identified and clarified or assumed without review.
- The needs and pressures of clienteles and constituencies.
- Resources available within the library, in money, personnel, space, time.
- Resources available outside the individual library, in the community and in other collections.
- The practices that have prevailed, formalized in many cases into official rules and regulations.
- Information that has been assembled on the matter, to some degree of completeness.
- Opinions of those who have been consulted, typically few in the case of specific decisions and many for a far-reaching choice.
- Thoroughness of consideration of options available.
- Values, ambitions, and prejudices of the individual decision-maker.

With all these and other factors bearing, is it a surprise that the decision may be less than forward-looking, balanced, prudent, practical, and politic?

Truth to tell, instead of the wise and considered decision arrived at with the counsel of colleagues and advisers, a conviction is reached by many a library director when going to the car in the morning or after glancing through the newspaper in the evening. Some directors used to say that they saw the answer in the mirror when shaving, but there may be just a bit of sexism in proposing that locale for decision-making.

The process in libraries is probably no more nor no less rational and systematic than in most other agencies. But there is one difference. All parties soon know if the wrong decision is reached in the sales organization or the engineering firm or the hospital consulting room or the locker room between halves. But the library official can be plain wrong without much discernible evidence turning up for a long time. This is all the more reason for careful and thorough consideration in each case.

In general, decisions should be made as low in the hierarchy as possible. This means that they are made by those closest to the matter, most informed and most immediately affected. It also means that the overload of problems going to the higher echelons is reduced, thus freeing time for overall evaluation and for planning ahead.

But for decisions to be made down the line, staff members and middle managers must have both responsibility and authority. Responsibility is widely dispersed in libraries, to workers at service stations who perforce must carry through the transactions before them. Authority is a different matter. This tends to be retained high in the structure, in or close to the chief librarian's office. The reference librarian, the department head, the branch librarian seldom have authority to modify policy to meet particular circumstances.

The point can be made by a comparison with the position of dean in a major division or school of a university. The dean—like the library director—is leader, planner, controller, and budget officer. But deans do not decide; they persuade and convince. They do not determine the curriculum; that is in the hands of the faculty. The dean does not set admission or graduation standards; again, these critical factors are determined by the faculty. The dean does not select or promote faculty members; that is done by peer groups. The only element of such collegial management that has taken any root in libraries is peer opinion on staff appointments and promotions, which has appeared in some academic libraries not as the result of a library movement in this direction but as a carry-over from practice in the rest of the college or university.

Library directors resent and challenge the criticism of centralized control. After all, as a group they are not particularly autocratic or dictatorial. Libraries are genteel establishments. But by tradition libraries have been run more like factories than like collegial agencies: there is a boss in a remote office, there is a dutiful middle management not disposed to make waves, there are the extensive regulations in the staff and procedure manuals. Like business firms, libraries have viewed employees not as sources of ideas but as sources of possible error on the job, which must be guarded against by supervision and regulation.

Paradoxically, despite a factory-type organization, libraries do not enjoy one of its prime benefits: productivity. By any measure the standard of productivity is not high at the cataloging desk or the reference desk or the circulation desk. And with good reason, the director responds, for we are an educational agency; our product is service and not bottle caps. If that is so, why not collegial-type management? The average library director would be frustrated by appointment to a deanship, and thus forced to lead by persuasion.

Group Participation in Decision-Making

Having alleged that most libraries follow a centralized pattern of administration, it must be noted, to keep the portrait in balance, that in some cases various devices have been used to involve staff more in decision-making. Usually there is little if any delegation of authority in such arrangements, so that the general characterization remains. These devices are more than a gesture, but they seldom amount in libraries to democratic management as it has come to be understood.

Some administrators consciously and carefully seek to use staff meetings to develop a genuine interchange with employees. This may occur within sub-units or in occasional meetings of the total staff, or at both levels. A good starting point is to encourage employees to express their concerns, for personal matters are more likely to strike a spark—but remember that some staff members will probably hold back for fear of burning themselves. A next step is to get staff to assess progress and stagnation in the service program, which will identify issues needing attention. Note that such efforts are preliminary to decision-making, not action itself, and staff members know this. It is essential that follow-up occur, or it would be better not to open up the dialogue at all.

Committees and task forces carry the process one step closer to resolution. Standing committees may deal with continuing issues, but they often become routine in their deliberations, the original moving spirits pass on to other works, and the groups then need re-invigoration—or termination. Both committees and task forces can be used to draw junior staff members into considerations beyond the tasks immediately before them.

Group decision-making has extended in some larger libraries to a small council or "cabinet." The members usually are general officers (assistant directors, division chiefs, coordinators), who are asked to review problems and who are free to offer suggestions and objections. This is a step in the right direction. But participation is limited and seldom extends to department heads, much less to workers along the line. As a consequence, the opposition may be driven underground or into labor unions, which simply leads to confrontation between the beleaguered director and a group of embittered employees.

The "cabinet" pattern could be applied at lower levels in the organization. Every manager, including department heads, should have a seasoned group to help consider problems and possibilities. There is no virtue in the manager trying to carry the burden alone. This is still not participatory management but at least it is two-way communication. This opportunity is examined in some depth in another volume in this series.[8]

Task Forces

Because task forces afford a means for decentralization of decision-making, they deserve further attention at this point. By a task force is meant a group of workers of different backgrounds and levels, brought together to reach conclusions and make recommendations on a clear and specific issue. The task force is distinguished from a committee in having a definite rather than a general assignment, and in particular in having a prescribed period and a terminal date for getting the job done. Both "pro" and "con" on this management device will be noted.

To begin with, a task force is purpose-oriented. There is no need to ask what the purpose of the group is; that is identified in the task that is the group's reason for being. This contrasts with much day-to-day service, where purpose is often vague and ill-defined, and with many continuing committees that wander from their original objective.

It follows that a task force is more solution-oriented. A given problem may have been on the minds of staff members for some time, there may have been formal or informal discussion about it, but closure is not reached and the problem remains. A team or task force is expected to produce, and in a sense has been placed in the spotlight to do so. Or, if such a group cannot reach a conclusion or solution, this is formally registered; inconclusiveness does not go undetected.

Another principle operating in the team or task force, in contrast with the typical hierarchical relationship, is that all members participate on an equal basis. All have their say, with "equal time." The chief executive's perception of the time required to search a particular data base may be contradicted by the experience of the librarian who actually does the searching; the circulation clerk's impression of who uses the library at night may broaden the perception of day-time managers. One input is not subordinate to the other; both contribute to understanding and solving the "task."

Still another characteristic of the task force is that it can more readily reach out and draw on all parts of the organization, for information, expertise, or judgment. When a line department requests information from another unit, or consults a staff member with different skills, questions arise and departmental rivalries may surface. Why do they want to know that—why should I share my special skill with a unit that has shown little interest in it to this time—what are they after? If an individual has a particular contribution to make, he or she may well be on the team. If not, then the request can come through another staff member from the same unit who is on the team, and who is viewed as a representative of the unit.

Also, the task force is more likely to reach a group conclusion, reflecting the views of all or most members. Within the hierarchical unit, staff meetings may be held, the views of staff members may be solicited, but the decision is more likely to be unilateral. This is not necessarily bad. We are comparing the two types of decision-making, but not advocating one over another. Most organizations, including libraries, properly have some of both.

The task force is more likely to have multi-vision rather than tunnel vision. Matters are seen not from one standpoint but from the several vantage points represented on the team. The process comes closer to taking the whole agency into account—for example, not just the views of the film librarian as to films needed by the library, but also those of the children's coordinator, the branch librarian in an ethnic neighborhood, etc.

Other things being equal, a team or task force is more open to new ideas and more flexible in considering change. The very fact that a "task" has been extracted from regular operating units implies that the matter has not been effectively or completely handled within regular line departments. For purposes of discussion, the established policies and procedures of the operating units have been suspended, and examination can proceed without routine constrictions. The nature and atmosphere of the task group encourages innovative ideas. Even representatives of the operating units most involved may express views that they hesitate to set forth within the department; the fresh view expressed within the operating unit takes on the character of a criticism or challenge, whereas in the task force the same views are considered as possible explanations or solutions. Put differently, the agency-wide team can break down the parochialism of separate units within the agency.

A final dividend. Teams provide educational opportunities, training grounds, for staff at various levels: the clerk with potential for supervisory responsibilities, the professional in a specialized service unit, the manager preoccupied with one part of the enterprise. Executives can better judge both workers and supervisors on the basis of their performance on a team. Some managers have learned to bring promising but restless junior staff into ad-hoc groups, where they gain a sense of participation and an outlet for bottled-up ideas and frustrations.

But task forces are by no means a panacea. Various aspects of human relations can get in the way of group decisions.

Ad hoc teams can be wasteful of time and effort. To begin with, the members have to take some time to get to know each other. A new set of working relationships must be developed. Some individuals must listen for a while before they are prepared to contribute, and others must have a chance to talk early on, to "establish" themselves, or they will feel insecure and may be defensive or belligerent. Anyone who has studied the deliberations of any group, whether the Congress of the United States or a meeting of the local parent-teachers association, is conscious that group discussion is often less than focused and logical.

The established structure inhibits group participation across departmental lines, even in team groups. Individuals have been located in one division within the organization, have developed a perspective from that angle, and also may have developed a special loyalty to the unit. Ideally, when they come together to deal with an organization-wide problem, they should drop the parochial view, but this is not easily accomplished. The hierarchy has conditioned them to cherish a partial viewpoint.

Further, authority relations carry over into group discussion. Everyone knows who the bosses are. Even if these individuals claim that they are just one of the group, their authority adheres to them. Members of the task force wait to get their opinion and exercise caution in what they say in their presence. The reality of the hierarchy prompts many participants to pull their punches.

At the very outset of a group parley it is likely to be superior officers who define the task before the group. Most manuals on group participation stress that the job to be done should be clearly defined, lest the group wander off in all directions. Thus those in command tend to lay out the course from the start. Any basic deviation from the assigned task arising from within the conferees may be dismissed by the chairperson on the grounds of irrelevancy, even though the proposed change may actually represent a deeper penetration into the problem on the table. Thus authority and open discussion can be in conflict, and it is usually authority that prevails.

Some contemporary managers have even learned how to manipulate the group process to their purpose. They set the agenda, select the conferees, influence the choice of chairperson, determine what information is distributed, and step into the discussion at strategic points, speaking, whether it is disavowed or not, with the voice of authority. The conclusions reached are likely to be those that management had in mind from the beginning. Participants from down the line have gone through the motions, and come away from the experience with a vague feeling of having been used.

Thus the task force is an imperfect instrument for decentralization of decision-making, but at least it is one available tool. Management has to learn on the one hand how to use the established structure to further the work of the library, and on the other hand how to overcome the tendency of organization toward inflexibility. The task force is one means for the purpose. Shortly we will carry this form of decision-making one significant step forward, in the form of Total Quality Management, TQM.

Staff Officers

In seeking to deal with the complexities of larger organizations, and to reduce the overload on the director, libraries have added staff officers, as distinct from line officers. These come in several different types and play roles that vary from central to marginal. There are the standard auxiliary officers: for personnel, for finance, for public relations, and for building maintenance. These in substance are extensions of the director, helping with parts of the responsibility that are intrinsic to the chief officer's job—in a sense, added arms and legs and ears and tongues. Then there are experts in one or another field who analyze aspects of the agency and feed information to the general officers, such as systems analysts, computer experts, and planning officers. Think of these as scouts who go out to check the territory, reporting back on what they have found and making recommendations for action. The first group helps directors to keep their agencies going; the second looks ahead to needed change and development.

A third type falls somewhere between staff officers in the usual sense and regular line managers, for they do not administer a service department as such but have responsibility and authority for part of the service programs. Examples here are the coordinators of adult service, of young people's service, and of children's service as used in public libraries; such positions will shortly be examined in a section on Coordination.

Staff officers theoretically have no authority or control. They keep the financial or personnel records, apply official standards and practices in their respective areas, prepare reports, and advise both department heads and individual staff members. They know the policies of the government unit or academic institution served and apply them within the library. They counsel with the director, who may or may not accept their advice. Once decisions are made, they may be designated as the official channel of communication within the field of their expertise. All of this is within the staff concept.

But in practice staff officers may drift into, or seek out, line authority. If it is not direct orders that they dispense, it may be more subtle but no less effective influence. The notable example in the national government is the power wielded by the Bureau of Management and Budget. Head librarians— whether in public, academic, school or special libraries—have learned to nurture relations with the budget offices in their respective jurisdictions.

Financial officers within libraries usually have limited influence, although this was not always the case. At an earlier time some larger public libraries had semi-independent financial officers, reporting directly to the board, but in most cases the professional director now controls this competing position. The financial officer does constrain expenditures through regular accounting and reporting, serving as the director's watchdog on outlays.

Personnel offices, on the other hand, have often grown in influence over a period of time, entering more into decisions in recruiting and selecting staff, in constraining managers in any activities contrary to civil-service or union agreements, even in assigning and transferring clerical employees. An effective and forward-looking personnel officer could lead a library toward what has been called "Workplace 2000."[9] In this case a thorough and accurate organization chart would show two lines leading to middle managers, one for regular line authority and a thinner or dotted line for prescriptions from the personnel officer.

A third line might lead from the head of buildings and maintenance, and this one would be thicker. Buildings and grounds, with its technical element and separate staff, can become an empire unto itself. Maintenance may not come up to department standards and repairs may proceed according to some secret schedule. Many a department head lives in a state of war, or at best a state of truce, with buildings and grounds.

The public-relations staff officer poses a different relationship. Here the task is to present the library in its most favorable light. Line officers may have to be educated on how to accomplish this, and may need help in preparing releases and contacting the media. This staff officer serves more as guide and expert, not just at the top but all down the line, and thus wields some influence by virtue of expertise. In most libraries total public relations have three dimensions: the contact that the director gains with strategic individuals in the civic or academic community, the impress that staff and service make on users, and communications emanating from the public-relations office. At times the latter even functions to counteract negative impressions made by the first two sources.

In some cases the dual relationship of middle managers with both line and staff officers violates the principle of unity of command. This is not necessarily harmful. The second group can bring to bear both information and skills not known in the line. The director may consciously promote certain policies through staff officers; for example, closer adherence to budget allocations, or regular evaluation of personnel, or better internal housekeeping without dependence on the maintenance department to put everything back in order. The conflicts that may arise can in the end result in better decisions. What is harmful is opposition between line and staff that eventually requires intervention by the director and very possibly an arbitrary resolution of the issue that is likely to displease one or the other party to that conflict. Joint effort is of course the aim, but some administrators have learned to use "constructive conflict" to achieve desirable ends.

The second group of staff officers, the specialized assistants in systems analysis or computerization or planning, set up a different group of cross-currents in the organization. These specialists examine aspects of the enterprise and report back to the director on recommended adjustments or changes. So long as they do not push too hard they are likely to be tolerated. If middle management and these staff experts are marching hand in hand, some improvements are likely to go through. But recommendations for revised procedures or for automation of additional functions of the agency can disrupt the established order and lead again to conflict.

In many cases differences can be resolved, but there is no doubt that as computerization proceeds, it is going to affect jobs and whole departments. Potentially the look-ahead staff officers may effect the greatest changes, and therefore cause the greatest friction.

A special word should be said about an office of evaluation and planning. This was the original purpose that initiated the concept of staff officers in the armed forces. In directing a complex organization, and in the heat of battle, the commanding general had little time or perspective either to look very far behind or very far ahead. The task of the staff officer was to evaluate past performance and to propose future action.

Libraries, even the largest, seldom have such an office. From one standpoint this can be understood, for directors recognize that evaluation and planning are essential parts of their jobs, and they therefore hesitate to delegate it to someone else. From another standpoint, the lack is surprising, for these are the tasks that executive officers find squeezed out under the pressure of the daily management overload.

In a study of the Philadelphia Free Library, it was proposed that a Planning, Development and Evaluation Office be established, as ". . . an intellectual scouting arm, to explore new territory, to bring back reports of what is over the horizon, thus enabling the command to order the next advance."[10] The office was established and promptly took hold of one of the recommendations in the survey, that the Central Library in Philadelphia become reference only (with a circulating Popular Library). The matter was thoroughly investigated by the Planning Office and brought to the point of action.

Some writers see staff officers as a kind of necessary evil. They often create tensions and conflicts, but are necessary to cope with complexity. This is a negative view. These staff officers are an asset in the organization, specialists in their fields, just as catalogers and reference librarians are professionals in theirs. The task of executives is to coordinate the efforts of line and staff. If the chief officers succeed, their lives in the end will be easier and they will accomplish some goals that they would not have without the "staff" aid. Once again we see the manager as a person who recognizes cross-currents in organization and who seeks to channel them in a common direction.

References

1. Likert, Rensis. *New Patterns of Management*. New York, McGraw-Hill, 1966.

2. Wilson, Louis R. and Tauber, Maurice F. *The University Library; the Organization, Administration and Functions of Academic Libraries*. New York, Columbia University Press, 1956, p. 140.

3. Gertzog, Alice and Beckerman, Edwin. *Administration of the Public Library*. Metuchen, N.J., Scarecrow Press, 1994, p.421.

4. Wheeler, Joseph L. and Goldhor, Herbert. *Practical Administration of Public Libraries*. New York, Harper and Row, 1962, p.80.

5. Cochran, J. Wesley. *Time Management Handbook for Librarians.* Westport, CT., Greenwood, 1992, p.4.

6. Metcalf, Keyes. "Departmental Organization in Libraries," in Joeckel, Carleton B., ed., *Current Issues in Library Administration.* Chicago, University of Chicago Press, 1939, p. 108.

7. Simon, Herbert A. *Administrative Behavior.* New York, Free Press, 1976.

8. Sager, Donald J. *Participatory Management in Libraries.* Metuchen, N.J., Scarecrow Press, 1982.

9. Boyett, Joseph H. and Conn, Henry P. *Workplace 2000: The Revolution Reshaping American Business.* New York, Dutton, 1991.

10. Martin, Lowell A. *The Free Library and the Revitalization of Philadelphia.* Philadelphia, Free Library of Philadelphia, 1981, p. 170.

X COORDINATION IN LIBRARIES

IF ANY ASPECTS of administration take precedence, they are decision-making and coordination. Much of internal organization is the assembling of parts, the positions and departments that will constitute the working units in the enterprise. Once the parts are in place, the critical test is to get them to work together, so the machine can move. And then the decision must be made as to where it will go.

Almost all that occurs in a library contributes to or detracts from coordination. Clear goals and definite plans help; staff members who know just what the library is after can better direct their own energies. Communication in all its variety is essential to coordination; staff members who know what is going on elsewhere can modify their actions in relation to other individuals and departments. Good morale contributes, for workers with a positive outlook seek to contribute to the joint effort. Each of these factors is dealt with at length in other volumes in this series, on planning, on communication, and on personnel.

In this volume the task is to view coordination as an element of organization; i.e., as a function of structure. The various elements already dealt with—defining positions, assembling departments, designating line and staff officers—contribute to joint effort. It remains to examine the role of the formal hierarchy in bringing parts of an enterprise together.

This brings us to organization charts. This presentation has purposely put charts toward the end in order to keep structure in perspective, as one factor but by no means the sole or even

251

primary factor in getting a group of people to work together. Although they show the anatomy of an agency, organization charts are seldom complete or up-to-date. More goes on than can be set down neatly with lines and squares. Nor is reading an organization chart very inspiring; one normally wants to know the living person, not just of his or her skeleton.

With this in mind, a moment of diversion is introduced in the form of a slightly irreverent chart of the organization of heaven (Figure 10). Various of the structural elements commonly found in organizations are pictured. Line divisions group related activities together, and—in adherence to limited span of control—are kept down to three in number. There are staff officers for personnel and research, and an office for control of expenditures. There is the "external" element in the form of an advisory council. Note that a considerable variety of management functions have been incorporated into a relatively simple structure, and that relationships can be readily traced. Naturally heaven has exemplary organization.

Coordinating Structure

For life here below, and specifically in libraries, it may be well to start with relatively simple structures, and then to move to larger and more complex arrangements. Watch the structure expand; see the bureaucracy grow. Harvard University has over fifty departments and units in its library system. The charts presented here will include coordinating officers and in some cases the departmental units, but not individual positions.

Figure 11 shows the organization in a small college library (Beloit College in Wisconsin, in this instance). The work of the agency has been divided into three groups, for public service (circulation, reference), for supporting technical services (acquisitions, cataloging), and for a group of materials that evidently posed special problems (serials, documents). There is an associate director but there are no staff officers as such. For a relatively small agency, the number of general officers is on the high side—i.e., the three Assistant Librarians in coordinating positions. In practice, this being a small library,

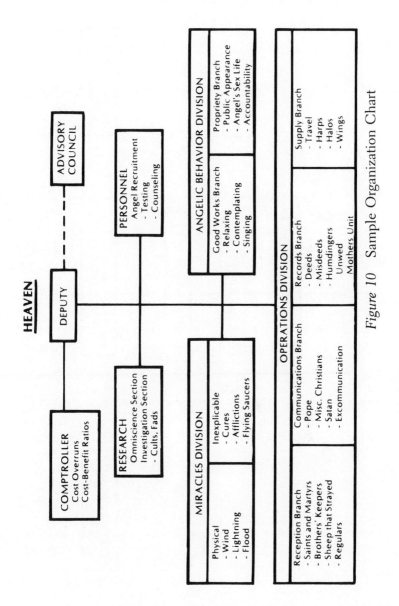

Figure 10   Sample Organization Chart

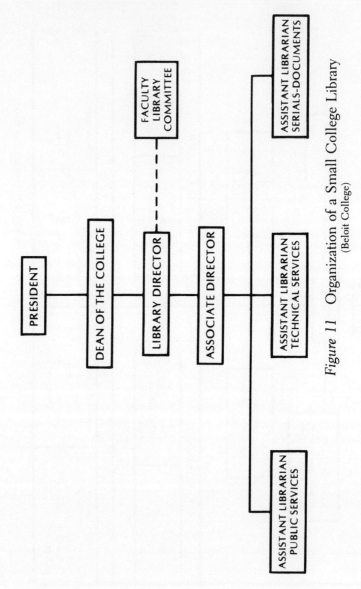

Figure 11 Organization of a Small College Library
(Beloit College)

they may also engage in as well as supervise services. It is a tight-knit structure, with a handful of managers carrying administration, and with limited demand for coordination by the Director. On the other hand, top heavy management provision makes for several authority levels in a relatively small agency, so that individual clerks and professionals are removed from the front office. It should also be noted that the Library Director reports to a Dean rather than directly to the President, thus adding further to the hierarchy.

A contrasting structure in a small agency is pictured in Figure 12. This is a county public library (Albany County in Wyoming, with headquarters in Laramie) serving 30,000 people spread over a large area. In this case, rather than services being grouped together into a few divisions, seven departments are maintained. Evidently, as functions came up, even "outreach," separate units were established for each. The load of coordination on the director is heavy in this plan, in order to mesh children's activities with public service, both of these with circulation, acquisitions with cataloging, and all of these with branches. Objective evidence indicates that the structure "works": the library spends only 51 percent of its budget for personnel (many public libraries are now over 66 percent) and it circulates eight books per capita annually (many public libraries do not circulate much more than half this amount). But without internal coordinating officers, and with only a "bookkeeper" as a staff officer, much depends here on one person for direction and coordination. In a small library, and with an energetic director, there is no reason why this plan would not work, but it is a safe bet that this individual has little time for external relations.

It would be a mistake to have any one model in mind and expect all agencies to conform to it. After all, in the foregoing pages in this volume, we have by no means come on the "perfect" structure. For the outsider, working only with an organization chart, it is often easier to tell what is wrong than what is right in an enterprise. In all cases there are forces that are invisible on any chart but that keep the agency functioning, and others, also invisible, that could destroy it if not thwarted.

Figure 13 charts the structure of a public library that serves

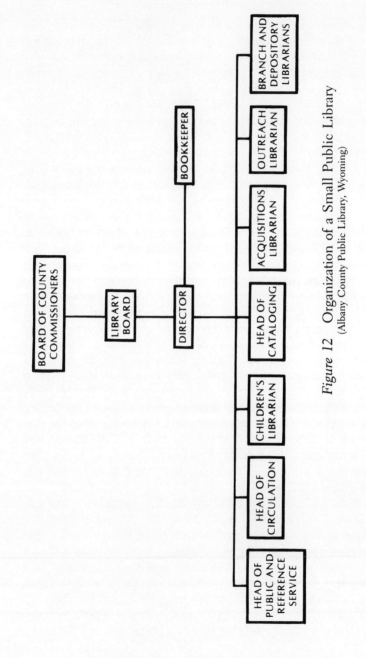

Figure 12 Organization of a Small Public Library
(Albany County Public Library, Wyoming)

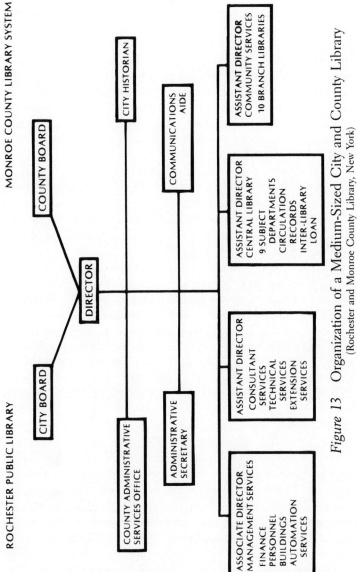

Figure 13 Organization of a Medium-Sized City and County Library
(Rochester and Monroe County Library, New York)

a city of 250,000 people (Rochester, N.Y.) and that functions also as the centrol unit of a federation of 19 independent public libraries serving a county (Monroe). The structure is unique in having two governing boards (one for the City and one for the County), with the Director employed by both boards. The advantage of the system is that library costs for a metropolitan region are shared by the region, while each municipality has its own library. To complicate the structure further, the Monroe County Library has contractual affiliations with four surrounding counties, comprising the Pioneer Library System, a federation of federations. The Director of the Rochester Public Library and Monroe County Library wears several hats while balancing several contracts in the air at the same time, an act that oddly enough seems to work; if some of the pieces were to drop, the performance might well fall flat.

Internally the Rochester Public Library is divided into four major divisions under Associate and Assistant Directors, two devoted to service in the Central Library and in community branches, one to support of service in the form of technical and consultation activities, and one to management functions. To help handle both internal direction and external relations, the Director has an administrative assistant and a communications specialist, the latter an uncommon position in libraries. The logic of the internal structure is evident, and span of control has been kept under control at the upper levels. Yet, given the dual role of this Library, and its web of governmental and contractual affiliations, the Director at the center can hardly sit and wait for results but must dash out on one strand after another. Whether pictured as a balancing act or as controller of a web, this spot is not the place for a passive administrator.

The Dallas Public Library, serving 1,000,000 people and with a staff of 500, can serve as an example of an even larger public library. Its organization is shown in Figure 14. Dallas is a council-manager city, with the Library Director reporting to the City Manager (actually directly to one of four Assistant City Managers), so there is no lay administrative board. An advisory board of eleven members is appointed by the City Council. The load down the line is carried by two Associate

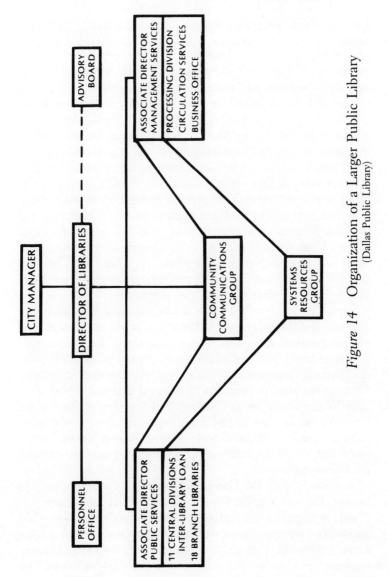

Figure 14   Organization of a Larger Public Library
(Dallas Public Library)

Directors, one for public services and the other for management services. Each of these combines a considerable number of units, the first being responsible for 12 central service departments and 15 branches, and the second for materials processing as well as business and financial affairs. Normally, in a library of this size there would be more divisions at this level; the smaller the number, the tighter the structure, the lighter the load of internal coordination on the Director, but the greater the load on the two assistant chiefs. The latter in turn do have middle managers handling coordination, one for central services and another for acquisitions-cataloging-binding. The chief needs and has staff officers, for personnel, for public and community relations, and for internal evaluation and planning, and the business manager serves in substance as a financial officer. Unusual features are the combining of business operations with materials processing under one Associate Director, and the use of two support groups for external communication and for systems development and evaluation.

One can see how the Director in this case has the senior aides to get the job done, without incurring an undue load of coordination at the top. At the same time, the plan should give the Director at least a little time for external relations with government, business and cultural interests, and communities. Only as the organization functions well will the Director be able to maintain these relations and to have at least some opportunity to plan ahead for the library five or ten years hence. Any loss or breakdown in two key positions would force immediate and full attention from the top just to keep operations going.

In contrast with the Dallas plan is that of the Memphis and Shelby County Public Library and Information Center, as shown in Figure 15. To quote the chief librarian in Memphis: "Instead of the traditional deputy or associate director, I have chosen to operate with a team management base. This administrative team consists of ten persons and meets each week for problem solving and policy recommendations." With a wide span of control, the Director must feel at times that he is running a ten-ring circus. Further, there is no one position that is logically in line to take over when the chief is away,

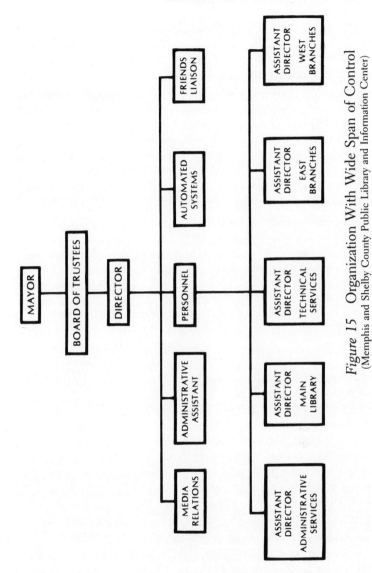

Figure 15 Organization With Wide Span of Control
(Memphis and Shelby County Public Library and Information Center)

whether for short or long periods. Some of the rings are devoted to distinctive characteristics of the Library, such as information service, media relations, and an active Friends group. One factor that helps is that the Memphis Library has an unusually definite statement of objectives and priorities, so that the various middle managers are clear on just what the agency seeks to accomplish, and therefore need less direction than normal.

A glance at Figure 16 shows how the structure grows in a public library serving twice as many people — the Philadelphia Free Library, in this case. A deputy director comes into the picture, and also six coordinating officers. Both the top two officials have staff officers reporting to them. An evaluation in 1981 made this observation:

> Thus two officers (Director and Deputy Director) seek to handle a very wide range of responsibilities, from broad planning to day-to-day crises, from budget making to external relations with the government and the public. In a time of limited funds, immediate and short-term problems tend to pre-empt management time and attention, while evaluation of performance and long range planning are short-changed.[1]

This last criticism has since been met by the establishment of a planning office.

In general it is difficult in a relatively large enterprise, with subject specialties and a wide territory to serve, to exercise internal control and at the same time reach out to the larger community. There is some point, not easily determined, where it may be advantageous to split up a very large library into separate entities. A study of three systems serving New York City (New York Public Library, Brooklyn Public Library, and Queens Borough Public Library) concluded that little would be gained by combining the three into a single system.

The plan of the University of Minnesota Libraries shows a fairly typical structure for a larger academic institution (Figure 17). Both a Director and Associate Director are needed, and also an echelon of three Assistant Directors, one for Resources, one for Processing, and one for Administration. The direct-services activities are under the Associate Director, and divided

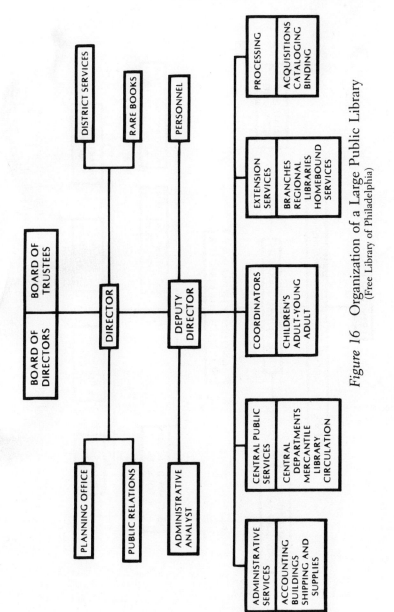

Figure 16 Organization of a Large Public Library
(Free Library of Philadelphia)

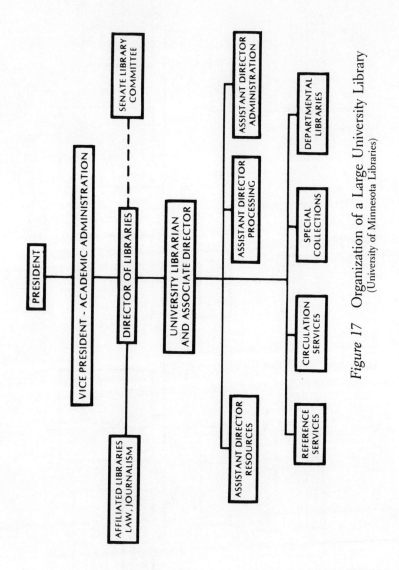

Figure 17   Organization of a Large University Library
(University of Minnesota Libraries)

into four units, for reference, circulation, departmental libraries, and special collections. Thus at least nine officers have purely managerial responsibilities, and under them are more than forty departments or units. The complex structure has grown up in response not to the needs of a uni-versity, if this means a cohesive institution with circumscribed objectives, but in response to the needs of a multi-versity engaged in teaching and research and service across much of the spectrum of human inquiry. All established structures are hard to move or change; a huge structure has that many more points of resistance. The test will come in these next years, as universities struggle to maintain quality in the face of the end of quantitative growth.

Various common characteristics are evident in these several samples. To a considerable degree the structures are basically similar, despite great differences in size and mission; one seldom comes on innovative organization in this field. The core in each instance is composed of functions, steps in the sequence from acquired book to satisfied reader. To this core are added units dealing with particular forms of publications: government publications, periodicals, films. The larger institutions develop a circle of subject departments, in substance as sub-divisions of the reference function. Because functional organization requires an extra measure of coordination, the structures tend to be top-heavy in general management positions, which is most evident in the larger agencies. And all leave a very heavy load on the Director, reflecting the centralized nature of library organization.

Innovative Proposals

Two proposals for less conventional structures are worth examining, one for a large public library and one for a large university library.

The proposal for the Chicago Public Library sought to identify and separate out four key activities: service, support for service, evaluation and planning, and budget and financial control (Figure 18).[2] This was an application of Drucker's

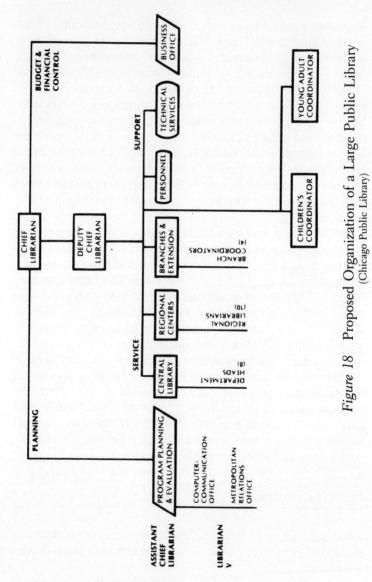

Figure 18 Proposed Organization of a Large Public Library
(Chicago Public Library)

principle of giving priority in organization to the purpose for which an agency exists, service to users in this case, and arranging functional groupings according to the kind of contribution made. For a library serving 3,000,000 people, the seven assistant chief librarians for line and staff functions could be justified, and there might well need to be additional coordinating officers for over 60 branches and for special services, as to children and young people.

The Columbia University Libraries were reorganized in general accord with a management study some years ago.[3] The study was one product of a "Management Review and Analysis Program" sponsored by the Association of Research Libraries and financed by the Council on Library Resources. The sticky question of to whom the university librarian should report was resolved by designating the position at the Vice President level. The library was re-structured into three broad groupings:

Resources Group: collection development and in-depth bibliographic and reference service.

Services Group: three subject centers:
Humanistic and Historical Studies Center
Social Science Center
Science and Engineering Information Center
and five distinctive collections (law, health science, Asian, architecture, and Special Collections).

Support Group: Business, records, processing, preservation.

This too is an effort to organize by the kind of contribution made to the work of the agency. The services group is there, and in addition a resources group, in recognition of the responsibility of a large university to build up collections in depth and to provide user assistance at the research level. This last is the more innovative aspect of the plan; libraries generally have dispersed collection building among professionals and subject librarians whose main function is user service, and then tried to gain coherence and balance in holdings by means of a book-selection policy statement. Collection building in depth and direct service to researchers have usually not been combined, although we will see a parallel development in the from of subject bibliographers, to be noted later.

Some university librarians have been skeptical about the Columbia plan. McAnally and Downs called it "unwieldy and cumbersome."[4] Ackerman more recently noted that ". . . the combination of advanced reference and collection building did not survive the revision process at Columbia."[5] Thus the time-honored and traditional structure tends again to prevail.

Organization in the Electronic Age

Few of the structures reviewed make direct provision for computerization, either of internal operations (acquisitions, cataloging, serials, circulation) or of on-line user services (bibliographic sources, direct information data). This profound development is usually left to the various separate units that are affected, even though the same system can serve more than one department, even though the different systems should be integrated, and even though regular staff members have only limited background in automation and computerization and may even have a bias against this trend.

Question any library of some size about current problems, and almost surely the matter of computerization will come up. For what should we go on-line—how far should we go—is this the time to start or to add to what we already have—how can we integrate the various systems? It is not too much to say that the answers to these questions will do more than anything else to determine how viable the library will be ten or twenty years from now. Yet the impression one gets in most directors' offices is one of uncertainty about the whole development; nor does the director in most cases have a staff expert to turn to who has an overall view. This leaves the chief at the mercy of the vendors of automated systems, and more than one library has been hurt by accepting the claims of one or another supplier in the marketplace.

In practice what provision is made for this kind of expertise within libraries? One or more middle managers in technical services may have picked up some background, because this is where automation usually starts. Then electronic control of circulation records appeared, and some other officer looked into this. More recently bibliographic data bases came online, the library uses them to some extent, and the person who knows most about them may well be an operator within the reference department. As to the great future of direct computerized information (separate from bibliographic data), the development that will transform the library, this has only recently come over the horizon, so no one in the agency has put much more than a toe into this large sea. The exceptions are libraries (relatively few in number) which have designated a senior officer in charge of on-line service.

It is a classic example of limited flexibility in a pre-existing organization. The structure evolved before the technology appeared. As it becomes practicable, pieces are parceled out within that structure. At best, what happens is that what the agency did before is now done with the help of the new technology. The greater potential is not perceived and the pieces may not fit together. At worst, what happens is that the agency actually resists a development that could rescue it from stagnation.

One of two results will occur in the next years. Libraries may learn to exploit computerization of data and will take their place in the so-called information age (what age has not depended on information?). Or libraries will make half-hearted and piecemeal applications, while commercial information systems come in to fill the void.

Along with electronic storage and access to information goes distribution by electronic means. Eventually readers will not come to the library but will have access to the central resource directly from their homes, offices, and classrooms. This does not mean the end of libraries but it does portend a profound transformation of the agency. Can the library organization of the 20th century be made to adjust to the 21st?

The closest the various organization plans previously reviewed come to making provision for the change appears in the planning offices specified in the Chicago, Philadelphia, and Columbia University structures. By focusing on electronic developments, these offices can chart the course and specify the necessary coordinating units. More than most new prospects this one calls for coordination, for computerization will affect every section of the library. And new line departments will emerge; the present corner in the reference room with a terminal will one day be one of the most important departments in the library, side-by-side with the departments built on printed publications.

The question is whether library organizers will grasp the nettle and move provision for on-line services to center stage, or whether pieces of the new technology will evolve almost by chance in the shadow of the traditional functions. This does not mean that libraries should become mechanized, with the tradition of printed knowledge submerged. But new automatic and communication possibilities should not be left to struggle to the surface. The library of tomorrow will be both off-line and on-line, a two-horse team, or it will be left behind.

Coordinating Officers

Administration can be viewed as a mixture of supervision, coordination, and leadership. Supervision predominates in the lower management ranks, and leadership in the upper. Coordination applies across the board, for administrators from the assistant department head to the chief librarian have responsibility for maintaining team effort among their subordinates. In addition, some positions may be interspersed explicitly for purposes of coordination.

Recognizing the need for joint effort in various services, public libraries in particular and academic libraries to some extent have created positions specifically for coordination; i.e., positions out of the line hierarchy. In the former these appear as Coordinators for Adult Service, for Young People's Service, and for Children's Service. In university libraries, where coordination is not the main purpose, the title is more likely to be subject bibliographer.

The children's coordinator in public libraries provides the most clear-cut and instructive example, and demonstrates what can be achieved with this approach. Children's service is provided in the main building, in branches, and perhaps in bookmobiles. Each of these has a line officer in general charge, usually not a children's librarian. The Coordinator cuts across these various lines and works directly with children's librarians, guiding collection development, selecting and training recruits for service to youngsters, setting the standards for service programs, analyzing causes when a particular program is failing, stepping in and making changes when necessary. All this is done with an aspect of service that is ostensibly under a line officer such as a branch librarian.

Children's service is a favorable candidate for this treatment. It serves a distinct clientele and works with a distinct collection. Librarians working with the younger age group have a strong sense of mission. They also have training and skills not possessed by other librarians. Effective techniques have been developed for stimulating and guiding the reading of youngsters. Finally, parents and the public in general applaud this service and feel convinced that it contributes to the younger generation.

But what is the effect within a department or branch when a line officer is in charge and another staff officer is calling the shots for part of the program? Is this not a violation of the principle of unified command? No doubt there are children's librarians and branch librarians who feel uncomfortable under the intrusion of an outside officer. However, many children's coordinators have gained such prestige, and are so sure of their ground in materials and program evaluation, that the line officer and the children's specialist both learn to fall in line and follow strong leadership. As to the youngsters, they benefit even if some rules are broken. "The chain of command is clearer without the introduction of the children's coordinator, but the expertise is certainly less."[6]

Children's coordinators have been among the most influential of public librarians. At an earlier stage there were Anne Carroll Moore and Francis Clark Sayers (New York), Frances Olcott (Pittsburgh), Effie L. Power (Cleveland) and Agatha Shea (Chicago), and the tradition has been carried forward by dedicated contemporaries in many public libraries. The fact that such names come readily to mind attests to the contribution these leaders made.

Adult service coordinators may not have as distinguished a record as the juvenile leaders, but the library historian cannot omit such individuals as Jennie Flexner (New York), Fern Long (Cleveland) and Marion Hawes (Baltimore). The impact of the adult coordinators may have been diminished because the target is so wide. Adult coordinators seek to influence activity not in distinct sub-units over which they have control, but over practically the whole service spectrum. In addition, responsibility for coordination of system-wide collection building falls on this office. New ventures in adult service—to low-education neighborhoods, to senior citizens, to handicapped persons—often emanate from the same source. With so wide a field to cultivate, no one part can be made to produce intensively. The adult coordinator has been a kind of jack-of-all-trades with a mandate to improve service across the board. Nonetheless, this officer in many instances is the source of what innovation and experimentation occurs in larger public libraries.

A different set of conditions limits the impact of Young People's Coordinators, and accounts for the decline of this service. The purpose (as developed by such leaders as Margaret Scoggin in New York, Jean Roos in Cleveland, and Margaret Edwards in Baltimore) is noble: to guide the reading of teenagers during their years of search and uncertainty. But young people prove to be too varied and unpredictable to fit into neat programs, and in this tolerant age they are not disposed to sublimate their urges and become compliant pupils. Who has learned how to lead this group during and after high-school years?

The "Young Adult" collections provided in libraries may actually have served to constrict rather than to liberate some growing adolescents. A small number responded to organized activities (drama groups, book-review clubs, sports seminars), but for the most part young spirits could not be so corralled. The problem was to connect with the vital interests of young people, and to bridge a generation gap between the established professional and the rebellious teenager, and neither effort has been successful. With response uncertain or declining, young-adult positions were often the first to be eliminated when funds became short, and the intermediate coordinator position itself has been absorbed either into the adult position or the juvenile one. One now finds in many libraries only a vestige of a once-hopeful service.

There may also have been a problem of organization here. The usual division between children's and young people's service is at age twelve or thirteen. This leaves all the teen years to the intermediate level. But thirteen and fourteen-year-olds are by no means the same as young adults at eighteen or nineteen. The first group is just reaching out while many in the latter group are overly sure that they have found the answers. Or the later teenagers have made decisions that will affect their whole lives: to be a doctor or an astronaut, to drop out of school, to get married, to try their hand at crime. Is all this to be met in a modest alcove in the library?

Perhaps children's work should be cut off a little earlier, say at eleven, with "young people" taken to be the transitional years of twelve to fifteen, and with service after that encompassed within the adult program. But who can say without careful experimentation? There is no limit to the human spirit when it breaks free of the restrictions of childhood.

The academic library coordinators have been oriented more to collections than to service programs. During the 1960s and 1970s with subject and research publication bursting its bounds, and with education-boom money in hand, subject bibliographers were hired and given substantial sums for acquisitions. Searching out faculty needs, and reviewing existing holdings, these specialists built a bridge from classrooms and research studies on the one side to library resources on the other. With this connection established, they were able to coordinate the two, at least to some extent. However, a competition sometimes developed between the bibliographer's office and the reference librarian's desk, with some faculty favoring the first because they felt that the bibliographer was more acquainted with their needs and also more familiar with resources. This did not sit well with other service professionals who had seldom made regular contact with faculty and graduate students. Then along came the 1980s and the 1990s with a downturn in both funds and graduate enrollments, and the subject bibliographer positions were often sacrificed. In most cases the pre-existing service structure carries on as before.

Yet the need for a bridge or connection with classroom and faculty may still exist. Much earlier Wilson and Tauber had recommended "library service coordinators" to:

> . . . relate the present or potential services of the public service units to the needs of clientele, especially undergraduates, solicit faculty advice in recommending new services and improving old ones, give instruction in library usage, and expedite the processing of materials needed for class use.[7]

While separate coordinators, whether in public or academic libraries, cut the cake in a way different from line officers, they have often made a distinct contribution. At the same time they have on occasion caused friction. Remember that conflict within organizations is not necessarily bad, that it can open new opportunities, and may even be resolved to the satisfaction of both sides.

The several kinds of coordinators, being neither fish nor fowl, not line officers with the duty of keeping a service department going, nor staff officers in the narrow sense of having always to work through the director, are in a position to explore and initiate outside the ongoing structure. They have built children's service and improved adult service in public libraries, and have strengthened collections in university libraries. The separate coordinating officer might well be considered as a means to meet the next great challenge, that of promotion and integration of computerization and on-line services in libraries. This development begs for attention, and in a framework that is not restricted by the past.

References

1. Martin, Lowell A. *The Free Library and the Revitalization of Philadelphia.* Philadelphia, Free Library of Philadelphia, 1981, p. 64.

2. Martin, Lowell A. *Library Response to Urban Change; a Study of The Chicago Public Library.* Chicago, American Library Association, 1969, p. 201.

3. Booz, Allen and Hamilton, Inc. *Organization and Staffing of the Libraries of Columbia University.* New York, Redgrave Information Resource Corporation, 1973.

4. McAnally, Arthur M. and Downs, Robert B. "The Changing Role of Directors of University Libraries," *College and Research Libraries,* Vol. 34, No. 2 (March 1973), p. 116.

5. Ackerman, Page, "Governance and Academic Libraries," *Library Research,* Vol. 2, No. 1 (Spring 1980–81), p. 20.

6. Gertzog, Alice and Beckerman, Edwin. *Administration of the Public Library.* Metuchen, N.J., Scarecrow Press, 1994, p. 130.

7. Wilson, Louis R. and Tauber, Maurice F. *The University Library; the Organization, Administration and Functions of Academic Libraries.* New York, Columbia University Press, 1956, p. 443.

XI LIBRARY WORKERS AND THE ORGANIZATION

IT REMAINS to look briefly at individuals within library organizations, both staff members and administrators. The usual view of an organization is from the outside, much as one might examine a machine. What are the parts, we ask, how well do they work together, does the organization accomplish the purpose for which it was designed? But a library is made up of people, which introduces the wonderful variety and idiosyncrasy of humankind. Viewed from the inside, from the staff member's station or the administrator's desk, the surrounding organization is not a machine but an environment, in which individuals thrive, drift, or burn out. What does the library organization do to its workers?

Staff members react to the library in which they find themselves in more ways than can readily be brought to mind: with enthusiasm, with skepticism, with apathy, with antagonism. Some seek to carry the library along, while others let the agency carry them. There is a two-way exchange here: what the organization does to the individual, and what the individual does to the organization. The exchange affects worker satisfaction and performance.

An insight that administrators will want to keep in mind is that morale is often determined by the relationship between expectations and the means available to achieve them. Effective managers seek to understand the expectations of staff at various levels and to provide the means to perform. If administrators doubt this relationship, they need only review their own experience, whether as underlings or masters. The connection between expectations and achievement applies in different ways at the several levels of employment.

Clerical Workers

In the study of organizations by social psychologists, attention has been given to the role of factory workers, of professionals, of managers, and to the satisfactions and frustrations of each within the hierarchy. But very little attention has been given to clerical workers. They tend to be the formless backdrop, or the muted chorus, against which the actual drama is played out by actors in the spotlights. Yet in many enterprises the clerical staff is more the foundation, holding up the rest of the structure; without this group the work of the agency would soon grind to a halt. In libraries such workers constitute half or more of the staff, and are likely to remain at this proportional level despite applications of new technology.

Organization puts the library clerk into a compartmented position, performing one specific and isolated part of a complex process. While this is true to some degree for every "organization man," the clerk performs a more circumscribed task, and does so with limited awareness of the end product. The clerk checks in acquisitions, or stamps books and inserts pockets, or records serials, or types lists, or shelves books, or files magazines. What is there to motivate clerks in such activities? How do they get any sense of mission? Some are assigned to the circulation desk, where they at least have contact with people. It is interesting to note their varying reactions to the contact: some derive satisfaction and proceed to sparkle on the job, a few seek to enlarge the assignment by trying to handle user inquiries for which they lack the requisite background ("look in the catalog and in the magazines on the shelves"), and a proportion still feel like cogs and perform in perfunctory fashion. In fact, discourtesy and resentment are not unknown at this service point.

What can be done? Certainly the library cannot be reorganized around clerical interests and preferences. Nor can staff be assigned to jobs for which they are not qualified. Both moves would violate organization principles. While there is no hype or pizzazz that will inject excitement into routine tasks, there are some psychological insights that can be of help.

Clerical workers, like others, initially take their jobs in order to get a paycheck. But as the work of Maslow and others has demonstrated, worker aspirations move to another level once salary is assured. They seek recognition and appreciation. It is not impossible to provide this within libraries.

The simple device of taking new clerks around the agency, introducing them to other workers, giving them a sense of the parts of the library and how they relate to each other, carries the message that they are members of an organization, not just movers of books or filers of cards in a corner. Staff-wide meetings should include employees at this level, whether the session has to do with as concrete a topic as adjustment in the pay scale or as speculative a topic as the future of electronic communication. In departmental discussions, get the opinion of the clerk on the line; it may have something the supervisors have missed. Consider exchanging assignments from time to time, to get the worker out of a single routine; this calls for an extra measure of training, but the payoff can be renewed interest and better performance.

As well as recognition as an individual, and as an individual who makes a contribution, the clerk seeks some feeling of group membership. While we tend to separate our working lives from our private lives, all organization workers, by force of circumstances, spend many hours a week in the society of the workplace; some even develop friends and outside companions from this source. Social life within the library should not be neglected. We sometimes say of a staff association that it is "just social," but providing activities in which clerical workers as well as others can participate can have benefits beyond an hour or two of relaxation and fun. Libraries do not have company baseball teams or bowling leagues or staff picnics—is this because professionals look down on such activities? The clerical group might see it differently.

How one instills a sense of educational mission in a group of workers who took a job in a library with about the same interest as they would a job in an office or factory is not easy to say. One lead that has hardly been explored is to draw this group into activities and programs put on by the library. The clerical staff constitutes an in-house source of potential participants in programs, for they are members of the public as well as employees. Public-library group activities are seldom aimed at clerical and semi-skilled individuals—audiences are more likely to be composed of "bookish" people—but focusing part of the offerings on non-users is worth consideration; the library clerical staff could constitute a start in getting response. For the most part they would be expected to participate on their own time, but is it too much to offer clerks the occasional opportunity to sit in on a program of particular interest to them, and to do so on library time? We expect the recruit to adjust to the organization—what adjustment should the organization make? Special services of the agency, such as educational counseling in independent learner projects, could be aimed in part at the in-house group. Such measures would provide a personal dividend for library employees, and at the same time would affect attitudes toward the agency. Workers who are stimulated to use some of the books they process would have a more positive conception of the library.

It would be unrealistic to assume that such steps will make all clerical workers happy and enthusiastic. Some recruits at this level have limited capacity and can only respond so far. Other recruits, unable to find a job in accord with their training, are over-qualified and give the job only a fraction of their ability. Inevitably some from both groups will feel alienated and there will be considerable turnover at this level. But some will respond. For these there should be a step of advancement, a senior clerk designation, even if this does not involve more advanced duties; the reward should be for steady, proven performance.

In this next period, with more and more young people getting at least some measure of special vocational training, it will become increasingly difficult to recruit and hold competent clerical personnel. Some people are attracted to the prospect of working in a library, but once on the job may find it little more appealing than working in a cheese factory, and the pay will probably not be as great. Library recruiters will have to consider unorthodox sources of help, such as part-time workers, senior citizens on Social Security, and even volunteers. And library administrators should be prepared to go an extra mile to make clericals feel like members of a team and not like cogs in a machine.

The first step in accomplishing this is for managers themselves actually to believe that non-professionals are members of the team. The administrator should recognize that organization looks very different to the person at the bottom. Directors see organization as opportunity and power; they can flex their muscles and seek to achieve great things by means of the hierarchy. To clerks, organization is at first a great unknown, and then as time goes on, and they come to recognize their lowly place on the totem pole, organization can mean an alien environment.

Managers who are unable to grasp their view from the clerical station are in for a rough time in the period ahead, because they will be unable to get and keep the troops they need in the ranks.

Professional Workers

Professional librarians, as was noted earlier, are inevitably creatures of an organization. Unlike doctors and lawyers and accountants and others, they do not have the option of setting up a private office. Most function within a structure that includes existing collections, established procedures, co-workers, and managers.

How do librarians fare in the hierarchy—what do they in turn do to the structure? In a sentence, they seek a little precinct suited to their aspirations and limitations, and once there they seek to protect their domain. This is not of necessity a criticism; it is the pattern followed by most people in many aspects of their lives.

We all seek a combination of two different and sometimes contradictory aims in our careers: an opportunity for accomplishment and self-expression, and a degree of security. Librarians arrive at their first professional job with an extra measure of the first aim. Their selection of a service profession, the bright prospect opened to them in library school, the standards of the profession they have joined, all combine to produce a personal goal of serving, and serving well. It is this positive attitude that will sustain them throughout their careers, even in some dark hours. If the library they join is effective, if it has definite institutional goals to match the personal goals of the recruit, and if it achieves those goals to a reasonable extent, the service attitude will be reinforced.

However, this same background and outlook prompt librarians to appraise with some care the agency they have joined. If they find a faltering institution, even for as downright a reason as limited funds, they are quick to criticize. It is painful to see an institution destroy the spirit of a professional, squandering one of the most precious of assets.

Librarians, again because of their training and aspirations, also expect a chance to participate in decision-making and to think about the welfare of the agency as a whole. But David Kaser has noted that the hierarchy puts staff members into separate slots. He calls for a "peer structure" for decisions on such matters as service priorities, collection-building policies, and staff promotions. He even raises the questions of election and interchange of department heads. "In this newer view librarians may no longer validly be thought of as 'working for' a library; rather they *are* the library, and they share equally in the responsibility for its services and failures wherever in the library system they happen to occur."[1] Responsibility as well as privilege.

Undue centralization and rigidity in the organization represses aspiring librarians. The effect is usually slow and not very visible, a gradual darkening of that extra spark, to the point where staff members settle in, keep their mouths shut, and, as Henry Ford asked, "do what they are told to do." A study of four university libraries found a negative relationship between innovation on the one hand and centralization and formalization on the other.[2]

On occasion the problem becomes more visible. It happened that the present writer returned from a publishing post to a library-school faculty position just after the student revolt of the 1960s. College graduates who were products of the period were coming through to library school. True to their upbringing, they were quick to speak up, to question, to criticize. Faculty had to learn to listen. What we heard, somewhat to our surprise, were the same questions that we ourselves were raising about the curriculum and the profession. The most outspoken of the students were the leaders, the shakers and doers, potential forces in librarianship. What happened when they graduated and took positions? They spoke up on the job—no doubt prematurely—and they were ignored or squelched or passed over for promotion. They stopped back at the library school after a few years to report that they were leaving the profession. The field lost some of its most promising recruits because it could not tolerate their making waves.

The response of many a settled administrator was: good riddance, we can get on with our job of rendering service. Libraries have done so, and have been increasingly called into question, by their users, by their financial sources, and by their own leaders. Of course it would be fantasy to claim that the rebels would have solved all problems. But libraries are in a period when fresh insights are needed. These will not come from those who fear to rock the boat.

Bureaucratic control discourages conflict. A monocratic system is followed in many libraries, and any challenge to it is considered disruptive of efficiency and production, and if continued consistently, is considered disloyal. The challenger is "not a team worker." Questioning of the prevailing ways is taken as criticism of those who devised and administer the system, and as an implication that there are unsolved problems that have not been given proper attention. It takes a confident manager to encourage the rebels to speak out.

But by no means does the pressure for conformity come solely from the administrator. Librarians themselves are looking for a measure of security, and find it in their place within the organization. The child reaches out, the teenager is uncertain, and the adult realizes that the world can be hostile. What starts out as great ambition can settle back into a search for a safe niche. What better place than an established library, with its opportunity to practice a profession, and even to cut out a little "turf" of one's own? Moreover, incremental salaries apply if one stays in line, pensions are common, seniority is stressed for promotion to the higher ranks. Many a librarian meets the bureaucratic structure more than half way, and directors may collide with both when they try to move the library forward.

New developments can be threatening to this security; currently, for example, the prospect of automation and computerization. New types of positions will arise. Staff members will come forward, or be brought in, to carry the new burden, while others may be left behind. It is natural that traditional staff members will be less than enthusiastic about the new technology, and may even resist when they can.

Thus professional and organization interact, each carrying the other along, providing opportunity for achievement, and each at times resisting change either in staff members or in purposes and practices. It is a symbiotic relationship that at its best benefits both parties.

Administrators and Leaders

Is the administrator the villain in the piece, or the victim? Both and neither. Again there is an interaction, with administrators seeking to move the organization and then finding themselves restricted by it.

The captain's seat is not always a comfortable one. Managerial positions lack the homely satisfactions of sound, skilled performance day-by-day. Persons low in the hierarchy can do their jobs and know that they have delivered what is expected of them. The upper echelons provide few opportunities for such concrete, daily accomplishments. At the managerial level the rewards are more in terms of power and prestige and salary. Workers may go home with a good feeling about what they have done, but also with a feeling of not being recognized or appreciated; while executives go home satisfied with the emoluments of the job but uneasy about the course and progress of the enterprise and unsure of their own contribution and performance.

The library director's day is filled with problems and deadlines. If the director succeeds in dealing with these various matters, and at the same time heads off some other issues, it can be considered a successful day. All the fires have been put out or prevented. At least the library is no worse off when the director leaves (often well after the rest of the staff) than it was in the morning.

But what of planning, what of progress and improvement, what of change to meet new circumstances? The task is not simply to preserve what previous administrators have built. Libraries cry out for leaders as well as followers.

Leadership is of two types. There are persons who move out front, breaking the trail, and calling others to follow. This is what is usually meant when we use the term "leader." Characteristics of such individuals are self-confidence, determination, dominance—and an objective which others may or may not share. The other type of leader keeps the enterprise on course, strengthening organization, methods, and personnel. The latter is likely to be adept at group leadership. The first explores new lands; the second keeps the store back home open and thriving. Libraries have need for both at different times in their evolution.

For either or both, effective organization is an essential tool or instrument. Tasks have been organized into positions, positions have been grouped into departments, duties and responsibilities have been assigned. Coordination has been established and authority delegated. The chain of command is clear. Communication is open, up, down, and across the lines. Staff members are seen as individuals within the structure. If all this is in place, the director has time and energy to lead, whether this means improving the present position or moving to new ground. The sound organization can respond, giving life and reality to dreams.

In his probing work, which won both the Pulitzer Prize and the National Book Award, James MacGregor Burns labels the two forms of leadership as "transactional" and "transforming."

> Transforming leadership, while more complex, is more potent. The transforming leader recognizes and exploits an existing

need or demand of a potential follower. But, beyond that, the transforming leader looks for potential motives in followers, seeks to satisfy higher needs, and engages the full person of the follower. The result of transforming leadership is a relationship of mutual stimulation and elevation that converts followers into leaders and may convert leaders into moral agents.[3]

He applies the concept to figures as diverse as Joan of Arc, Hitler, and Franklin D. Roosevelt. While his focus is on political leadership, he shows how the two modes also apply to institutional executives. Throughout he stresses the relationship between the objectives of leaders and the motives of followers; unless the two join and coalesce, little of permanent value is accomplished.

Application of the Burns' formulation to librarianship raises some problems. Where are the leaders who transform? What are the motives of staff which the administrator can energize? Not often does the current spark and move from the front office to the service desk, and back again. But many a library director does have goals; many a staff member has ideals. Make the connection between the two and mountains—or at least institutions—can be moved.

Leadership in our time has come under harsh criticism. Asks James Reston: "Is the life of the world really changed by the rise and fall of presidents and prime ministers these days? Are they the shapers or the casualties of events, the authors of history or the prisoners of geography?"[4] A study of how leaders are chosen by Senators in the U.S. Congress concluded that ". . . the highest priority is somebody they feel comfortable with."[5] Thus social critics say that the times are out of joint and that institutions drift.

Certainly libraries have settled into a bureaucratic form for a half-century or more. There has been relatively little basic change in either objectives or organization for several generations. By the turn of the century the several types of libraries had appeared, and their functions remain much the same to this day. Very early the method of organizing collections was established, along with the means of gaining bibliographic access to them. The service pattern was in place by World

War I or soon after, with reference stations, subject divisions, children's units, processing departments, and circulation desks.

The unique strength of the library is the collection, the heritage which the institution preserves. But this same resource inhibits change, for the collection must be continued and it imposes a methodology based upon past decisions. A library can't start fresh, like the American Telephone and Telegraph Co. (which is no longer concentrating on either telephones or telegraphs) or a corporation that diversifies and moves into new endeavors. The collection, for all its primacy is more an anchor than a driving force.

Librarians of the 1930s and 1940s could come back into most libraries after a 50-year absence and fit into the system with very brief orientation. The two adjustments of any import that they would have to make are to the computer terminal in the minority of libraries that have made any substantial strides in automation of information provision, and to cooperative relations with other libraries in those agencies active in systems and networks (although even here they would be familiar with cataloging from a central source, interlibrary loan, union catalogs and lists, joint selection agreements, and the other components of networks).

The various common threads have persisted despite the fact that this same half-century has seen profound changes in the provision of the product that libraries purvey, recorded knowledge and information. Compared to the time when the public-library service structure was formed, this is a specialized, information-dependent, multi-media, and questioning age. Compared to the time when the school-library service program came into place, this has been a period of experimentation back and forth, up to the present pointed criticism of the schools. Compared to the time when the academic-library organization appeared, this is a time of declining income and of an effort to preserve quality. Yet libraries continue serenely on their appointed path. Either they possess remarkable clarity of purpose and unusually effective organization, or they are drifting out of the mainstream as new channels of knowledge and information form.

At the least, critical self-examination would be wise and

salutary. Libraries, like other enterprises, need periodic renewal. But where in library-land is the voice that challenges, the figure who strikes for new ground, the lodestar that beckons?

The Current Test: TQM

The test now confronting libraries has to do with library reaction to Total Quality Management (TQM), which was described in Chapter III. Are libraries taking advantage of this new means for increasing quality, effectiveness. and customer satisfaction? An opportunity is not just on the doorstep; it is in some of the very books the agency has on its shelves.

A survey of the professional literature of recent years shows relatively few sustained efforts to apply TQM in the library field. Two books on library administration recently off the press give no attention to this culmination of the humanistic trend.[6] The 1993 revision of another recognized text dismisses TQM as the "latest management fad."[7] This may be the natural reaction of an administrator who has struggled through such phases as Management by Objectives and Zero-Based Budgeting, and seen them fade from the scene, but there is a human element in Total Quality Management that may give it longer life and greater impact. Further, TQM should be suited to and appeal to professionals, who by definition have a commitment to the improvement of service and also have training which enables them to envision new approaches to the dissemination of knowledge. But to date the applications in the library field have been sporadic and inconclusive.

It is true that library literature has examined the possible utilization of TQM by libraries as a means to increase user satisfaction and also the job satisfaction of library workers. A book of some substance has suggested various applications.[8] A symposium on the topic appeared in the *Journal of Library Administration*,[9] including utilization of TQM at the Harvard College Libraries and the Oregon State University Libraries; both reports stress the time and effort required to get this management technique under way, and both conclude that in

time it leads to a new and promising "organizational culture."
Three academic librarians have analyzed the relationship[10].
Of particular interest is an example of the application of TQM
at Bowling Green State University Library[11].

The opportunities for improvement in libraries are readily
at hand, in this institution that depends on many items for
use (actually miles of stacks in the larger agencies), on extensive
record keeping (catalogs, bibliographies, and circulation files),
and on experts in various complex fields (book selectors, reference librarians, subject bibliographers, and computer-access
specialists). It is not difficult to identify possible problem areas
in libraries that would stand to gain from quality review.

Starting right at the point of acquisition, various time questions arise:

- time required to decide on and order books
- length of time before arrival
- length of time before items stand on shelves ready for use
- if requested item not held, how long to get through interlibrary loan

In TQM, fairly specific matters are dealt with; it is such specif-
ics together that add up to service or lack thereof.

Going on to the collection on the shelves, additional questions arise:

- how many books mis-filed on the shelves
- missing titles
- items not selected
- mis-filed folders
- material "at the bindery"

Expanding to broader questions, many come readily to mind
that might well be analyzed in a push for consistent quality:

- appropriateness of format, as among books, pamphlets,
  videos, CD Roms, etc.
- clerical tasks in professional positions
- exchange of information among departments

- follow-up on clients served by reference librarians
- reaction of users, and their appraisal of services

And on through a litany of possible problem areas.

Don't library staff members possess the outlook and attitude requisite to quality management? The clerk at the circulation desk sincerely tries to direct users asking questions to the next steps to reach their goals. The reference librarian seeks to understand just what the user is seeking, directs them to appropriate materials, and might check to see if customers were satisfied. Have librarians been practicing TQM these many years even though the term was not used?

Yes and no. Yes in the sense that the interests of users were kept in mind. But no in at least two important regards: staff members are not encouraged and expected to watch for problems and to suggest solutions, and there seldom was an explicit check on the end product, whether users really got what they wanted. The library has had no direct competition, so that the old ways could be tolerated—but this is changing.

In libraries there is not even an old-fashioned control unit to catch deficiencies. Nor is there an evaluation form or a suggestion box at the exit, as in many restaurants and supermarkets.

Take as obvious a development as computerized catalogs—how many users find it a benefit, how many consider it frustrating, and how many avoid using it if possible? The present author was surprised recently, in talking to a well-informed friend, to have him say that he no longer used the public library because he could not make the computerized catalog work. How many are there like this?

It is interesting to note the satisfaction some users experience in small one-person libraries (in small communities, schools, and some special libraries). They find a librarian who knows resources thoroughly, who is acquainted with the user, and who follows up to determine if the material sought has been found. Built-in quality control.

If Total Quality Management is to be brought to bear, certain principles must be kept in mind:

- must start at the top, with the director and middle managers
- must involve all staff members
- must have goals and objectives clearly in mind
- must be prepared to empower workers
- provide necessary training and re-training all along the way
- pick specific operations or problems and concentrate on them
- pick soluble problems in the beginning, in order to give TQM a promising start
- check back, evaluate, to determine effect, and use findings as feedback
- don't think of TQM as short-term; stay with the process until it is built in

The articles cited on applications of TQM in libraries are straws in the wind, while much of library organization stands as before and day-to-day management is still organized around traditional (albeit civil) authority. Most professionals still lack the challenge and stimulus of tackling new problems, and fall back into routine performance. New recruits lack the challenge and stimulus of being brought into an improving and evolving organization.

Total Quality Management provides a means to strengthen the library as it stands today, to improve the services it has been giving. But a larger question—and a larger challenge and opportunity—looms with the prospect of a shift to both information and text in machine-readable form and to computerized delivery of content at a distance. How fares the institution in the age of the Electronic Library?

References

1. Kaser, David. "Modernizing the University Library Structure," *College and Research Libraries*, Vol. 31, No. 4 (July 1970), pp. 227–228.

2. Howard, Helen A. "Organizational Structure and Innovation in Academic Libraries," *College and Research Libraries*, Vol. 42, No. 5 (September 1981), pp. 425–434.

3. Burns, James MacGregor. *Leadership*. New York, Harper and Row, 1978, p. 4.

4. New York Times, August 30, 1983, p. A35.

5. New York Times, September 4, 1983, p. A25.

6. Coughlin, Caroline M. and Gertzog, Alice. *Lyle's Administration of the College Library*, fifth edition, Metuchen, N.J., Scarecrow Press, 1992, and Gertzog, Alice and Beckerman, Edwin. *Administration of the Public Library*. Metuchen, N.J., Scarecrow Press, 1994.

7. Stueart, Robert and Moran, Barbara. *Library and Information Center Management*. 4th ed. Englewood, CO., Libraries Unlimited, 1993, p. 223.

8. Jurow, Susan and Barnar, Susan B. *Integrating Total Quality Management in a Library Setting*. New York, Haworth, 1993.

9. Clark, M. E. "Organizational Development and TQM." *Journal of Library Administration* 18, no. 1, 1993, pp. 29–43.

10. O'Neil, Rosanna M., Harwood, Richard L., and Osif, Bonnie A. "A Total Look at Total Quality Management: a TQM Perspective from the Literature of Business, Industry, Higher Education and Librarianship," *Library Administration and Management* 7, no. 74 (Fall,1993), pp. 244–53.

11. Miller, Rush G. and Stearns, Beverly. "Quality Management for Today's Academic Library," *College and Research Library News* 55, no. 7 (July-August 1994), pp. 406–9.

XII THE ELECTRONIC LIBRARY

ONE OF THE MOST insightful critics of our times Peter F. Drucker, has pointed to a "Post-Capitalist Society," which he believes is emerging at the present time.[1] This new structure he sees as a "Knowledge Society", in which knowledge industries dominate in the economy and knowledgeable people dominate in the society. The knowledge industries are the professions, the communication agencies, the computer enterprises, and what he identifies as endeavors based directly on knowledge, such as the pharmaceutical industry. Everything from finance to education must be transformed and held accountable for producing workers and citizens with the background to contribute to the new society.

Drucker examines this prospect from many angles and admits that the structure and sources of the Knowledge Society cannot yet be clearly discerned. Interestingly enough, he does not once mention libraries either as agencies of transformation or as the source of recorded knowledge. Evidently information and understanding will come from the heavens, perhaps in the falling rain—or will be somewhere on the Internet.

We surely are moving into a new period in which knowledge will play an even greater role than in the past. Included in this future will be the electronic library. What will be its role—how will it relate to present-day libraries—how will it change the organization of libraries.? It is too soon to make any exact and didactic predictions, but a few relevant observations can be ventured.

293

The Demise of the Book?

Many people react instinctively against the prospect of an electronic library in which all material is in machine-readable form to be accessed by means of the computer screen. They have grown up with the printed page, in hard binding, in paperback, in journals. They find this form convenient and friendly. The organization of the book is familiar, with its table of contents and its index. It can be read rapidly or slowly, as the individual prefers, and one can readily turn back to review earlier pages. It can be put down and picked up again as needed. The primary advantage of the book is its portability; you can take it with you, but you have to have access to a computer to consult a database.

The properties and advantages of the book have enabled it to prevail for centuries. More recently it has survived movies and radio and television and CD-ROMs and E-journals and will probably continue doing so. The electronic library does not mean the end of the printed page; books will continue to be in the library of the future. This is not a matter of the new versus the old, but of the probable relationship between the two.

But the book has built-in limitations and disadvantages. The user has to gain access to the individual copy. This may be readily at hand on the desk or on the nearby shelves. If not, the seeker must go to the library—down the hall in a school, to another floor in the corporation, across campus in a college, across town in a community. Even there it may not be available. Someone else may be using the title desired; the book can be used by only one reader at a time. Or it may be misplaced or "missing" or "at the bindery." Or not in the collection at all. One study in an academic library showed that a document sought was available only 60 percent of the time.[2] Another study showed the portion of satisfied users at 48 percent.[3] In contrast, if it is in the computer data base, a book can be retrieved 100 percent of the time.

Beyond that, books are bulky in size. One has only to walk the bookstacks of a good-sized collection to realize the storage space required. And libraries in the same city or area duplicate each other to some extent, with the same titles sitting on the shelves of agencies within a few miles of each other. This is not likely to be the infrastructure that will continue into the future.

Finally, books are for the most part one-dimensional or uni-media in a multi-media age. Computerized knowledge can combine print, illustration, and sound. And books are not reactive; they stay the same and do not respond depending on the needs and background of the user, whereas a well-designed computer program can test the searcher along the way, repeat material if necessary, and suggest new avenues to search. Reading therefore takes more motivation on the part of individuals; they are on their own with the finished text. Children often respond more readily to digital content than to reading because the computer speaks back to them, keeps their attention, and moves them forward. For them it is easier—they might say "more fun"—to sit down at the computer terminal. In planning ahead, one must take into account the different generations with different ways of gaining knowledge.

In terms of overall organization, libraries rest on the strategy of separate collections assembled for a particular group of users, a very convenient structure—and very expensive. Also, each collection can only go so far in coverage. Much effort in recent years has been directed to systems and networks designed to provide each library with access to the content of other collections—the making of a super-facility out of the myriad of libraries in a region, a state, or even the nation. Substantial effort and expense are devoted to this coordination of scattered resources.

Note the role of the factor of *convenience* in determining the present organization of library service. Collections are placed as close as feasible to potential users. If distance to the center is too great, departmental libraries are established in the university and branch libraries in the city, adding substantially to the cost of maintaining the system. This factor of convenience will continue to play a deciding role in the future organization of knowledge provision, and once again computerized content has a definite advantage.

Despite the various advantages of the machine-readable form, books will be held in future libraries—for older material, for little-used material, for readers who prefer to handle material physically when making their selections, and for traditional book readers. But the present trickle of machine-readable documents will increase into a flood. Some items may be issued both in printed and computerized form. Building collections from both forms will be the challenge of the future, getting the right proportion, taking cost and convenience into account.

Libraries as Sources of Information

If one shifts emphasis from the library as book provider to the library as a source of information, the picture changes. Many people today go to the library for a discreet piece of information (from per capita income in a foreign country to the side effects of a prescribed medicine) and obtain what they seek without reading a book. They will continue doing so in the future and the agency to which they turn will increase in strength in the computer age.

The provision of information is a traditional function of the library. The high-school student seeking a historical date and the business person seeking data beyond his or her office resources will go to the building or get on the telephone. In the future they can gain access to the Internet, or other data structure through the same agency, thus providing information for the "have-nots." Further, the library will continue its role of guiding and leading seekers through the sources. And, as far as possible, the librarian will seek to ensure that the information is reliable and authoritative. Who else or what other agencies will serve these functions?

Think of the library as an information source and the future seems less uncertain. The test for library managers will be to continually reorganize and restructure the library to most effectively use the new technology for information provision. The agency will be in a continual state of transition with continuing changes, retraining of staff, and rethinking the structure of the organization.

Next Stages

The electronic library should not be confused with the automated library. Many libraries today use digital methods in
acquisition records, circulation transactions, and the catalog
of holdings. These are all methods or operations of libraries,
which the computer has helped them perform. The advantages
accrue to the libraries themselves more than to the users of
the agencies. There are, it is true, dividends in the information
provided searchers.

The electronic library takes the next quantum step and has
all the content of its collection in machine-readable form,
CD-ROMs in house, or through networked computer sources.
In the not so distant future this could include text as well as
reference data. Theoretically, the history, the science text, the
poem, and the novel could all be brought up on the computer
screen. Dictionaries, encyclopedias and other reference works
are already available in CD-ROM form.

In digital form, the material is readily at hand, through the
machine on the desk—at home, in the classroom, and in the
office. Computerized access appears to surpass most of the
limitations of the printed page. Many users can obtain the
material at the same time—it is always "in stock"; it is in
compact form; it is multi-media; it is reactive. These are the
characteristics that have prompted several recent laments in
Publishers Weekly about the future of book publishing, starting
early in the decade with an article entitled "Toward the Electronic Book."[4] Since then more books in traditional form have
been published than ever before, circulation has increased in
all types of libraries, and new, huge bookstores have appeared.
It is too soon to cry "havoc."

The traditional book-lover reacts to the unfolding prospect
with repugnance, pointing out that all contents—data and text
and illustration—will come back on a computer screen. How
long will viewers want to read text from the screen? To this
reaction it can be pointed out that the computer has an
attached printer, the words can be set down on a page, and
in time there will be a mechanical means to attach the pages

together. Thus we have come full circle, back to the printed book. At this point the distinction between printed text and machine-readable text is removed; the dichotomy becomes artificial.

When will the electronic book and the electronic library come into place? Well within the lives of many librarians now on the job—indeed in some form by the advent of the new century.

Future Organization of Libraries

What effect will the electronic library have on the organization of the libraries—and on librarians? No one can be positive about the answers at this point. We can only look into the glass and detect some indistinct and changing images.

The present-day library may evolve into the electronic library; certainly some first steps have been taken, by incorporating digital databases into the arsenal of resources. Or a separate and distinct structure may emerge, leaving traditional libraries in a kind of backwash. Or some combination of these two alternatives may evolve.

The existing library has a head start in this perspective development. It has an infrastructure in place, it has thousands of locations within regions and across the country, and it has a goodly measure of support by individuals, communities, and government. The argument to build on an existing institution will carry weight. But the library also has its set ways, its patterns, its traditions that may stand in the way of basic change. At least one thoughtful attempt has been made to sort out short-term and long-term effects and to venture predictions for the middle term, five years to ten years ahead.[5]

One can readily foresee some of the probable adjustments in organization. The networking of resources, already well under way, will go forward. As this develops, the pressure to expand local collections will decrease. As it becomes easier and faster to gain access to material within and between regions, there is no need to add marginal and infrequently-used items to the collection in the community, the school, the college, or the corporate enterprise. Smaller nearby collections, aimed specifically at the local user group, and rejecting the temptation to add marginal items, are on the road ahead. Yet overall the resources that the user can command will increase.

Similarly, because machine-readable documents require less storage space, the pressure to build and expand buildings will be lessened. Think of the recent rash of new, large and traditional central public libraries in cities around the country, a look back to prior conditions rather than a look ahead. These buildings of the 1990s will be antediluvian in twenty years.

Now the Library of Congress has announced a massive program to convert the text of a million volumes a year to machine-readable form, and to incorporate the material into a "virtual" library accessible by way of computers.[6] Even as the provision of centralized cataloging entries by the Library of Congress many years ago led to a revolution that transformed the control of resources within libraries, so this new development could lead to transformation of local collections themselves across the country. The technology is there, although methods for converting printed text into digital form are still slow and inaccurate.

What about the personnel in the electronic library? The need for clerical workers to record and file and retrieve information and documents will decrease, as the machine does the work. But the same is not likely for professional personnel, for the need for guidance—help in locating resources—will continue and may well increase. The structure and possibilities and limitations of resources at a distance will be no simpler than the structure of an individual library, so that the searcher will need assistance. Even today the average library user has more familiarity with the library he or she can see and touch than with a complex system beyond the walls; most would throw up their hands at the mention of simply turning to the Internet.

Searchers who need guidance in the future may not go to the library but can make contact from their desks and get the help they need—even as they do so today by consulting a reference librarian. To handle the complex variety of demand for resources, a human being will still be needed, and this won't be an "electronic librarian"—that is, some kind of automated response such as one sometimes gets in making a telephone call to a large enterprise—but a specialist some steps beyond the typical librarian of today. Currently the best of reference librarians knows more about the range of digital resources then most knowledgeable workers, including the dabblers on the Internet. New York State, which now provides access to Internet from its public libraries, calls these agencies "Electronic Doorway Libraries."

The key to future developments will be what happens to the Internet system. Now having grown for a decade or more, and grown with few if any standards or regulations, Internet is a vast conglomerate, with everything from obscure scientific data to trivia; there is even a section for women only where they can record what they like or don't like about men ("I like the smell of men after they exercise"). One librarian has called the system a "seething and growing organism".[7] A less polite characterization is to say that it contains much garbage.

Currently the federal government, which has subsidized the Internet since its inception, is seeking to pull out and "privatize" various sections of the system. The prospect is for increased growth under uncoordinated segments aimed primarily at commercial interests. The goal is to make it commercially self-sufficient in five years. The effect on access and costs is most uncertain.

Issues such as privacy, affordability, and public access must be addressed. We must make sure that the electronic superhighway is just as accessible through libraries as the printed word has been.

Librarians themselves are exploring the possibilities.[8] An encouraging development has been the appearance of "Free-Nets" in various regions. Librarians have been at the center of local efforts to provide free access to the Internet.[9] This removes the barrier of a fee of $10.00 a month or more to be connected to the huge computer files. The local public library may be the access point to the portion of the infrastructure now in existence. Whether local, volunteer efforts of this kind, with uncertain financing, will be the wave of the future is unclear. It may well require more to turn the highway into a freeway.

The advantages of computerized resources—access, convenience, cost—have already, and will increasingly, impact library service and library organization. This will not only change but will go further and transform the agency.

But this does not mean that it will eliminate the library. There will still be books and collections—to be selected, acquired, organized and serviced. And there will be computerized data bases, text and pictorial material—also to be selected, acquired, organized, and serviced. The question is the relationship of the two channels of provision.

And who will build, organize, and maintain the future machine-readable collections? Will users simply depend on the output of vendors, as though today we were to depend on the output of publishers and dispense with libraries? Professionals of the highest order will be needed to provide plans and blueprints for the Information Highway, and to maintain the road once it is designed and constructed. Call them intermediaries, consultants, counselors, or whatever. These may or may not be librarians, depending on the flexibility of existing professionals and on the extent to which library administraters will release the potentialities of their staffs.

In the end the future pattern will be determined by the reaction of library users. If the visceral affection for the printed page will predominate, the library will remain much as at present, a book agency backed up by digital data bases. But if coming generations of users will turn readily to computerized text (as seems likely), the agency will be transformed into the electronic library, unless new enterprises will arise to organize the world of digital communication and to guide people in its use. By the third edition of this work a less qualified prediction can be made.

The interval will be the most exciting, challenging, frustrating time for librarians since the concept of "library" came into existence several centuries ago.

References

1. Drucker, Peter F. *Post-Capitalist Society.* New York, Harper, 1993.

2. Buckland, Michael. *Book Availability and the Library User.* New York, Pergamon, 1975.

3. Saracevic, T., Shaw, W. M. and Kantor, Paul. "Causes and Dynamics of User Frustration in an Academic Library," *College and Research Libraries* 38 (January, 1977), p. 7–18.

4. Lande, Nathaniel, "Toward the Electronic Book," in *Publishers Weekly,* Vol. 238, No.42, September 20, 1991, p. 28–30.

5. Buckland, Michael. *Redesigning Library Services: a Manifesto.* Chicago, American Library Association, 1992.

6. *New York Times.* September 12, 1994, p. A10.

7. Walker, Leonard D. In the Introduction to "Libraries and the Internet." *Library Trends.* Vol. 42, No.4, Spring, 1994, p. 585–758.

8. Potter, William G. "Access to Electronic Information; Exploring the Options," in Godden, Irene P. (ed.) *Advances in Librarianship.* Vol. 17 (1993), p. 61–77. San Diego, Academic Press, 1993.

9. *New York Times.* August 4, 1994, p. B1.

BIBLIOGRAPHY

This is a very selective list; additional references appear at the end of each chapter. Every title listed here has something to say, and they seldom duplicate each other. It is not too much to claim that every library administrator, and every aspiring administrator, would find benefit in spending at least a few hours with each of these authors, absorbing their particular insights and considering their particular prejudices.

Barnard, Chester I. *The Functions of the Executive*. Cambridge, MA., Harvard University Press, 1966.

Boyett, Joseph H. and Conn, Henry P. *Workplace 2000; the Revolution Reshaping American Business*. New York, Dutton, 1991.

Brocka, Bruce and Brocka, M. Suzanne. *Quality Management*. Homewood, IL. Business One Irwin, 1992.

Buckland, Michael. *Redesigning Library Services; a Manifesto*. Chicago, American Library Association, 1992.

Burns, James MacGregor. *Leadership*. New York, Harper and Row, 1978.

Coughlin, Caroline M. and Gertzog, Alice. *Lyle's Administration of the College Library*. 5th ed. Metuchen, N.J., Scarecrow Press, 1992.

Crosby, Philip B. and Creech, Bill. *The Five Pillars of TQM*. New York, Dutton, 1994.

Drucker, Peter F. *Management: Tasks, Responsibilities, Practices.* New York, Harper and Row, 1974.

Drucker, Peter F. *Post-Capitalist Society.* New York, Harper, 1993.

Fayol, Henri. *General and Industrial Management.* London, Pitman, 1967.

Gertzog, Alice and Beckerman, Edwin. *Administration of the Public Library.* Metuchen, N. J., Scarecrow Press, 1994.

Gulick, Luther. *Papers on the Science of Administration.* Dublin, Institute of Public Administration, 1937.

Holroyd, Gileon. *Studies in Library Management.* London, Linnet Books and Clive Bingley, 1974.

Ladenson, Alex. *Library Law and Legislation in the United States.* Metuchen, N. J., Scarecrow Press, 1982.

Likert, Rensis. *The Human Organization; Its Management and Value.* New York, McGraw-Hill, 1967.

Line, Maurice B. *Academic Library Management.* London, The Library Association, 1990.

Lynch, Beverly P. [ed] *Management Strategies for Libraries.* New York, Neal-Schuman Publishers Inc., 1985.

Maslow, Abraham. *Motivation and Personality.* New York, Harper and Row, 1970.

Metcalf, Henry C. and Urwick, L. *Dynamic Administration; the Collected Papers of Mary Parker Follett.* New York, Harper, 1941.

Pfiffner, John M. and Sherwood, Frank P. *Administrative Organization.* Englewood Cliffs, N. J., Prentice-Hall, 1960.

Prentice, Ann E. *Financial planning for Libraries.* Second Edition. Lanham, Md., N. J., Scarecrow Press, 1996.

Rogers, Rutherford D. and Weber, David C. *University Library Administration.* New York, H. W. Wilson, 1971.

Sager, Donald J. *Participatory Management in Libraries.* Metuchen, N. J., Scarecrow Press, 1982.

Simon, Herbert A. *Administrative Behavior.* New York, Free Press, 1976.

Stevens. Norman D. *Communication Throughout Libraries.* Metuchen, N. J., Scarecrow Press, 1983.

Taylor, Frederick W. *Scientific Management.* New York, Harper, 1947.

Veaner, Allen B. *Academic Librarianship in a Transformational Age.* Boston, MA., G. K. Hall & Co. 1990

Weber, Max. *The Theory of Social and Economic Organizations.* New York, Free Press, 1947.

Wheeler, Joseph L. and Goldhor, Herbert. *Practical Administration of Public Libraries.* Revised by Carlton Rochell. New York, Harper and Row, 1981.

Wilson, Louis R. and Tauber, Maurice F. *The University Library; The Organization, Administration and Functions of Academic Libraries.* New York, Columbia University Press, 1956.

INDEX

ABOUT THE AUTHOR

Lowell A. Martin (B.S., Illinois Institute of Technology; Ph.D., University of Chicago) has worked in libraries, library schools, and in publishing. He was branch librarian and assistant to the chief librarian, Chicago Public Library; professor and associate dean, School of Library Service, Columbia University; and organizer and dean of the library school at Rutgers University. Dr. Martin was vice president of Grolier, Inc., a publisher of reference books. In recent years he has conducted administrative surveys of several city libraries in Chicago, Los Angeles, San Francisco, Atlanta, Dallas, Philadelphia, Baltimore, and Portland. He is the author of *Library Response to Urban Change* (American Library Association, 1969).